OPEN-ECONOMY MONETARY ECONOMICS

Also by M. L. Burstein

MONEY
THE COST OF TRUCKING: Econometric Analysis (*with others*)
ECONOMIC THEORY: Equilibrium and Change
*RESOURCE ALLOCATION AND ECONOMIC POLICY (*editor with
   Michael Allingham*)
*NEW DIRECTIONS IN ECONOMIC POLICY
*MODERN MONETARY THEORY
*STUDIES IN BANKING THEORY, FINANCIAL HISTORY AND
   VERTICAL CONTROL

Also published by Macmillan

Open-Economy Monetary Economics

M. L. Burstein
York University, Canada

MACMILLAN

First published 1989

Published by
THE MACMILLAN PRESS LTD
Houndmills, Basingstoke, Hampshire RG21 2XS
and London
Companies and representatives
throughout the world

Printed in Hong Kong

British Library Cataloguing in Publication Data
Burstein, M. L. (Meyer Louis), *1926–*
Open–economy monetary economics
1. Monetary policies
I. Title
332.4′6
ISBN 0–333–49616–7

For
Eugene Mitchell

My English text is chaste,
and all licentious passages are left in
the decent obscurity of a learned
language.

Edward Gibbon, 1737–94

Contents

List of Illustrations

Preface

This book evolved from a course in open-economy monetary economics at York University (Toronto) from which I at least have learned a lot. The book is an idealized, polished-up version of the course, preserving the problem sets around which the course pivots – along with some of the flavour of 'live' classroom dialogue. The *Study Guide* (Lecture One) shows readers how to use the book; how to grip the controlling logic of a perplexing subject; and, perhaps, to have fun doing so.

Just as I emulate my distinguished teachers of open-economy subjects – Milton Friedman, Earl J. Hamilton, Arnold Harberger and Lloyd Metzler – my towering exemplars *comme* writer of a text (teaching) book are J. S. Mill and Alfred Marshall. Mill and Marshall stretched themselves, doing some of their best work, while *teaching* their readers; they extended the frontiers of economics as they taught economics. The expository mission of this book is reflected by the way its compact space is utilized, not by dilution, let alone distortion, of its substance. Thus some chapters devote more space to exemplifying the lecture – often by variations on lecture themes based on leading political–economic stories of the day – than to the lecture itself.

The book completes my conceptual traverse to a financially-innovated open economy. And it shows that I have come some further distance in my long struggle of escape from habitual Keynesian modes of thought and expression:

The ideas which are here expressed so laboriously are extremely simple and should be obvious. The difficulty lies, not in the new ideas, but in escaping from the old ones, which ramify, for those brought up as most of us have been, into every corner of our minds.

J. M. Keynes (1936, p. viii)

Ironically, science embodies the central myth of *The Golden Bough*. For the land to be renewed, the king must be slain. Keynes taught us that.

****

I am indebted to my colleagues John B. Beare, S.-H. Chiang and John Evans; to Lester Telser; and to my students Craig Penney and Joel Polan.

Toronto   M. L. BURSTEIN

Acknowledgement

The author and publishers wish to thank the following for permission to reproduce copyright material in the text: the University of Chicago Press for the quotations from M. Friedman, *Essays in Positive Economics* (1953a).

1 Lecture One: A Study Guide to the Book

This book is based on a case, or problem, method of instruction: many of its principal points are embedded in analyses of problem sets rather than in formal lectures.

The book supplies economic logic controlling analysis of open-economy financial economics within a compass of some 280 pages. And, indeed, a price must be paid for its compactness and density. Empirical and institutional detail is often elided. The reader should consult other sources: it would be preposterous for anyone to claim to supply a self-contained encyclopaedia of open-economy monetary economics.

There is another cost of compression. From time to time, concepts like tabular standards, European Currency Units, the *J*-Curve, Euro-dollar markets and the Laursen–Metzler effect appear, to be fleshed out only later. But any such fault is repaired on second, or third, reading of the short book. Readers of novels know all about this. Charles Swann enters, in *A la recherche du temps perdu*, as:

> M. Swann . . . apart from a few passing strangers . . . almost the only person who ever came to the house at Combray, sometimes to a neighbourly dinner (but less frequently since his unfortunate marriage [to Odette Crécy], as my family did not care to receive his wife) and sometimes after dinner, uninvited.[1]

As for Baron Charlus, in *Within a Budding Grove*, Robert Saint-Loup awaits a visit from his Uncle Palamède who is greatly addicted to physical culture.

The point can be made more simply! Examinations demand review (revision); readers should also review, and review – again, and again. That done, the work will be seen as a whole before long.

1.1 THE RÔLE OF THE PROBLEM SETS

Examples must both cement analytic development and illuminate the practical context – so important in economics, an applied subject. The problem sets and their annotations do the necessary work. If the rather austere lectures supply only desiccated thrills which can be got from contemplation of abstract reasoning (to paraphrase the *New Statesman*'s review of *Value and Capital*), the problem materials are quite earthy. So to speak, a gregarious tutor ornaments the lecturer's spare harmonies and shows how his complex phrases are in fact based on the music of the folk. Indeed much of the theory evolves from pondering on widely-reported, politically-charged events like the twin American deficits, gyrations of exchange rates defying the 'law of one price' (never a robust idea), the widening scope of options-writing creating virtual, but not statistically accessible, financial assets, reversals in the international rôles of Japan and the United States, the impending financial integration of Europe, etc. Nor is that all. In recent years spontaneous, intricate (sometimes seemingly bizarre) developments in financial markets have shown the way to theorists. Theorists must explain perplexes not dreamt of in their philosophy. Options-writing and the currency cocktails and other intricate transnational modalities of the Euro-markets supply examples. It would be a fatal blunder today for theorists to lose contact with innovative market practice.

1.2 SOLVING THE PROBLEMS

Correct choices are indicated by upper-case letters: **(A)**, right!; **(b)** wrong!. *Why* is **(A)** right and **(b)** wrong? Working through the *raisons d'être* reconstructs the lecture's logical chains. The reader's assessment, and re-assessment, of the problems imitates the way a discerning viewer maps a cubist painting into three-space – pleasing the head and the heart. The reader should repeat these exercises; and then again. And *then* she should read the whole book *again*, uninterruptedly – as musicians go through a score continuously after having taken it to pieces. In a college course, much of this happens automatically. If the auto-didact (the 'single copy sale' authors yearn for) follows the recommended drill, I am quite sure he will master the material – and so find it easy to go on to understand more, and more. Some of the 114 problems are not taxing intellectually; they concern quite straightforward applications of the logic of the lectures to sometimes famous episodes in political economy. Nor are the tales of Mr Heath's and M. Mitterrand's economic policies (and contrasting political fates), of the Japanese 'miracle', etc. suitable for compact, snug lectures; but they accommodate happily to the looser, more congenial, problem set/annotation framework.

1.3 SOME COMMENTS ON THE MATERIALS

1.3.1 Chapter 2

Just as the quantity theory of money is generated by an accounting identity which yields falsifiable implications if velocity-behaviour is specified, the accounting framework for an open economy can be transformed into a powerful analytical engine. Lecture Two describes the transformation quite informally. The problems apply the theory to effects of changes in tax policy or in global preference for 'our' assets – e.g. the twin American deficits are confronted; as is the more-intense stringency of longer-run (vs short-run) constraints on an open economy – thus illuminating the third-world debt problem (and its shrouded dual, the international bank 'liquidity' problem). The algebraic method of comparative statics is put into place straight off, permitting a sensitivity analysis (i.e. a qualitative assessment of the ways in which equilibrium values change in response to par- ameter shifts) to be made. The problems can, from an economic point of view, be solved at a number of levels. True, some results cannot be extracted without mathematics; but, once extracted, they can be explained 'intuitively'. Finally, possibilities for *drill* are es- pecially extensive – and should be exploited.

1.3.2 Chapter 3

Lecture Three like Lecture Two, first describes properties of econ- omic concepts and then builds economic models around the concepts – specifically interest parity and overshooting. Perhaps the lecture's key word is *arbitrage*; and rational-expectations theory has expanded the scope of the idea of arbitrage to include invisible occurrences – i.e., forecasts. Overshooting has deeper mathematical and historical roots than is typically realized; the lecture expands on this point, before specializing the analysis to foreign-exchange markets.

The Euro-currency market discussion anticipates Lecture Ten's analysis of innovated money markets in which *A* banks 'create' *B* dollars (Uncle Palamède makes a shadowy appearance).

Mundell–Fleming theory is touched upon, pending the quite thorough exegesis in Lecture Five of the work of Lloyd Metzler, the basis for *M–F* theory – theory that the book shows has become very tired.

The problem set for Chapter 3 (Problems **13–31**) is both important and acutely pertinent for ongoing commercial and political affairs. Problem **16** explains overshooting in the context of a putative American (Presidential) political shock. And the modalities of forward markets are rather fully developed through exploration of a number of practical, and indeed provocative, situations.

Problems **23–28** are amenable to the new classical macroeconomics; they develop the implications of economic agents' forward-looking ('rational') strategies – and concern preannounced currency depreciations that may be aborted and unanticipated exchange-rate-target changes that may reflect more general unanticipated monetary displacement. Looking back on the substantial work accomplished by the annotations of Problems **23–28**, one sees that macroeconomic theory has become much more sophisticated and much less general; the ideal of the general field theory that so attracted the best minds in macro-theory *circa* 1935–65 has receded, if not disappeared.

Problems **29–31** delve into a number of Euro-market corners. A commanding theme of this book, as well as my 1986 and 1988 ones, concerns denationalization of money, and so owes much to Hayek (1976). And a corollary theme of equal importance concerns 'quasi-banking' – i.e., the distribution of financial-market action over a continuous field rather than concentration of financial intermediation and 'money creation' at relatively few nodes.

1.3.3   Chapter 4

Lecture Four seeks to clear up endemic confusion of criteria for choosing targets (and so control-levels) in a context requiring equilibrium with criteria for paths to be followed after being blown off course. Roughly – the former analysis is statical and the latter dynamic. The resulting model is then specialized to the 'Japan Problem' – i.e. to a collective decision to accumulate foreign assets over a protracted interval. The upshot reminds us that a set of economic policies comprises an equilibrium only in a game-theoretic sense; here *equilibrium* has little in common with an equilibrium state of a gas, for example.

As for dynamics, this is the principal point. Instruments are *not* properly exclusively assigned to particular targets; exclusive assignment is appropriate only in mathematically-degenerate cases. Optimal-control theory, concluding the lecture, drives this point home.

Problems **32–34** and **39–43** concern 'static' policy theory, applying Tinbergen's (1963) famous model to fiscal policy.

The annotation of Problem **35** both elucidates the distinction of static from dynamic policy analysis and elaborates on the futility of 'assignment rules'. And the lengthy annotations of Problems **44** and **45** carry us much farther along that azimuth, while properly introducing *official* (international financial) *transactions*.

The annotation of Problem **38** comes back to the way in which 'policy equilibrium' entails 'wilful' elements absent in physical processes.

The problem set *cum* annotations for Chapter 4 is more or less a reprise of the lecture. The lecture *propre* establishes key ideas that become the basis for the economically-motivated, more discursive, discussion of the problem set and its annotations. The problem sets are meant to stimulate lab work; this is especially obvious in Chapter 4.

1.3.4   Chapter 5

The work of Chapter Five Lecture Five is especially well defined: a number of Keynes-based paradigms are closely analysed. And the lecture may be speciously precise, since Keynesian modelling, going back to Metzler (1942), has long been mechanistic. A modulation of the Keynesian analysis, making it tenable for game theory, may be quite novel – see Section 5.3. And the Canada/US problem of Section 5.4 points up properties of trade between economies of different orders of magnitude. Section 5.5 glosses Metzler's brilliant development (1942) of stability properties of open-economic systems modelled along Keynesian lines. Until recently, stability of economic systems was not much distinguished from that of physical ones; Metzler's analysis looks rather brittle now.

The book largely eschews 'ISLM', for a number of reasons I gave in 1986 and 1988 – and, indeed, in 1963. For one thing, ISLM cannot be dynamized unless it is continuously 'redrawn', so that it is no longer even convenient. But Section 5.6, also based on Metzler's work, displays a schema closely related to ISLM, leading to a number of comparative-statics exercises of considerable interest.

Much of the 'lab work' for Chapter 5 – see Problems **46–52** – is quite routine: the lecture, based on rather mechanistic modelling, includes many specific derivations. So Problems **46–52** and their annotations are valuable for review but break no new ground. Problems **53–56**, concerning tax-policy in open economies, are much more ambitious (also see Chapter 7). The annotations of Problems **53–56** *precede* the problems and so comprise a short lecture on tax-policy – putting into play concepts of the after-tax rate of return and after-tax cost of capital. Problems **53–56** review this miniature lecture, specializing a Keynesian paradigm to tax-policy. Effects of changes in marginal tax (or, better, net-transfer) rates in open economies are analysed, and the analysis is complicated by the extent to which non-resident investors in *A* securities are more sensitive to before-tax than to after-tax *A* yields (they pay taxes at home). In the upshot, stimulus to savings from tax cuts is indirect: *effort* may be stimulated by lower marginal rates, leading to greater wealth (and income) and so to increased saving.

1.3.5   Chapter 6

The primary mission of the lengthy Chapter 6 is to consolidate analysis of established topics before sailing into more or less uncharted waters (see Chapters 7–10). The most prominent subject concerns properties of fixed and flexible (floating) exchange-rate régimes. And the most famous feature of fixed-rate régimes is the *specie-flow mechanism*, quite deeply probed by the lecture. Then, along lines established by Friedman (1953b), the equivalence of fixed and floating rate régimes under perfect price flexibility is studied – so that *differences* when prices are sticky become salient. Reflection erodes these differences: 'speculators' acting, for their own reasons, as quasi-officials supply *devisen* to finance trade deficits induced by transient factors. And on further reflection, transient distortion of relative prices under fixed rates would be greatly reduced if the 'money of account' were transformed into a synthetic unit (denoted the Aureus in Chapter 6) so that our prices would not have to be revised if values of various monies change: prices would not be expressed in money, to start with.

Section 6.4 concerns interest rates under fixed-exchange rates and harks back to the salad days of Bank Rate at London *circa* 1874–1914.

Section 6.5 studies the standard proposition that, under fixed rates, central banks cannot control 'local' money supplies. After the proposition is studied, it is countered by examples based on more sophisticated financial systems in which money yields interest – and by others that hark back to the canonical model of economic policy of Lecture Four.

Section 6.6., in which Friedman (1953b) is important, assigns the properties of floating-rate régimes to six 'boxes', which are then studied quite intently. Criticism pivots on various facets of *expectations*, and so on *speculation*. Much exchange-rate variation seems unrelated to 'fundamentals', in share-market parlance. Another interesting point concerns *capital flows*: 'speculators' – i.e. forward-looking transactors prepared to take open (unhedged) positions – substantially imitate national authorities defending fixed rates. And forward-looking tactics smudge distinctions between fixed and floating rates in another, related, way: if Economy A's real-growth rate temporarily surges, it might seem that the A-dollar will depreciate relative to the C-dollar (Economy C being A's most important trading partner) – at least if we make the fragile assumption that 'trade events' dominate exchange-rate fluctuations. But, if the episode is transitory, the A-dollar would then be an attractive buy.

Is speculation apt to be destabilizing? The lecture probes into this issue, distinguishing *instability* in its mathematical sense from erratic behaviour of essentially convergent processes.

The massive problem set for Chapter 6, and its annotations, is especially important. Thus the 'Bretton Woods and Aftermath' topic is almost entirely covered by annotated Problems **67–73**. The material – including corollary discussions of the Triffin, Harrod and Bernstein plans of the 1950s and 1960s, the IMF's *domestic credit expansion* (DCE) idea and Britain's traumatic 1977 Letter of Intent, along with the contrasting fates of Mr Heath and M. Mitterrand – is much more suited to a case study method of instruction than a formal lecture.

The 17 problems *cum* annotations are arranged under seven heads and, *inter alia*, accomplish reprises of small open-economy properties and Keynesian adjustment mechanisms while studying optimal-currency-zone criteria, the European Currency Unit (ECU), the 'Dutch disease', 'stagflation', the Marshall–Lerner condition and the Laursen–Metzler effect.

The extensive annotations use no mathematics except for a proof of the Marshall–Lerner condition; the texture of the analysis is quite light. The annotative material looks two ways: it reviews the lecture, partly by applying its concepts to a number of practical situations; and it opens up new ground described above. So the annotations operate at both the intensive and extensive margins.

1.3.6   Chapter 7

Economists like to say that the primary distinction between neoclassical and Keynesian economics lies in the former's reliance on price adjustments and the latter's on output adjustments. And there is a rather tenuous link to the dynamic paradigms of Walras and Marshall (Keynes's teacher). The Walrasian 'dynamic law' is:

$$dp/dt = \dot{p} = f[q^d(p) - q^s(p)] \tag{1.1}$$

And the Marshallian one is:

$$dq/dt = \dot{q} = g[p^d(q) - p^s(q)] \tag{1.2}$$

In truth, both 'dynamic laws' belong to the pseudo-dynamics of tâtonnement; neither paradigm permits *false trading*, i.e. trading outside of equilibrium. The price-motions of the Walrasian schema and the quantity-motions of the Marshallian one are purely notional: Walras contemplates a price displacement and studies a hypothetical price-motion relative to notional demand and output plans – actual output not being initially displaced; Marshall contemplates a quantity displacement and studies a hypothetical quantity-motion relative to the disparity between notional demand price and notional supply price – actual price not being initially displaced. Surely a dynamical system that can be interpreted in real time and whose variables are potentially observable is preferable to either pseudo-dynamic. Cf.:

$$\dot{p} = \phi(p, q) \tag{1.3}$$

$$\dot{q} = \psi(p, q) \tag{1.4}$$

Lecture Seven aims to do just that: the processes of the lecture concern motions of observable quantities in real time.

The system comprising equations (1.3) and (1.4) is not, in principle, biased towards preponderence of price- or quantity-adjustment; and it is properly neoclassical. So some other distinction must be found – readily owning that price-movements accomplish adaptations in neoclassical systems, but so do quantity-movements. And the proper distinction is near to hand: neoclassical economics is based on *disaggregation; many* quantities and *relative* prices are in motion. In particular, 'labour' is disaggregated into many categories and 'capital' is perceived to be a vector of many, many 'instruments', including cumulants of investments in people – so that the vectors have many, many components.

The lecture discharges a corollary burden; it deepens and clarifies the idea of *saving*, going back as far as Adam Smith's *Wealth of Nations*. Special heed is paid to *consumer durable* accumulation.

The lecture also analyses a rather novel concept, the *relative* wealth of nations. After discussing Hirshleifer's (1987) interesting analysis of 'political versus natural economy', the lecture harks back to a Lecture Three theme – on human wilfulness, making schemae based on the theory of gases, for example, untenable for economics in ways long anticipated by Frank Knight – and so introduces *emulation* as well as rivalry among nations. And that is not all: the idea of the nation is antithetic to the neoclassical world-view. This point is made particularly clear by elaboration of Lecture Two's sharp distinction of GNP from GDP. In the model open economy of the lecture, supplemented by elaborate flow charts and studied further in the problem set, it is quite plausible that declining demand for our exports affects non-residents more than residents, due to cross-ownership of resources. And one asks *how* the labour force is deployed, not whether some are unemployed; labour switches between 'services' and the export-industries. But in the worst-case scenario, the economy implodes so that its residents simply take in each other's washing; poverty, but not involuntary unemployment, may be a persistent difficulty in a neoclassical economy, an economy that is highly disaggregated and brought into equilibrium by the motion of numerous relative-prices and quantities.

The lecture concludes with a reprise of the 'Say's Law' literature centring on the nature of financial entrepreneurship, along with the rôle of consumer durables in savings behaviour. Excess demand for money is thus properly perceived as excess demand for financial-intermediary paper, issued by a banking industry seeking seigneurage profit. If an economy's demand for money increases, neoclassical theory calls for a wider intermediary spread, increasing the flow of seigneurage profit (which may flow to non-resident owners of bank capital). In the upshot, the economy's quantity of money, along with its specie reserves, will correspondingly increase (see Lecture Eight).

There is unlikely to be even a transient crisis, or turndown, in the real economy – as *ante-bellum* 19th-century American experience makes especially clear. (See the extensive annotation of Problem **79(c)**.)

Problems **74–83**, attached to Lecture Seven, and their sometimes lengthy annotations, are especially important. For the most part, the annotations develop variations on the lecture's themes, while reviewing its principal points. But the annotation of Problem **74** deepens analysis of 'comparative fiscal policy', describing 'tax games' played by groups of national and local authorities. And Problem **78** breaks new ground – unveiling the Banana Republic (*BR*), a society that could have been invented by Graham Greene. *BR*'s technical features are related to the investment/profit theory of Keynes's *Treatise* (1930). In the model, imitating life, the disjunction of GNP and GDP, enforced by the fact that the planters do not make net investments at home, is so complete that fluctuations in activity levels of wretched home-goods industries are independent of fluctuations in banana prices and crop yields.

The annotation of Problem **80** covers much ground. In Problem **80(a)**, our marginal productivity of capital falls; will adverse effects be countered if our propensity to save falls at the same time? No(!): in neoclassical theory the principal response shifts investment expenditures overseas, so that effects of the shift (or shock) on GNP are apt to be slight–although workers' real incomes will fall. It would be highly counterproductive to respond by abandoning thrift, making certain that our living standards will fall in future.

The annotation of Problem **80(b)** does a reprise on the fundamentally real neoclassical theory of real interest rates vs the fundamentally monetary Keynesian theory of real interest rates.

The annotation of Problem **80(c)** analyses the specious 'cheap foreign labour' and 'deindustrialization' themes. *A* economy labour indirectly displaced by cheap *B* labour is *redeployed*. And the cheaper is the *B* labour, the less need be the value of the marginal product of redeployed *A* labour for the *A* economy to benefit from the *opportunity* to utilize cheap foreign labour. That said, distributional effects in *A* should be assessed, and perhaps corrected relative to a consensual ethic. The scenario's balance-of-payments effects partly hinge on *who* owns relevant *B*-sited capital. Indeed, American MNCs have increased the relative weight of foreign assembly operations: negative trade-account effects are largely offset by positive effects on factor income earned abroad(y')in reckoning the current account. What if non-*A* resident capitalists own the relevant capital deployed in *B*? The answer takes us back to Lecture Four's 'Japan Problem'. Indeed ex-*A* owners of *B*-sited capital may buy *A* capital with export revenues. But *A* residents can construct valuable capital assets on highly favourable terms – using imports from *B* and the product of redeployed *A* labour. The scenario, if properly understood, describes an opportunity for *A*, not a threat to *A*. Total capital deployed in *A* may substantially increase, along with total *A* wealth. True, *A* residents and their government may go on a consumption binge, selling their patrimony to finance it. But that would not be *B*'s fault.

Problems **82** and **83** ring changes on the partition of GNP and GDP in neoclassical theory and in innovated modern practice.

1.3.7   Chapter 8

Lecture Eight is compact, if not dense; and it carries most of the chapter's weight. Associated Problems **84–88** do little more than organize 'lab work' and review – except for Problem **87** which leads to an analysis of the Gibson paradox, concerning positive correlation between interest rates and price *levels*. The Gibson-paradox literature – going back to Keynes (1930) – concerns historically interesting data but is not tenable for contemporary analysis, since the idea of a normal price *level* is long gone. But the explanation – in the annotation of Problem **87(a)** – of *why* this is true is highly instructive, going to the bottom of the logic of fiat-paper (vs commodity) standards. In the upshot, expectations of general price levels have been replaced by ones about price inflation . . . Without doubt, the *money-and-interest* perplex is as important as it seems to be intractable.

The lecture is so painstakenly organized that no précis is called for. Suffice it to say that 'a dynamic analysis of a generic commodity-money standard' (Section 8.1) is followed (in Section 8.2) by study of a theme going back at least as far as Adam Smith and associated with Nassau Senior (1830): 'the purchasing power of money as determined by the cost of obtaining money'. Factors such as exploration activity, shifts between monetary and non-monetary gold (including industrial gold and jewellery) are explicitly modelled. The analysis is quite formal and indeed I try to supply a few desiccated thrills. But the models' variables are observable and the theory is operational. What is more, the formal structure is easily reinterpreted in terms of the crude-oil industry, for example.

Section 8.3 opens up new territory – properties of sophisticated financial systems in gold-standard régimes. It introduces a deposit rate and so a *spread* between the deposit rate and Thornton's 'mercantile rate of profit'. Comparative-statics operations are performed: intensity of demand for non-monetary gold is to shift; or the liquidity preference parameter shifts. The upshot is especially interesting because monetary assets (liabilities) typically *did* yield interest under the classic gold standard – and do so *now*. Finally, the analysis deepens understanding of Wicksell's (1898) famous cumulative process (see Burstein, 1988b).

Section 8.4, strongly supported by the problem set, develops a network or matrix approach to the theory of the gold standard. Properties of the distribution of specie across economies are developed in a specialized general-equilibrium context through comparative statics in the Hicks–Samuelson mode. Inevitably some of the invariance quandaries studied in Lecture Six reappear, but are not resolved.

1.3.8 Chapter 9

Perlman (1986) explains a conceit of Ricardo, challenged by Malthus and Thornton, that reappears in the monetary theory of the balance of payments (MTBOP): 'a necessary and sufficient condition for a balance of trade deficit is a redundant currency' (Perlman, 1986, p. 745). Lecture Nine explores the sequel in some depth – and by the close of its companion Lecture Ten (and the book) it becomes clear that financial, including monetary, displacement is mostly corrected within financial channels so that exchange rates and balances of payments are not disturbed. (Of course, if A's secular inflation rate exceeds B's, moving equilibrium requires secular decay of the A/B exchange rate; MTBOP is better defined under fixed exchange rates.) Lecture Ten develops Lecture Nine's hints about how options and Euro-market dealings continuously reconstruct virtual 'currency' positions so that switches in asset preferences are accommodated by balance-sheet reconstruction (through the agency of professional dealers, including 'speculators'). And Lecture Eight shows that in fact Economy E's authorities are more able to influence E's equilibrium specie holdings – *via* their influence on the E central bank deposit rate, for example – than the literature suggests; another facet of the theory of interest-bearing money. In modern theory, 'demand for money' is subsumed by 'demand for intermediary assets (liabilities)'. Initial excess supply of money in Economy E can be corrected by narrower E-bank spreads (higher deposit rates relative to Thornton's mercantile rate of profit for example), together with 'disintermediation' (so that banks sell assets to the public, redeeming deposit-liability). Similarly, excess demand for money is accommodated by wider spreads and increased mediation by banks and other financial institutions.

Many analysts mistakenly associate expansion (contraction) of financial-intermediary balance sheets with 1:1 expansion (contraction) of fresh lending to deficit spending-units. No! Financial institutions must obtain resources in order to expand their lending – they must sell liabilities (deposits, for example) unless they increase share capital. Even if a bank hands over notes (as it would in the 19th century) or writes up deposits in exchange for borrowers' IOUs, the public must be induced to *hold* the fresh bank liabilities: incremental bank deposits reflect fresh lending by depositors – the source of the *real* finance supplied to the bank's clients. It is *so* necessary to distinguish the essentially monetary function of financial intermediaries from the real-credit processes they mediate (see the interpolation in Section 10.2).

Lecture Ten shows how MTBOP conflates Ricardo's conceit with the Humean specie-flow mechanism, subject to three qualifications. First, 'specie flows are . . . produced not by discrepancies in prices but by differences between [nominal] demand for output and the supply of output at world prices' (Friedman and Schwartz, 1982, p. 28). Secondly, *money* is not precisely defined in MTBOP: the Red Queen tells us that, whatever it is, it is *very* important. Third, direct impact on international capital flows by monetary imbalance is *not* ignored by MTBOP.

Anticipating Lecture Ten, the lecture describes a stark alternative to MTBOP – a *fiscal* theory of the balance of payments, anticipated by Thornton (1802) – cf. Section 9.3. Section 9.3 establishes a definitive counter-example to MTBOP: purely fiscal phenomena drive balance-of-payments fluctuation in the lecture's thought experiment. Secondly, it is shown that Economy E's external finance requirement does *not* imply corresponding excess supply of E-dollars: E securities may be denominated in j-dollars; E-dollar-denominated assets may be a popular foreign investment. In any case, capital inflow into E by *no means* corresponds 1:1 with demand for E-dollars; just as E's finance requirement does not mirror supply of E-dollars seeking j-dollars. These simple points shatter the MTBOP paradigm.

Section 9.4 leads into Lecture Ten. Four events are studied. All influence balances of payments but none entails properly-monetary causation. The controlling discipline is the theory of *finance*.

The problem set, comprising Problems **89–96**, merely guides 'lab work' facilitating review of the lecture, while modulating towards the material of Lecture Ten.

1.3.9   Chapter 10

Lecture Ten buttressed by its massive problem set/annotations, makes a general portfolio analysis in an amorphous financial space in which monetary disequilibrium is like disequilibrium in *any* asset market. An analogy to securities markets is telling: forward and futures transactions, together with options writing, affect virtual supplies independently of the firm's board, comparable to a central bank.

Section 10.4 summarizes the 'preferred theory', contrasting it with MTBOP. This may be the most important result. In the preferred theory, spontaneous free-market processes swamp out official-sector monetary actions and freely cross national borders – often with unobservable effects: what if a real British asset is monetized by purchase of an option to put the asset for x^* US dollars (USD)?

Lecture Ten's coda anticipates the practical work of the problem set. First, a Dutch guilder exercise by McKinnon (1979) is reworked; and quite different results are obtained. Then consequences of an increase in A's monetary base are studied from the angle of the preferred theory, applied to open economies. The most interesting result concerns 'second round' exchange-rate effects not explained by MTBOP.

Annotation of the eighteen problems (Problems **97–114**) attached to Lecture Ten begins with Problem **103**; earlier problems guide lab work by way of review – an objective that directs all eighteen problems to varying degrees. The annotations emphasize practical applications of lecture material.

The annotation of Problem **103(b)** develops two more counter-examples to the 'Ricardian conceit' that only money-market disequilibrium affects the current account of the balance of payments. The second counter-example delves, at thought-experiment level, into the real world of trade and finance – describing how a big London bank may alter its lending profile in order to offset an open short position in USD created by accommodation to a global increase in demand for USD sensitive holdings.

The annotations move on to *laissez-faire banking*, controlling five choices among Problems **103–114**. Five practical illustrations are studied. The fourth displays the thrust of the analysis: financial houses o'er the world satisfy increased French demand for liquidity: *inter alia* options equivalent to guaranties to indemnify French holders in French francs (FF) or in currencies worth FFx^* on the day (i.e. FF equivalents) are sold. Banks may raise capital by selling equities in France.

The annotation of Problem **107(b)** discusses an economy's possible (US) 'dollarization'. The controlling insight is based on the partition separating choice of payment-medium from choice of monetary measure (money of account). A further example is supplied by annotation-material for Problem **110(a)**.

The annotation of Problem **110(a)** includes four practical variations on the theme 'interaction of industrial/commercial with financial modalities'. In a typical instance, a British company imports inputs from America; it typically owes USD. So it raises Euro-sterling capital, investing the proceeds in USD-based assets, thus shortening its sterling position and lengthening its USD one.

The annotation of Problem **111(a)** draws the stark contrast between American foreign debt, largely dischargeable by the American 'printing press', and Brazil's, payable in USD it cannot print.

The lengthy annotation of Problem **113(d)** *cum* **114(c)** shows how ongoing innovations sap the ability of central banks to control credit flows and money-supply within their jurisdictions. Banks anywhere can issue A-dollar monetary liabilities for borrowers' IOUs, covering resulting open positions by selling securities, including their shares, in A's security markets. And that is not all. Gigantic MNCs, like IBM, are likely, the day after tomorrow, to go into banking overtly (they are quasi-bankers now). Obligations will be backed by vast global holdings, including highly-liquid receivables.

Note

1. Marcel Proust, *Remembrance of Things Past* (New York: Random House, 1981) vol. 1, p. 14 – a translation, by C. K. Scott Moncrieff and Terrence Kilmartin, of *A la recherche du temps perdu*.

2 Lecture Two: The Accounting Framework and Extensions

2.1 THE ACCOUNTING FRAMEWORK

2.1.1 Preliminaries

The *foreign-exchange nexus* is much more ambiguous in innovated than in conventional settings. For example, on an innovated financial network foreign-exchange-rate changes may not have trade effects: the controlling value standard may be tabular; or the standard of value may be based on an ECU-like measure. (Under a tabular standard, the accounting unit is based on tiny fragments of many goods, perhaps including foreign currencies. A debt valued at one new pound is then discharged by tender of, say, British currency exchanging for a unit quantum of the complex imaginary substance.)

The themes controlling these opaque remarks are quite fully developed later, but their flavour is captured by Luigi Einaudi (1936/1952):

> The difficulty of finding a satisfactory definition for 'money of account' results from its history. Money of account was not created by decree but grew almost spontaneously out of man's habit of keeping accounts in monetary units, some of which corresponded in the time of Charlemagne to real coins . . .
>
> Today each country has but one monetary unit: the lira, franc, etc. This is the system established by the French assemblies at the end of the 18th century . . . Furthermore, if in the country in question convertibility is suspended the fact remains that the monetary unit is defined in a real physical quantity of gold, silver . . .
>
> There was then a monetary unit used only as a standard of deferred payments or for the purpose of keeping accounts. This was the function of imaginary or ideal money . . . Although it was

17

possible to make contracts or keep accounts in imaginary money, it was impossible to make actual payments in these monetary units, since they had not been coined for centuries.

The discovery of imaginary money . . . was not the work of a theorist, but the result of a long process of historical change, However, . . . one should mention the longing of medieval men for the eternal, the immutable. They stubbornly looked for an invariable standard of value and called it the pound; they pretended that it was immutable in the monetary chaos in which abraded, clipped and adulturated foreign and domestic coins circulated side by side.

From the Middle Ages down to the end of the 18th century, men saw much better than we do that money is a negotiable commodity like any other . . . In former times, because of the existence of money of account, men every day set a price on the florins, doubloons, etc. which they received and paid out . . . It was made clear . . . that the money which they paid, even bank money and paper money, was a commodity like any other, that its price was governed by the market and, like any other price, was the result of an infinite number of economic and noneconomic forces which determine the general equilibrium of all prices.

Einaudi (1952, pp. 229–61, esp. pp. 233ff)

Einaudi's discussion illuminates the disjuncture of *depreciation* of a currency from an inflation process. Contracts calling for consideration valued at x imaginary units are immune from effects of depreciation of the substance actually tendered.

Gross National Product vs Gross Domestic Product

We must distinguish an economy's *Gross Domestic Product (y)* from its *Gross National Product*:

GNP = y + (service income earned abroad, including capital and labour services) − (service income earned 'here' by non-resident-owned capital and alien workers)

i.e.:

GNP = y + y₁ − y₂

Denoting y' as $y_1 - y_2$

$$GNP = y + y'$$

In Chapter 2, but not in Chapter 7, savings are defined so that finance available from GDP is isolated; finance available from, or required by y' (cf. $y' < 0$), is picked up by the *capital inflow* concept (see equation (2.5)). And it is convenient to assign a common dividend rate, or repatriation coefficient, b, to y_1 and y_2, so that repatriated service income is by' – always positive in Chapter 2 operations, but not in those of Chapter 7.

2.1.2 Sources and Uses of Goods

Equation (2.1) is an accounting identity linking real variables.

$$C + I + G + X = y + J \tag{2.1}$$
$$\text{(uses)} \qquad \text{(sources)}$$

where:

C = consumption, defined so that expenditures on consumer-durable sources are classified as investments

I = investment – ignoring public-sector capital accumulation for expository convenience

X = exports

J = imports, absorbed by the 'uses' of the right-hand side of equation (2.1)

If the variables are defined *ex ante* – i.e. as planned quantities – equation (2.1) defines 'goods market equilibrium – as does equation (2.2), obtained by dividing through by y – an operation yielding proportions like $C/y = c$, $I/y = i$, etc.

$$c + i + g + x = 1 + j \tag{2.2}$$

Now define the proportion borne by voluntary saving to y as s'. Similarly, the proportion borne by *involuntary saving* – net negative transfers to the public sector (i.e. 'tax-payments') – is denoted τ, so that $s = s' + \tau$. By convention, $(1-c) = s = s' + \tau$.
And:

$$s' + \tau = i + g + x - j \tag{2.3}$$

$$(i-s') + (g-\tau) = j-x \tag{2.4}$$

(Company-income is tacitly imputed to households so that all saving is household saving.)

The left-hand side of equation (2.4) defines private- and public-sector finance requirements (relative to y); and its right-hand side shows that the economy's net internal finance requirement is reflected 1:1 by its deficit on trade account; the internal finance requirement is structurally linked to the balance of payments.

The *external* finance requirement is defined by equation (2.5) in which capital inflow $= \phi$.

$$(j-x) = \phi + by' \qquad y'' = y'/y \tag{2.5}$$

If y' is positive, necessary resort to aliens for finance is reduced by repatriation of claims against foreigners – i.e. by by'. In the upshot,

$$(i - s') + (g - \tau) = \phi + by'' = (j - x) \tag{2.6}$$

(In the annotations of the problem set, repatriated foreign earnings are ignored, so that the current- and trade-account positions are identical. Indeed the accounting framework is built so that the *current account of the balance of payments* is virtually elided throughout the book.)

2.2   SHIFTS, SHOCKS, DISTURBANCES, ETC.

Accounting *pur et simple* has been exhausted. Behavioural relations must be supplied.

Examine equation (2.6), which is indeed a pair of equations. Effects of internal events are to be distinguished from those of external ones; and effects of shocks to import/export structural relations should be distinguished from those of asset-preference shocks. But this work is deferred until we analyse effects of income (or, better, real-growth) changes – leading to study of 'auto-finance' in Keynesian systems.

2.2.1 Auto-finance (or Not) in Keynesian Models

Closed Keynesian Models

The following simple schema makes our point:

$$S(y, \gamma, \tau) + T(y, \gamma, \tau) = A \tag{2.7}$$

where, in an especially simple case, the parameters of the 'tax function' deploy as follows:

$$T = \gamma + \tau y \tag{2.8}$$

Obviously, y adjusts so that total available finance is unaffected by a tax change. Voluntary saving, encompassing saving induced by income changes, precisely offsets tax-take changes in equilibrium – where the finance requirement, A, is given.

Open Keynesian Models

$$A - S(y, \gamma, \tau) - T(y, \gamma, \tau) = J(y) - X = \phi \tag{2.9}$$

For $dA = d\gamma = dX = 0$,

$$-dT = d\phi + dS \tag{2.10}$$

Equation (2.10) shows that the change in tax revenue is partially offset by a change in capital inflow. Common sense supports this conclusion. A tax-cut, stimulating aggregate demand, leads to increased imports that must be *financed*. How? In financially-primitive modelling, gold and foreign assets must be transferred. More sophisticated analysis encompasses sales of domestic assets to foreigners. And short-run possibilities are much less circumscribed than long-run ones.

Common sense is a problematical guide to the intricacies of capital-account theory. It may seem obvious that, if foreigners are to increase their relative holdings of our assets (underlying preferences unchanged), yields of our assets must increase (e.g. our shares must sell at lower P/E ratios). But beware of *speculation*.

Consider Keynes's classic discussion of speculation in asset markets – exceptionally important for this book.

Speculation [is] the activity of forecasting the psychology of the market, and . . . *enterprise* . . . the activity of forecasting the prospective yield of assets over their whole life . . . When the capital development of a country becomes the by-product of the activities of a casino, the job is likely to be ill-done . . . These tendencies are a scarcely avoidable outcome of our having success-fully organized 'liquid' investment markets. It is usually agreed that casinos should, in the public interest, be inaccessible and expensive, and perhaps the same is true of Stock Exchanges.

Keynes (1936, pp. 158–9)

The following primitive scenario shows how 'speculation' may upset 'common sense'.

Say that Economy *A* installs a tax-cut, leading to a higher external finance requirement and, more uncertainly, to improved terms of trade (calling for appreciation of the *A*-dollar). If expectations are elastic, so that the market (casino) expects the *A*-dollar to continue to appreciate, capital inflow will be further stimulated; asset prefer-ences become endogenous in a dynamic process. Ambiguity is in-trinsic to open-economy analysis; and is heightened by the volatile and unfocused consequences of speculation.

2.2.2 Sundry Shocks

Preliminary Comments

The discussion pivots on the following query: *Is the source of the disturbance rooted in international asset markets*; *or in factors affect-ing 'our' aggregate demand for goods in our economy?* Two scen-arios, loosely based on American experience in the 1980s, are developed around the pivotal query.

Scenario One The *A*-dollar appreciates; and *A*'s trade account deteriorates, accompanied by increased capital inflow. Unemploy-ment declines in *A*'s generally-buoyant economy. Inflation-adjusted *A* asset prices rise.

Sources of motive power include the following. (1) *A*'s fiscal policy – or some other source of aggregate-demand stimulus or con-traction. (2) Changes in global asset market preferences. (3) Switches in preferences for foreign-traded goods, in relative production costs and in trade barriers.

Compound, putatively causal, events are examined. Is a particular 'compound event' logically a source for the scenario?

Source (3), in isolation, is rejected. It implies a falling *A*-dollar, rising *A* unemployment and falling asset prices in *A*.

Source (2) is plausible, but the case is not airtight. Aggregate demand in *A* becomes subject to opposing forces: asset-market buoyancy has expansionary effects; appreciation of the *A*-dollar is contractionary. (The more powerful are effects of asset-market buoyancy, the less need there is for *A*-dollar appreciation; then demand for imports is strongly stimulated by wealth effects.)

Source (1), in isolation, is not tenable *sans* 'speculation' (see Burstein, 1986, pp. 144–7). The *A*-dollar should *depreciate*. But, if expansionary impulses trigger a stock-market boom in *A*, foreign capital will be attracted – perhaps leading to an *A*-dollar bubble (i.e. a self-sustained rise in the *A*-dollar).

A compound (1)/(2) event is quite plausible. Its analysis makes clear that 'loss of competitiveness' is a baseless explanation of the first scenario.

Scenario Two   The *A*-dollar depreciates. *A*'s trade account deteriorates. The economy is buoyant.

Buoyancy of the *A* economy is inconsistent with the hypothesis that the prime mover is an adverse switch in (or shock to) global demand for traded goods. But Scenario Two is consistent with a compound event comprised of fiscal stimulus (buttressing aggregate demand) and adverse 'trade' events, together with upward pressure on real interest rates in *A*.

A variation of Scenario Two – call it Scenario Two* – may be especially *à propos* for the United States *circa* January 1989. Say that Scenario One has been in place for some time; and that asset preferences, which had switched towards *A* assets, revert back to 'neutral' positions. As the *A*-dollar depreciates, *A*'s trade account deteriorates[1] and *A*'s economy is buoyant. In Scenario Two*, *A*-dollar depreciation is triggered by 'asset market events'. A *once-and-for-all* fall in the *A*-dollar, all else the same, stimulates *A* share prices: the equivalent to unit distance on a foreign value scale entails a larger number of *A*-dollars. But speculative forces can engender a cumulative decline in A share prices. Or there may be a Crash (see 19 October 1987); share prices may *overshoot* (see Lecture Three) so that recovery of *A* share prices may run parallel to further deterioration of the *A*-dollar so that total return to foreign investment in *A* shares, in foreign measures, is buttressed (i.e. losses on the foreign-exchange swings are recovered on the share-price roundabouts).

The fall (or plunge) in the A-dollar will stimulate aggregate demand in A, although living standards may fall. Resulting eventual improvement in A's trade account facilitates accommodation to reduced capital inflow, or to foreign divestiture of A assets.

The upshot of Scenario Two* can be schematically displayed by the accounting paradigm. The following is a short-to-medium-term outcome that conforms to conventional wisdom and, perhaps, to Virtue.

$$\overset{\downarrow}{c} + \overset{\uparrow}{i} + \vec{g} + \overset{\uparrow}{x} = 1 + \overset{\downarrow}{j} \tag{2.11}$$

An alternative paradigm, less rooted in demand-side absorption bias, reduces to:

$$\overset{(?)}{c} + \overset{\uparrow}{i} + \overset{\downarrow}{g} + \overset{\uparrow}{x} = 1 + \overset{\downarrow}{j} \tag{2.12}$$

Absorption-based reasoning lies behind the proposed switch from public-sector spending to investment. Supply-side reasoning suggests that total production may rise above projected trends so that private-sector consumption is supported by resources released by the public sector and by increased output.

The outcome of Scenario Two* may quite plausibly be:

$$\overset{\downarrow}{c} + \overset{\downarrow}{i} + \overset{\uparrow}{g} + \overset{\uparrow}{x} = 1 + \overset{\downarrow}{j} \tag{2.13}$$

Equation (2.13) projects a dismal prospect (for hedonists, at least) that, when translated into American terms, would prompt historians to describe the Reagan years as a prolonged consumption binge, financed abroad and forcing the Administration installed on 20 January 1989 to cope with the equivalent to a Reparations crisis. And that Administration is likely to be hopelessly committed to substantial increases in public-sector spending.

The controlling model is rather shaky in at least one respect for both American and British conditions. American growth has been importantly based on immigration; the analysis masks this significant relaxation of binding constraints. Nor is Britain constrained as heavily as the model seems to suggest: labour-slack exists in Manchester, if not in Chichester.

2.3 IMPERIALISM, ANCIENT AND MODERN

The accounting framework accommodates an array of 'imperial' relations, some more authentic than others. Thus Rome's commercial balance with its dependencies was characteristically negative (but hardly adverse), save for a balancing entry, 'sales' of uncovenanted government services. The amoral calculus classifies Roman slave-acquisitions as imports of capital goods, offset by sales of government services. And the Church of Rome's otherwise negative current account has long been importantly pumped up by communicants' contributions. Both economies absorb more goods and services than they produce.

The British imperial economy operated quite differently. Agents resident in the Mother Country ran commercial surpluses with her dependencies, building up huge asset positions, yielding correspondingly large income flows (cf. y'), once substantially reinvested but, by 1914, supporting British absorption of goods and services in excess of British production.

The skeletal logic controlling the economic framework is revealed by a hypothetical example in which the Mother Country is stipulated to be in balanced-growth equilibrium so that, at any time,

$$(j-x) = by'' \tag{2.14}$$

where *all* capital grows at the common rate $(1-b)\varkappa(100\% \ p.a.)$, 'the' rate of return being $\varkappa$; and the dividend rate, b.

Exploitation (?)

Payne (1985) seems well based in writing that British overseas investment, which 'rose from £235m in 1854 to £2b in 1900, yielding annual income in 1900 of £100m' (p. 273) paid off.

> Overall, the yield from overseas investment was higher than the domestic market would offer . . . These investments were directly responsible, too, for much of the buoyancy of the service sector of

the economy in which . . . a very high proportion of the employed population was engaged.

Payne (1985, p. 274)

This remark hardly perturbs bourgeois economists, who go on to point out that inhabitants of the imperial domain demonstrably benefited from capital inflows. Indeed the United States continued to absorb massive inflows of British and Dutch capital for years after Independence. And Payne points out (p. 274) that the 19th-century debate (and the 18th-century one, according to Adam Smith) centred on the possibility that capital outflow caused capital shortage in Britain. (Payne concludes there was no such shortage, whatever that may mean.) Not surprisingly, Marxist–Leninists give this history a different twist. Thus, citing Lenin (1933), Sweezy (1942/1970) writes:

Imperialism may be defined as a stage in the development of the world economy in which (a) several advanced capitalist countries stand on a competitive footing with respect to the world market for industrial products; (b) monopoly capital is the dominant form of capital; and (c) the contradictions of the accumulation process have reached such maturity that capital export is an outstanding feature of world economic relations. As a consequence of these basic economic conditions, we have two further characteristics: (d) severe rivalry in the world market leading alternately to cutthroat competition and international monopoly combines; and (e) the territorial division of 'unoccupied' parts of the world among the major capitalist powers (and their satellites). With minor qualifications, this is the definition of imperialism favoured by Lenin.

Sweezy (1942/1970, p. 307)

Nor is this all! Sweezy goes on (pp. 308ff) to describe 'nationalism, militarism and racism' as spin-offs from imperialism. But Payne (1985, pp. 274–5), reflecting the vast bulk of competent empirical work, writes that: (1) 'during the 19th century efforts to subvert the sovereignty of the consumer by market-sharing schemes and price-fixing arrangements tended to be brief and ineffective'; (2) the merger wave of the late 19th century 'affected only a small part of the entire range of British industry'. And the 'capital shortage' debate has already been referenced.

This much can be said for the policy of the *Soviet* empire. The Russians have absorbed goods from their dependencies (*à la* Rome) rather than press gimmicky gizmos upon them; nor have they force fed their allies with capital infusions. *Sic eunt fata hominum*?

A Postscript to Imperialism, Looking Ahead to Later Lectures

Repeal of the Corn Laws in 1846 (after the modifications of 1828 and 1842) led to indirect production of British food: overseas suppliers took back manufactures, financial and managerial services, etc. Now such nations as Britain, Canada and the United States may be moving towards indirect production of *manufactures*. We study properties of such putative post-industrial trade in Lecture Seven. And the analysis inevitably intersects the discussion, in Lecture Four, of *optimal paths of foreign-asset accumulation*: Japan has thus exchanged vast quantities of manufactured goods for foreign assets. Techniques of such analysis are derived from optimal-control and dynamic-programming literature. (See Dixit, 1976, Chapters 9–11, and Kamien and Schwartz, 1981, by way of two examples from a huge population.) It suffices now to make two remarks. (1) Attitudes of adults towards their progeny – indeed, unborn progeny – matter, as does intertemporal tussle in general. (See Barro, 1974 and Barro, 1984.) (2) In a full economic–political–strategic analysis of national (or imperial) policy, gold and foreign assets comprise treasure chests for possible conflicts and may confer freedom of political action. Indeed, geopolitical motivation for entering asset positions into the equivalent of indirect utility functions has been already made quite clear. And one can go further: proper macroeconomic studies are inevitably exercises in political economy.

An Annotated Problem Set For Lecture Two

1.1 PROBLEMS

1. In the correct theory of a fully-employed economy, a tax increase leads to:

(a) a higher trade deficit;
(B) increased capital outflow (reduced capital inflow);
(c) higher interest rates, unless money supply is contracted;
(d) all of the above choices are correct;
(e) none of the above choices is correct.

2. And an increase in planned private-sector investment leads to:

(a) a higher trade deficit;
(b) increased capital inflow;
(c) higher interest rates;
(D) all of the above;
(e) none of the above.

3. Open- is distinguished from closed-economy analysis by:

(a) the requirement that, in open economies, absorption must equal gross domestic product;
(b) the requirement that in open economies the trade surplus must equal the public sector's borrowing requirement, while in closed economies, '$s = i$';
(c) a narrower range of possible outcomes in open economies;
(d) all of the above;
(E) none of the above.

4. Increased global preference for our assets:

   (A) may lead to reduced demand for our goods;
   (b) raises our interest rates;
   (c) leads to higher unemployment in equilibrium if ours is a small open economy (SOE);
   (d) all of the above;
   (e) none of the above.

5. In our model of imperialism:

   (A) the Mother Country runs a trade deficit in long-run equilibrium;
   (b) the Mother Country's y' value is typically negative;
   (c) in equilibrium, capital flows are nil across the board;
   (d) two of the above choices are correct;
   (e) choices **(a)**, **(b)** and **(c)** are correct.

6. In our model of imperialism:

   (a) the Mother Country's position in 'long-run equilibrium' pivots on the cumulative effect of long sustained capital inflow (excluding y') towards 'Mother';
   (B) the Mother Country's current account is more positive due to 'y''';
   (c) in equilibrium, the Mother Country is still accumulating foreign assets ('equilibrium' refers to a rest point in a dynamic process);
   (d) two of the above choices are correct;
   (e) none of the above choices is correct.

7. As for relationships in long-run equilibrium between foreign-held debt, real growth, the trade account, etc.:

   (A) if the rate of interest exceeds the economy's growth rate, and it is a debtor, it must run a trade surplus;
   (b) short- , but not long-run, equilibrium is consistent with a debtor economy continuing to increase its debt when its growth rate exceeds the interest rate;
   (c) a creditor nation in long-run equilibrium typically runs a trade surplus;

(d) all of the above;

(e) none of the above.

8. Choose the correct statement:

(A) the transfer problem's solution requires the debtor economy to run a trade surplus;

(b) the logic controlling Problems **7** and **8** strictly depends on the assumption that the debtor economy's debt is denominated in foreign currencies;

(c) to the extent that oil-exporting economies tend to prefer to invest in American securities and buy German goods, the dollar will appreciate against the mark in the long run but will fall against the mark near term – following a large permanent increase in the real price of oil;

(d) two of the above choices are correct;

(e) choices **(a)**, **(b)** and **(c)** are correct.

9. In a fully-employed open economy, if autonomous expenditures increase:

(a) living standards fall in the long run unless taxes are permanently cut;

(b) net foreign asset accumulation increases if the terms of trade do not change;

(c) improvement of the trade account of the balance of payments is the key to improved living standards in the short run;

(d) all of the above;

(E) none of the above.

10. Choose the correct statement:

(a) persistent American trade deficits in the 1980s were at the expense of American living standards;

(B) a process in which the American trade account turns positive and the Japanese one negative is equivalent to that governing successful French discharge of the reparations imposed by Prussia in 1870;

(c) fiscal contraction, accompanied by currency depreciation, leads to lower living standards in the long run because of the cumulative effects of capital outflow from the economy;

(d) all of the above;

(e) none of the above.

11. Choose the correct statement:

   (a) nontraded goods are goods that are not marketed;
   (b) in order to calculate GDP, net factor income from abroad is added to GNP;
   (C) in 1982, the Kuwait GNP exceeded its GDP by more than 20%;
   (d) all of the above;
   (e) none of the above.

12. Choose the correct statement:

   (a) the trade balance contains merchandise imports and exports;
   (b) the current account picks up service income;
   (c) statistical discrepancy in balance-of-payments statistics is only slightly larger than that pertinent to measurements in quantum physics;
   (D) at least two of the above choices are correct;
   (e) none of the above choices is correct.

SELECTIVE ANNOTATIONS

Problem 1

In what follows *terms of trade* are designated by ξ; so the analysis is tenable for fixed *and* flexible foreign-exchange régimes.

The underlying model is of the form

$$f(r, \xi, \tau) = y^* \tag{2.15}$$

$$\phi(r) = \psi(\xi) \tag{2.16}$$

$$\begin{array}{ccc} (-) & (-) & (-) \end{array}$$
$$f_r dr + f_\xi d\xi = -f_\tau d\tau \tag{2.17}$$

$$(+) \qquad (+)$$
$$\phi_r dr - \psi_\xi d\xi = 0 \tag{2.18}$$

$$\Delta = (+) \tag{2.19}$$

$$dr/d\tau = [(+)(-) - (0)(-)]/(+) = (-)/(+) = (-) \tag{2.20}$$

(Remember that the tax-rate is *cut*. And the reader should prove that the terms of trade will 'improve' ('deteriorate') if there is a tax-cut (increase).)

Comments on the Scheme (related to that of Burstein, 1986, Chapter 10)

Function $f(\cdot)$, equation (2.15), determines aggregate demand; aggregate supply is specified to be y^*. Planned capital inflow is determined by $\phi(r)$; the trade deficit by $\psi(\xi)$. (As has been explained, repatriated income from services of capital and labour sold abroad is picked up in 'capital inflow' *here*, in order to simplify the discussion.) Equation (2.16) simply requires that the trade deficit be financed.

Subsequent steps are obvious to the mathematically initiated; and completely opaque for others. So some readers will elide this exercise.

Since the tax-rate, τ, is parametric, equations (2.15) and (2.16) comprise a system of two equations in the unknowns (r, ξ). We stipulate the existence of a unique solution $(\bar{r}, \bar{\xi})$. Now differentiate the system totally in the neighbourhood of the solution point. This work yields a pair of *linear* equations whose coefficients are the gradients at the solution point; and whose unknowns are the differentials $(dr, d\xi)$. Common economic reasoning assigns *signs* to the gradients (partial derivatives). Equation (2.19) establishes that the linear system's determinant is positive. And so the table is set for equation (2.20). The work lies in the domain of the technique of *comparative statics*, developed by Hicks and Samuelson.

1(c) At one level, this choice is trivially easy to assess. Common City, or Wall Street, reasoning concludes that faster money-growth leads to *lower* interest rates. At this early stage of the course, the reader is most unlikely to conclude that monetary contraction induces *lower* interest rates. At another level, the problem is both deep and knotty; and is splendidly elucidated by Friedman and Schwartz (1982, Chapter 10). Thus only *real* interest rates are proper to the analysis; at a deeper level, the choice's second clause is a red herring.

By the time the course ends, the reader will conclude, I hope, that lower rates of liquidity-base growth (say, money growth) *do* indeed associate with lower market (nominal) rates of interest; market rates of interest, at least retrospectively, comprise real and inflation-premium components; the real component tends to be roughly invariant against secular monetary trends; and the inflation-premium is positively correlated with money-growth. (Again see Friedman and Schwartz, 1982.)

Problem 2

The analysis easily accommodates effects of changes in public spending. And this remark leads to another. Especially in the cases of mixed economies, like those of Sweden, Italy and France, it is important to distinguish expenditures of government agencies *propre* (*cf.* defence expenditures) from those of Crown corporations (*régies*) generating electricity, producing cars, operating railroads, etc. The latter expenditures concern *investment*. Traditional distinctions of above-the-line from below-the-line expenditures are in order.

The second preliminary remark is this. How do intensified 'animal spirits' of accumulators of real capital transmit to the balance of payments? Increased demand for finance pushes up 'the' interest rate, encouraging capital inflow. (For simplicity's sake, we elide share-market phenomena.) Resulting increased demand for our currency (in the financially primitive model we are compelled to operate at the beginning of the course) pushes up our exchange rate, causing trade-account depreciation. So they acquire the consideration necessary to pay for securities and other capital assets by increasing their trade-account surplus. In a régime of fixed rates, instead of the flexible-rate régime so far discussed, our currency rises to its upper gold point; and specie, and specie-convertible, assets flow in. Resulting price-inflation in our economy (or, perhaps better, resulting higher prices) 'improve(s)' the terms of trade, as in the mathematical model that follows. In the fixed-rate mode, capital inflow operates in two stages. In the first stage, offers of foreign 'currency' for our 'currency' drive the exchanges to the gold points; realized (*ex post*) flows may be slight. In the second stage, the entire accommodation is borne by realized flows.

Turning to the model underlying Problem 2, insert a shift parameter for investors' animal spirits into the function of equation (2.15); and proceed in the usual way:

$$f(r, \xi; \tau, \alpha) = y^* \tag{2.21}$$

$$\phi(r) = \psi(\xi) \qquad \text{repeating equation (2.16)} \tag{2.22}$$

$$\overset{(+)}{f_r dr + f_\xi d\xi} = -f_\tau d\tau - f_\alpha d\alpha \tag{2.23}$$

$$\phi_r dr - \psi_\xi d\xi = 0 \qquad \text{repeating equation (2.18)} \tag{2.24}$$

$$dr/d\alpha = [(-)(-) - (0)(-)]/(+) = (+) \tag{2.25}$$

Finally, an extreme case in which capital flows are perfectly elastic at a globally-uniform riskless rate of interest (so that each economy is assigned a risk-premium factor) is frequently deployed in economic literature and has surprising utility.

Problem 4

We must insert more shift parameters. Parameter ε concerns *asset preferences*. It indexes intensity of demand for our assets, including paper ones. And parameter λ similarly concerns foreign preferences for our goods. The next exercise concerns a shift in asset preferences; the reader should also work out implications of shifts in foreign preferences for our goods; and then implications of simultaneous shifts in preferences for our goods and our assets.

$$f(r, \xi; \tau, \alpha) = y^* \qquad \text{repeating equation (2.21)} \tag{2.26}$$

$$\phi(r; \varepsilon) = \psi(\xi, \lambda) \tag{2.27}$$

$$f_r dr + f_\xi d\xi = 0 \tag{2.28}$$

$$\overset{(+)}{\phi_r dr - \psi_\xi d\xi} = -\phi_\varepsilon d\varepsilon \tag{2.29}$$

$$d\xi/d\varepsilon = [(-)(-)(+) - (+)(0)]/(+) = (+)/(+) = (+) \tag{2.30}$$

Completing discussion of Problem 4, choice **4(c)** anticipates fuller discussion of *small open economies* (SOEs). 'Full employment' is assured in an SOE if wages and prices are flexible. Keynes (1936) develops this point in a way that contradicts much 'Keynesian' instruction:

> If we are dealing with an unclosed system, and the reduction of money-wages is a *reduction relatively to money-wages abroad* . . . it is evident that the change will be favourable to investment, since it will tend to increase the balance of trade. This assumes, of course, that the advantage is not offset by a change in tariffs, quotas, etc. The greater strength of the traditional belief in the efficacy of a reduction of money-wages as a means of increasing employment in Great Britain, as compared with the United States, is probably attributable to the latter being, comparatively with ourselves, a closed system.
>
> In the case of an unclosed system, a reduction in money-wages, though it increases the favourable balance of trade, is likely to worsen the terms of trade, Thus there will be a reduction in real income, except in the case of the newly employed, which may tend to increase the propensity to consume [*pace* later work on the consumption function by Friedman and Modigliani].

Keynes (1936, pp. 262–3)

Problem 7

Problems **7** and **8** rely heavily on Burstein (1986, Chapter 10:§3, pp. 151–3). Equation (2.31) states the *fundamental relationship* between foreign-helt debt, real growth and the trade account in long-run equilibrium, where

z = the proportion borne by foreign debt to y
r = the rate of interest
ϱ = the long-run rate of growth of the economy
q = the proportion borne by capital inflow to y, in a certain sense (shortly to be explained)

$$r + q/z = \varrho \tag{2.31}$$

$$(\varrho - r)z = q \tag{2.32}$$

The left-hand side of equation (2.31) supplies the relative increase in foreign debt. In long-run equilibrium this corresponds to the relative increase in national product.

The variable q is framed quite obliquely. First assume that *all* interest on existing debt is financed. Then note that, in long-run equilibrium, the relative increase in foreign debt must equal that of national product. So q is a balancing term; and is *negative* if all interest cannot be financed. Thus for $z = 1.0$, $r = 0.02$ and $\varrho = 0.01$, only half the interest bill can be defrayed by additional borrowing: $q = -0.01$.

Observe that, for $\varrho = 0$,

$$rz = -q = x-j \qquad (2.33)$$

More generally, if the interest rate exceeds the growth rate, so that $\varrho - r < 0$: $(q/z) < 0$. In other words, $(x-j) > 0$.

Searching for a cross-over point at which the trade account is precisely balanced in full equilibrium: we find it when the growth rate and the interest rate are equal, interest-requirements are fully financed and the trade balance nil in balanced moving equilibrium.

Another 'cross-over' finds fresh foreign borrowings for all purposes *nil*:

$$r + q/z = 0; q = -rz \qquad (2.34)$$

We rediscover that, in the nil-growth case, there is no net borrowing.

Problem **7** reflects essential characteristics of open-economy modelling. In the short run, an open economy is only weakly constrained. If absorption exceeds output, goods can be sucked in from abroad. If output exceeds absorption, the surplus can be exported. If uses of finance exceed domestic finance-sources, capital can be borrowed from abroad; if the economy generates more finance than it absorbs, it can export capital. The accounting framework establishes irrefragible linkage between the financial and product accounts; the controlling analysis is dualistic. The theorist, surely an immature theorist, may well find this 'freedom' untidy, if not chaotic. Surely the clear-cut properties of closed-economy modelling dissipate. However, in longer runs, open economies are indeed sternly constrained; the feasible data space becomes quite strictly bounded and its contours quite stark. Configurations that are feasible in short runs, but unsustainable, are excluded. A prime example is embodied in the prolonged external-debt crisis that challenges the stability of Mexico,

Brazil, Argentina *et al.*, and that of huge multinational lenders. Finally, from a formal point of view, the properties of long-run, or full, equilibrium are obtained in the way actuaries obtain properties of demographic processes. All of this is familiar to students of equilibrium macroeconomic growth. (See Dixit, 1976, for an excellent introduction. Also Allen, 1967.)

Problem 8

8(b)   Choice **8(b)** is at the watershed (great divide) of modern monetary theory. There is no intrinsic reason for the agents of the jth economy to denominate their debts in j-dollars; nor for its members to require that proceeds due to them either be denominated or paid in j-dollars. Nor has the contrary been true in life – although, as Einaudi explains, larger modern economies, surely continental ones like that of the United States, tend to order their monetary arrangements inwardly, so to speak egotistically. And it is important to understand that this book's formulations are neutral both for the choice of accounting units and of means of payment (debt-discharge); there are no preferred coordinate systems in the theory.

8(c)   As for Choice **8(c)**, see Krugman (1983, pp. 179–90). On the usual assumption that goods markets adapt more slowly than asset markets, short-run effects of the oil shock favour the dollar over the DM. But, in a longer run, the DM recovers lost ground: expenditure will be directed towards German goods; aggregate holdings of 'dollar' assets will stabilize – and, indeed, accumulation of dollars may cease.

   The 1973 and 1979 oil-price shocks led to 'creation' of a great mass of *petro-dollars*. Before a number of oil-exporting states became, or thought that they had become, financially sophisticated, low absorbers, accumulating financial surpluses, committed vast inflows of funds to major banks (including Citicorp, Chase and Morgan of New York). The banks invested the funds. The intermediate claims against the banks were called petro-dollars. Two remarks may be made. (1) the resulting huge increase in virtual monetary liabilities was accompanied, obviously, by increased demand for virtual monetary liabilities 1:1. (2) to the extent that oil exporters directed their massively-augmented inflows into US dollar securities, the oil shocks led to excess demand for American securities on net – so that there was downward pressure on American interest rates and upward pressure on the foreign-exchange rates commanded by the US dollar. Choice **8(c)** shows that, in a longer run, pressure on Germany, for example, diminished, as propensities to purchase German goods came into action.

Problem 9

The following crude model underlies Problem **9**:

$$y^* = C(y^*; a) + a + X(\xi) - J(\xi; y^*) \tag{2.35}$$

For a change in autonomous expenditure,

$$0 = \overset{(-)}{C_a} da + da + X_\xi d\xi - J_\xi d\xi \tag{2.36}$$

$$(1 + C_a) da = (J_\xi - X_\xi) d\xi \tag{2.37}$$

$$d\xi/da = (1 + C_a)/(J_\xi - X_\xi) = (+) \tag{2.38}$$

Interpolation

1. As for $\partial C/\partial a = C_a = (-)$, Barro (1984) interestingly develops implications of the fact that public-sector expenditure will substitute for otherwise-planned private expenditure to *some* extent.
2. In general, such substitution is imperfect.

Resumption of the Mainstream Analysis

Equation (2.38) shows that the terms of trade will improve: imports will increase. And effective or virtual consumption must increase: (1) some expenditure on imports will promote consumption; (2) the *raison d'être* for any decrease in private-sector consumption-expenditure is that public-sector expenditure has provided for private-consumption purposes to that extent.

Turning to choices **9(a)**, **(b)**, **(c)**:

9(a) We have established that, at least in the short run, living standards will *increase*.

9(b)   Increased imports must be financed.

9(c)   Surely in this full-employment version, the contrary is true. Lecture Four will show how very important is this conclusion: diversion of resources towards exporting, at the expense of private and public sector consumption, may permit accumulation of capital promoting higher living standards in future. ·

Problem 10

Study of the following Keynesian scheme promotes understanding of choice **10(c)**. Terms of trade are parametric; unknowns are (r,y):

$$f(r;\xi,a,\tau) = y \tag{2.39}$$

$$\phi(r;\varepsilon) = \psi(y;\xi,\lambda) \tag{2.40}$$

$$f_r dr - dy = -f_a da - f_\xi d\xi = (?)$$
$$f_r=(-);f_a=(+);da=(-);f_\xi=(-); d_\xi = (-) \tag{2.41}$$

$$\phi_r dr - \psi_y dy = \psi_\xi d\xi = (-)$$
$$\phi_r=(+);\psi_y=(+);\psi_\xi=(+);d\xi=(-) \tag{2.42}$$

$$\Delta = (+) \tag{2.43}$$

Commenting on the sign analysis of equations (2.41) and (2.42), recall that $\psi(\cdot)$ defines a *deficit*: $\partial\psi/\partial\xi$ and $\partial\psi/\partial y$ are indeed positive. The ambiguity of equation (2.41) is inescapable: the fiscal action is contractive; and the change in the foreign-exchange rate is expansionary:

$$dr = [(?) (-) - (+)]/(+)] = (?) \tag{2.44}$$

$$dy = [(-)(-) - (+)(?)]/(+) = [(+) - (+)(?)]/(+) = (?) \tag{2.45}$$

Of course, if $\partial f/\partial\xi$ is sufficiently negative, equilibrium output increases. In the upshot, the pervasive ambiguity of open-economy analysis, discussed in the commentary on Problem **7**, is revealed again.

10(c)   Choice **10(c)** is nonsensical. But it would be difficult to formulate a well-defined outcome that is in any sense ineluctable.

Problem 11

As for *non-traded goods*, *import substitution* is as important as increased exporting. Hair cuts are not part of foreign trade; they are not *traded* goods. But changes in terms of trade affect the 'hair cut market'. Thus 'devaluation' encourages consumers to import less cheese and cut their hair more often (and accept options proffered by barbers). Not surprisingly, proper open-economy theory nests in general-equilibrium theory.

Notes and References

1. See the famous *J-curve*. Inertia of demand and supply of traded goods makes A's trade balance worsen in the short run as a result of depreciation of the A-dollar.

3 Lecture Three: Topics in Open-economy Financial Mechanisms: Interest Parity; Overshooting; Euro-currency Markets

3.1 INTEREST PARITY

3.1.1 Introductory Comments

Kindleberger (1958) explains *interest arbitrage* more transparently than is now the fashion.

> The link between the forward and spot rates of exchange is the rate of interest in the two markets involved and . . . interest arbitrage . . . If the three months interest rate is three per cent per annum in London and one per cent in New York . . . three months' sterling should sell at a discount equivalent to two per cent per annum. This rate . . . is $2.786, given a spot rate of $2.80 and a discount of $0.014. If forward sterling is sold at any higher price, it would be profitable for banks in New York to put more spot funds in London and sell these forward.
>
> Kindleberger (1958, p. 591)

(For an excellent more recent, and more technical, discussion supporting the covered interest arbitrage hypothesis, see Clinton, 1988, pp. 358–70.)

Some of the most fruitful developments in modern financial analysis centre on arbitrage formulae. Important open-economy-theoretic examples are explored in this lecture.

3.1.2   Deriving the Formula

(See Rivera-Batiz and Rivera-Batiz, 1985, Chapter 2, for a more complete treatment.)

Terms are defined as follows:

CD = covered interest differential
r^* = a money-centre yield
r = another money-centre yield
θ = the forward discount on currency*

(The assets in question must have congruent risk characteristics. And it must be possible to ignore risks of default.)

Call the asterisked market *London*; and the other *New York*. If there is not to be a riskless (covered) interest differential between London and New York, gains obtained from higher yields at London must be offset by losses due to the discount on forward sterling so that proceeds generated by higher London yields are coughed up in the forward-exchange market. (Commitment to London funds is *simultaneously* accompanied by sales of forward sterling, married to purchases of forward dollars.)

The algebra carries its own weight:

$$CD = [(1-\theta)(1+r^*)] - (1+r) \tag{3.1}$$

$$CD = 1 + r^* - \theta - \theta r^* - 1 - r \tag{3.2}$$

$$CD = (r^*-r) - \theta(1+r^*) \tag{3.3}$$

$$CD = r^* - r - \theta - \theta r^* \tag{3.4}$$

As the investment period becomes very short, so that r^* and θ become very small, θr^* goes to zero first; cf. Marshall's 'second order of smalls'. This precarious line of reasoning leads to deletion of the $r^*\theta$ term.

For $CD = 0$,

$$\theta = r^* - r \,(!) \tag{3.5}$$

3.1.3   Gold Points and Fixed Exchange

Say that transactions-costs factors, including shipping costs, measured in physical units of gold, are 0.02 units per unit of gold transferred from London to New York. And assume that the dollar and the pound 'contain' equal amounts of gold of specified purity. Then the pound may trade in a \$0.98–\$1.02 range. Britain's *gold-export point* is \$0.98, its gold import point \$1.02. The gold points limit feasible interest-rate differentials between money centres. If, in a fixed-rate régime, in which Treasuries are prepared to exchange gold for their 'currencies' freely, annualized British interest rates exceed American rates by more than 2%, the pound will rise to \$1.02; and gold will flow to London (in life, this may be accomplished by bookkeeping entries). Excess supply of dollar offers for sterling at \$1.02 per pound does *not* cause the dollar to fall further: it is more profitable to ship gold than to pay more than \$1.02 per pound.

Supplementary Remarks

A gold-outflow state may be incompatible with equilibrium; it may be unsustainable – reserves may be quickly exhausted. But, *par contre*, an economy may mine, and export, gold indefinitely.

Excluding devaluation possibilities, potential exchange risk on uncovered positions is bounded by the gold points. So forward-exchange manipulation (cf. *infra*) is bootless if exchange risk does not inhibit uncovered arbitrage (i.e. portfolio switching stimulated by interest rate differentials, the portfolio managers *not* hedging their positions, relying instead on their *expectations* that exchange rates will not change against them; uncovered 'arbitrage' is risky and is accordingly really not arbitrage at all). The upshot led Keynes to advocate more-widely-spaced gold points. (See Application 4, Section 3.1.5 below).

3.1.4 Motivation

Modern exchange-rate theory stresses agents' motivation. If the forward pound goes to a discount against spot sterling, it must be *expected* that the spot pound in future will be 'that low'. Otherwise agents will bet against the market's implicit forecast – and will surely be unwilling to sell pounds forward at the discount against spot sterling mandated by interest parity. True, we are masking important complexities: there never is perfect consensus in exchange markets in life!; opinions about the veiled future may not be held sturdily; and *susceptible funds* may not be abundant – a possibility that is rapidly eroding as markets becomes more heavily capitalized, and more sophisticated. So *motivation* is a principal component of a correct analysis.

3.1.5 Applications

1. The market may conclude that nominal French money stocks will accelerate over the next year, so that the FF will fall 30% against sterling. Interest parity requires, if this figure for the spot franc one year out becomes a fixed end point in the analysis, that the spot franc fall 30% against the spot pound, so long as interest rates are held in place.
2. The first application illuminates ways in which *asset-market events* make exchange rates much more volatile than was expected when Bretton Woods collapsed, giving way to a 'dirty floating' régime, in August 1971. And the paradigm controlling the first application was (largely improperly) prominently cited in the aftermath of the 19 October 1987 stock-market crash. *En principe*, short selling of stock-market-average futures at Chicago can induce a plunge in spot prices along lines just established.
3. (See Section 3.2 below) *E* increases its secular rate of monetary growth. And *E* interest rates temporarily *fall* as the monetary spigots open up. Interest parity requires that the forward *E*-dollar go to a *premium* against the spot *E* dollar. But rational expectations – and, indeed, common sense – require a consensus expectation that the spot *E*-dollar will *fall* overall. So the current spot *E*-dollar must immediately fall *below* the level it will touch later. A depreciated spot-*E*-dollar level must be approached from below. There is *overshooting*.
4. Keynes (1923) suggested that forward exchange rates be manipulated so that British authorities, for example, wishing to attract short-term capital, push prices of forward sterling above interest parities. (Formerly, susceptible funds were limited, so that it was plausible to posit bounded response to departures from interest parity.) Assume, counterfactually in modern markets (again see Clinton, 1988), that this is done; the hypothetical scenario helps solidify comprehension of the logic of the controlling theory. Speculators will sell sterling forward, offering to buy other currencies forward. These transactions, massive as they may be, entail no current payments. *Arbitrageurs*, however, are immediately important. They will buy spot sterling, planning to invest the proceeds at London while simultaneously selling sterling forward.

3.1.6 Arbitrage Without Flows

The delphic title of this sub-section is based on the following point. Correction of a discrepancy (say between the price of *A* wheat at Chicago and at Kansas City) can be accomplished without a measured flow of the commodity between the various points (cf. Chicago and Kansas City). Thus, if the Chicago price 'improperly' exceeds the Kansas City price, selling orders at Chicago and buying orders at Kansas City will unbalance specialists' books in both markets. Specialists will mark up Kansas City prices, and mark down Chicago prices, restoring equilibrium before dealings are accomplished. But flows based on arbitrage *do* occur; arbitrageurs earn profit on the substantial capital they employ by *exploiting* discrepancies – 'exploitation' that restores equilibrium relationships.

Indeed quite miniscule financial flows may accomplish correction of quite substantial price disparities. Thus, if agents insist on covering capital movements out of their 'preferred habitats', an increase in Bank Rate in the *i*th economy may lead only to very slight capital inflow: the interest parity will be restored by a corresponding discount on the forward *i*-dollar – brought about promptly by market makers seeking to balance their order books.

Remarks on Bank Rate (Interest Rate Policy) and Flows of Funds

First assume that portfolio managers insist on hedging capital (funds) movements. And note that restoration of the interest parity then requires that forward sterling go to a discount against spot sterling, so that the time-profile of 'the' sterling rate displays a contango (think of a downward-sloping yield curve). If 'speculators' – who might be huge banks – do not expect spot rates in future to conform to the profile mandated by the interest parity, they will buy sterling for forward delivery; they will 'marry' interest arbitrageurs, sellers of forward sterling. The upshot depends on the capitalization of 'speculators' and the intensity, and various pseudo-stochastic properties, of their beliefs. If they are timid or nervous, miniscule capital movements may restore the interest parity; if their views are strongly held, and strongly backed, restorative capital movements may be massive.

Similar reasoning governs the analysis of uncovered transfers (cf. 'Hot Money'). In this scenario, in some circumstances, the Bank of England would supply sterling to foreigners offering *devisen* in order to take advantage of higher rates at London. Or the Bank may raise the interest rates it controls in order to promote a rise in spot sterling – as does the Bank of Canada. If beliefs are timid and precarious, small inflows of funds could push up sterling, or Canadian dollar, rates very substantially in thin markets. (The time-profile of the exchange rate is described by a slope parameter as well as an 'altitude' parameter; the curve is subject to torsion generated by interest-rate differentials.) If well-financed 'speculators' have strong, definite views about 'true' exchange rates, Bank Rate policy may induce massive flows of funds before traders are prepared to accept an exchange-rate profile reconciliable with the interest parity – which mandates a slope, not a base-line value.

3.2   OVERSHOOTING

3.2.1   Generalization of the Problem

Solutions of mathematical/scientific problems frequently entail overshooting. The brachistochrone problem of John Bernoulli (1696) is an example

> A brachistochrone is the characteristic curve along which a particle slides from one point to another under the influence of gravity in the least possible time, friction being neglected. The solution-curve for Bernoulli's problem is a cycloid, a special case of a trochoid.

Following Allen (1938 Figure 104, p. 524), Figure 3.1 graphs the solution. There is overshooting: points belonging to the curve, and for which $t < t_1$, have x co-ordinates for which $x < x_1$. That is to say, Point A is approached from below. (The 'approached from below' conclusion follows from the curve being a cycloid, not from perfectly general reasoning.)

Along less transparent lines of development, consider any problem entailing the solution of a second-order, or higher, linear differential equation whose characteristic equation has imaginary roots. If the real part of the dominant root is negative (in the second-order case, if the real part of *the* root of the form $\alpha \pm i\omega$ is negative), then the integral is of the form shown in Figure 3.2 and Figure 3.3.

Figures 3.2 and 3.3 display overshooting in the sense that the variable exceeds its trendline solution value before becoming confined to an 'epsilon interval' around the solution. See a related

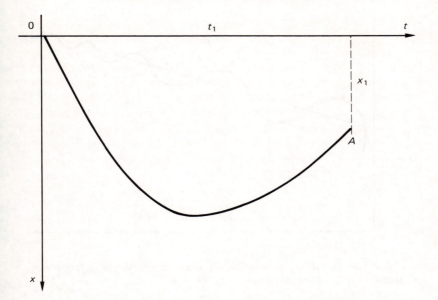

Figure 3.1   The brachistochrone problem of J. Bernoulli

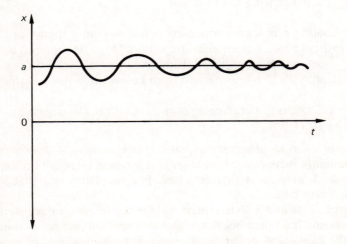

Figure 3.2   A cyclic general solution where the particular solution is a steady state

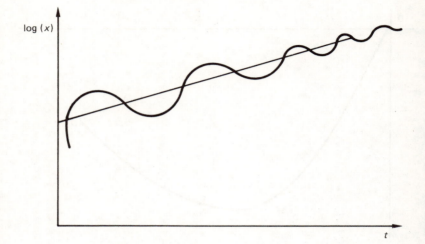

Figure 3.3   A cyclic general solution where the particular solution is a 'trend'

problem studied by Friedman (1969) in his essay 'The Optimal Quantity of Money'.

3.2.2   Particularizing the Problem

Overshooting problems in open-economy monetary theory are typically rather crude. The equilibrium value x^* is to be replaced by x^{**}. If $x^{**} > x^*$, and is approached from above, x has overshot; just as it has overshot if x^{**} is approached from below when it is less than x^*.

A Typical Overshooting Scenario in the Context Developed by Dornbusch (1976)

There is a shock. Monetary expansion in Economy A unexpectedly permanently increases. Shorter-term A interest rates fall on impact, as, indeed, may all A interest rates. For simplicity, say that *the* A interest rate falls.

Figures 3.4a and 3.4b tell the story. On the interval on which the A interest rate has fallen below the global norm, interest parity requires that the forward A-dollar be at a premium. And, since the equilibrium A interest rate exceeds the global norm (because of the higher inflation premium; in equilibrium *real* risk adjusted interest rates are

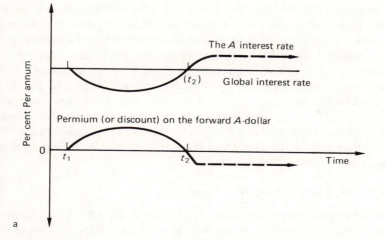

Figure 3.4a   Interest-rate and exchange-rate premia behaviour

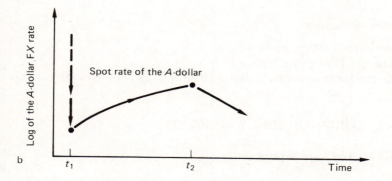

Figure 3.4b   Behaviour of the spot *A*-dollar

assumed uniform), the forward A-dollar is at a discount. Figure 3.4a displays these points.

Figure 3.4b tracks performance of the spot A-dollar. And remember this. Under *rational expectations*, abstracting from random shocks, forward rates correctly anticipate subsequent spot rates; behaviour of the forward rate is implicit in the chart of the spot rate. The unexpected change in régime occurs at date t_1: interest rates temporarily fall, remember. The witch's brew comprised of adherence to interest parity and rational expectations requires that the spot A-dollar increase over a significant time-interval; and that the spot-rate attained when the spot rate begins its 'permanent' descent be below its t_1 level. The latter value is approached from below: *overshooting is mandated*. *Now* the Prince comes on stage. The puzzle is solved by an *immediate* plunge in the spot rate upon announcement (or discovery) of the new régime – along lines interestingly explored by Sheffrin (1983, p. 74ff). The plunge takes the spot rate below the level that will be reached when the spot rate regains its equilibrium trend line.

Terms of Trade Effects; Non-neutrality

The change in monetary régime is obviously inconsistent with *neutrality*: the real economy *is* affected. In particular, the initial plunge in the A-dollar rate entails a radical fall in A's terms of trade; just as the subsequent rise in the A-dollar, while prices are accelerating in A, entails increasing (improving) A terms of trade.

Some References

Dornbusch (1976, pp. 1161–76).
Krueger (1983, pp. 77ff).
Rivera-Batiz and Rivera-Batiz (1985, pp. 289–92, 396–401).

3.3   EURO-CURRENCY MARKETS

3.3.1   The Modus Operandi

See Einzig (1969) and Einzig (1970). Also McKinnon (1979) and Rivera-Batiz and Rivera-Batiz (1985, pp. 79–104).

The material is not fully developed until Lectures Nine and Ten. But the following provisional construction is useful. *B* bankers, comprising sector (B), subject to regulation and operating competitively in a régime in which all bank liabilities flexibly yield interest (see Burstein, 1986, Chapter 3), operate, at the margin, at spread β. Financial houses ex-(B), comprising sector $(\bar{B})$, operate at spread $\alpha(<\beta)$ in dealings through which they obtain resources redeemable in the same media that the *B*-dollar obligations of (B) are redeemable. These 'resources' need not be claims against (B) and, indeed, need not be redeemable in B-dollar consideration: a $(\bar{B})$ house may swap its promise to pay B-dollars at a certain time for a C-dollar claim; or it may guarantee the B-dollar value of a C-dollar deposit, redeemable in C-dollars, thus essentially monetizing the C-dollar claim in a B-dollar measure. (The $(\bar{B})$ house will decide whether it will in the upshot be short B-dollars, etc.) Some such claims against $(\bar{B})$ are called *Euro B-dollar* claims.

One reason for the '$\alpha < \beta$' relationship is that (B) houses must maintain low-yielding (perhaps zero-yield) reserve positions with B's central bank. At the same time, (B) has privileged recourse to B-central-bank credit; and we assume that such credit is an ultimate source of redemption of obligations to pay B-dollars; (B) has a privileged status in the B-dollar domain. And there are other 'transactional' reasons for (B)'s viability, despite its inability to offer as much for resources as can $(\bar{B})$.

$(\bar{B})$'s reserve principle is quite different from (B)'s; $(\bar{B})$ relies on its holdings of marketable securities and lines of credit with members of (B); the set of *de facto* eligible reserve assets for $(\bar{B})$ is virtually open-ended.

It follows that the quantity of $(\bar{B})$'s actual and virtual B-dollar liabilities is a function of *demand*: the model's specifications lead to a perfectly elastic $(\bar{B})$ supply curve, relative to a competitively established spread. *And* it follows that 'Euro-dollar-multiplier' schemes are quite chimerical.

Remark

(B)'s demand price for deposits, transformed into deposit rate, r_B will fall if, say, (B) must increase its reserving against various liabilities (including deposits). Then demand for $(\bar{B})$ liabilities will increase (assuming unchanged open-market yields): $(\bar{B})$'s liabilities will increase correspondingly. Shifts of conventional monetary-policy instruments – mostly contrived for hypothetical closed economies – are likely to trigger large, but imprecisely measurable, counterforces whose parameters are subject to large standard errors of estimation.

An Annotated Problem Set For Lecture Three

PROBLEMS

13. Overshooting:

- **(a)** confirms purchasing power parity (PPP);
- **(B)** is linked to the interest rate parity;
- **(c)** is inconsistent with portfolio-manager effort to reduce exposure to foreign-exchange risk;
- **(d)** all of the above choices are correct;
- **(e)** none of the above choices is correct.

14. In a typical description of an overshooting episode:

- **(a)** domestic money supply increases;
- **(b)** depreciation of the currency runs beyond the long-run equilibrium level (the 'typical description' is more naive than the lecture *supra* in this respect);
- **(c)** interest rates on domestic assets decrease in the short run;
- **(d)** two of the above choices are correct;
- **(E)** choices **(a)**, **(b)** and **(c)** are correct.

15. In our overshooting model:

- **(a)** interest parity is observed;
- **(b)** over a certain interval, the terms of trade are above their norm;
- **(c)** when equilibrium is regained, the forward *A*-dollar is at a premium;
- **(D)** two of the above choices are correct;
- **(e)** choices **(a)**, **(b)** and **(c)** are correct.

16. In our overshooting modelling of a 'monetary expansion at the outset of the *X* presidency':

    (a) interest parity is violated;
    (B) *A* terms of trade deteriorate sharply at the outset of the adjustment process;
    (c) on the interval on which *A* interest rates fall, the forward *A*-dollar goes to a discount;
    (d) two of the above choices are correct;
    (e) choices **(a)**, **(b)** and **(c)** are correct.

17. If there is substantial short selling of the pound:

    (a) there is immediate downward pressure on spot sterling;
    (b) the interest parity can be maintained only by huge capital flows;
    (c) effects on spot sterling may be at least partially offset by higher Bank Rate at London;
    (D) two of the above choices are correct;
    (e) choices **(a)**, **(b)** and **(c)** are correct.

18. As for efficiency, speculation and tests for efficiency:

    (a) speculation is consistent with efficiency;
    (b) speculators promote efficiency to the extent that they aim to fix discrepancies between the forward rate and the spot rate expected when the forward contract matures;
    (c) efficient forecasts may have high standards of estimate;
    (d) two of the above choices are correct;
    (E) choices **(a)**, **(b)** and **(c)** are correct.
(See especially Caves and Jones, 1985, pp. 398–407, McKinnon, 1979 and Sheffrin, 1983, Chapter 4.)

19. Choose the correct statement:

    (a) the forward exchange rate is not a highly accurate predictor of future spot exchange rates;
    (b) when the required rate of return on invested capital is taken into account, it becomes clear that foreign-exchange advisory services make it possible to beat the market definitively;
    (c) futures contracts are more liquid than forward contracts;
    (D) two of the above choices are correct;

(e) choices (a), (b) and (c) are correct.
(See especially Rivera-Batiz and Rivera-Batiz, 1985, pp. 28–37; Telser, 1981; and Working, 1948, 1962.)

20. Choose the correct statement: (See especially Einzig 1961; Keynes, 1930, II, pp. 319–27; McKinnon, 1979; Rivera-Batiz and Rivera-Batiz, 1985, Chapter 2.)

   (a) the concept of a covered interest differential involves assets of categorically-different risk characteristics;
   (b) Keynes's early suggestion for using the forward market to affect spot values of currencies ignores interest-rate parity;
   (c) deviations from covered interest parity are based on errors in foreign-exchange forecasting;
   (d) all of the above;
   (E) none of the above.

21. Which of the following may explain deviations from covered interest parity?: (See especially Rivera-Batiz and Rivera-Batiz, 1985, Chapter 2, and Clinton, 1988.)

   (a) transactions costs;
   (b) costs of gathering and processing information;
   (c) government intervention and regulation;
   (d) political risk;
   (E) all of the above.

22. Choose the correct statement:

   (A) actual exchange-rate changes consist of random and systematic components;
   (b) absence of an exchange-risk premium invalidates the uncovered interest rate parity as a general condition;
   (c) the Euro-mark and Euro-dollar markets are intrinsically different;
   (d) all of the above;
   (e) none of the above.

23. A preannounced depreciation (lowering of target values of the currency) in a fixed-exchange régime:

- **(A)** leads to immediate increases of many prices;
- **(b)** exerts downward pressure on nominal domestic interest rates;
- **(c)** triggers capital inflow, since vast profits will be reaped just before prices shoot up, when 'devaluation' takes effect;
- **(d)** all of the above;
- **(e)** none of the above.

24. As for stagflationary effects of unrealized depreciation:

- **(a)** until the depreciation aborts, the economy behaves as it would in Problem **23**;
- **(b)** derivative inflationary pressure persists after the abortion;
- **(c)** real interest rates increase; (In the controlling script, see annotations below, higher prices and faster inflation drain liquidity, forcing up interest rates.)
- **(d)** two of the above choices are correct;
- **(E)** choices **(a)**, **(b)** and **(c)** are correct.

25. As for effects of unanticipated depreciation:

- **(a)** at impact the effects are stagflationary;
- **(B)** in the controlling (more or less new classical macro-economic) script, the economy is temporarily stimulated by lower real wages;
- **(c)** if expectations are formed adaptively, demand, but not supply, will be temporarily stimulated;
- **(d)** all of the above;
- **(e)** none of the above.

26. In the controlling script (see annotations below), which of the following are effects of an unanticipated increase in money supply under floating exchange rates?:

- **(a)** nominal domestic interest rates fall;
- **(b)** 'our' currency depreciates;
- **(c)** 'our' real wages fall;
- **(D)** all of the above;
- **(e)** none of the above.

27. Continuing discussion of unanticipated monetary changes:

    (a) in the aftermath of an unexpected monetary contraction, 'our' currency will appreciate above its long-run value;

    (b) in the aftermath of an unexpected monetary expansion, the interest parity tends to be violated, so that the real exchange rate first depreciates and then appreciates – thus overshooting;

    (c) an unanticipated permanent increase in money-growth leads to a permanent increase in the rate at which the currency depreciates, and to permanently higher nominal interest rates;

    (D) two of the above choices are correct;

    (e) choices **(a)**, **(b)** and **(c)** are correct.

Remark: Problem 27

Recall the dynamics of the process that finally attains the equilibrium path described in Problem **27**; cf. Figures (3.4) and (3.5). So long as our nominal interest rate is below the global rate, our foreign-exchange rate must appreciate, so that it approaches its equilibrium path from below; thus *overshooting*. In a counterpart overshooting process, a *higher equilibrium value is approached from above*.

28. Choose the correct statement:

    (A) if more expansionary monetary policy leads at once to higher interest rates, the foreign-exchange rate may approach a new equilibrium path from above so that there is no overshooting;

    (b) in the controlling script, see annotations below, anticipated monetary changes affect output more than unanticipated ones;

    (c) and in the controlling script falling interest rates unequivocally reflect more-rapid monetary expansion;

    (d) all of the above;

    (e) none of the above.

Remark: Problem 28

Happily, monetary theory now tends to accept that anticipated sustained increases in money-growth should lead to higher, not lower, interest rates – as expectations of inflation are reworked. So monetary/macro theory has retreated from the malignant proposition that real interest rates are significantly, let alone predominantly, determined by monetary events. But the temple of theory is far from being thoroughly purged.

(In connection with Problems **29–31**, see especially Einzig, 1970 and McKinnon, 1979.)

29. It is conventionally maintained that the Euro-dollar market:

   (a) deals in time deposits denominated in US dollars but placed outside the US;
   (b) tends to expand when the Federal Reserve tightens its policy;
   (c) expanded as a result of recycling during the oil shocks of the 1970s;
   (d) two of the above choices are correct;
   (E) choices **(a)**, **(b)** and **(c)** are correct.

30. Choose the correct statement:

   (a) a drastic fall in the crude-oil price is apt to lead to faster short-term growth of the Euro-dollar market;
   (b) if American sales become more important for risk-averting Company *C*, *C* will increase the volume of its purchase contracts expressed in non-dollar currencies;
   (c) reduction of capital employed by foreign-exchange *speculators* will make the markets more liquid;
   (d) all of the above;
   (E) none of the above.

31. Choose the correct statement about the economic rationale of Euro-currency market: (See especially Rivera-Batiz and Rivera-Batiz, 1985, pp. 89–101.)

   (a) the nomenclature, and the market itself, have Soviet-based origins;
   (b) one reason for the growth of the Euro-currency markets is the ability of Euro-banks to offer higher yields;
   (c) petro-dollars are generated by lending to high-absorber petroleum exporters;

(D) two of the above choices are correct;
(e) none of the above choices is correct.

SELECTIVE ANNOTATIONS

Problem 16

This is the script for Problem **16**, written in May 1988. The Democratic convention at Atlanta nominates the radical, Mr X. X is committed to dramatic acceleration of the American money supply. It is
universally believed that the Republican nominee, Mr B, will beat X
at the November polls. But, in the upset of the century, completely
unexpected right up to the vote tallies, X wins. So it is established
that, come 20 January 1989, American monetary expansion will
increase dramatically (X is swept in with crushing Democratic Con-
gressional majorities, committed to abolishing the independence of
the Federal Reserve). And it is anticipated that American interest
rates will temporarily fall as the monetary spigots are opened up;
later to increase markedly as American prices overcome inertial
resistance. So there will be an interval on which American interest
rates fall below world levels *and* the dollar sinks. We have seen that
this parlay can be achieved in markets obedient to the interest parity
and rational expectations only if the dollar plunges to deep lows *at
once*; and then rises over the interval on which American interest
rates are below global norms. In this way the interest parity is
preserved and no exploitable riskless profit opportunity is preserved.

The scenario compels reference to the Crash of 19 October 1987.
Thus if traders on the stock-markets experienced a sordid epiphany
on 19 October revealing that earnings on invested capital are to trend
downward, but open-market yields are to be 'stable', so that total
returns can be aligned only through capital gains on share holdings,
share prices must plunge *at once* and then rise over the interval on
which the rate of return on capital is falling – a fanciful picture that
may evoke useful insights.

Problem 18

The most useful definition of an asset market's *efficiency* is *weak* in
that it does *not* entail solution of a conjugate problem in optimization
(e.g. Pareto Optimality). Thus, in the simplest case, market-action is

efficient if one cannot expect to outperform random share selection – implying that forecast errors are random.

Two further remarks are called for. (1) an efficient market's standard error of estimate may be 'large'; efficiency implies that errors are random, not 'small'. (2) the definition's spirit (to commit a pathetic fallacy too!) is consistent with one expecting to 'beat the market' if one deploys sufficient resources – so long as the resulting expected rate of return, taking account of resources spent on 'enhancement' of performance is 'normal'.

Problem 19

As for choices **19(a)** and **19(b)**, see the annotation of Problem **18**. The following material makes the distinction necessary for proper assessment of choice **19(c)**:

> A *forward contract* is for deferred delivery of a given quantity . . . at a given price between two parties named in the contract . . . Forward contracts are in fact more common than futures contracts and are the ancestors of futures contracts.

> Telser (1981, p. 5)

> A *futures contract* is a financial instrument traded on an organized futures market such that all contracts of the same maturity date are perfect substitutes for each other . . . The validity of a futures contract is independent of the identities of the buyer and seller. It is a creation of the organized exchange and its clearing house. A futures contract is . . . fungible . . . A given futures contract stands on its own almost in the same sense as currency.

> Telser (1981, p. 5)

Problem 20

This annotation extends Example 4, Section 3.1.5. Also see Burstein (1963, pp. 262–5).

Bank Rate, Interest Arbitrage and Forward Exchange

Recall that, as far back as 1923, Keynes suggested that forward exchange rates be manipulated so that, for example, British authorities seeking to attract short-term capital, would push prices of the forward dollar above interest parities. (Also recall that Clinton, 1988, establishes that violation of the interest parity is much more problematical now than it was then. This exercise is now quite hypothetical.)

Switching from London to New York, assume that the forward dollar is supported at prices overvaluing it relative to its interest parities. Speculators will sell forward dollars for forward marks (lire, francs). Arbitrageurs will plan to buy spot dollars, simultaneously swapping forward dollars for forward marks. Hot money flows to New York, countering a deficit in the American balance of payments.

True, the remedy is transitory, containing as its antithesis, potential reverse flows. But conventional bank-rate policy is in the same position.

In the example, the authorities buy forward dollars and sell forward marks; interest arbitrageurs and speculators sell forward dollars and buy forward marks. Each transaction consummates a marriage. To the extent that the United States will need marks to fulfil its contracts, others will need dollars to fulfil theirs. The scale of forward operations is not pivotal for the feasibility of the policy. (The analysis elides possibilities, probed in Lecture Ten, for American authorities to make virtual mark issues.)

And Spraos (1959) cogently suggests that forward arrangements tend to be renewed:

> Operators who had sold sterling 'short' are in the nature of things compelled to reverse their initial deals. Whilst those who possessed convertible sterling but chose to cover it by a forward transaction . . . would also be expected to reverse their initial deals if they were rational. For just as in the first place the authorities support of the forward rate made spot conversion less desirable than forward cover, so their continuing support would make conversion more costly than reversal of the initial deal combined with renewal of forward cover.
>
> Spraos (1959)

Also see *The Economist*, 10 February 1962, pp. 541–2; 28 April 1962, pp. 366–8. And Jasay makes a valuable contribution, Jasay (1959, III, pp. 132–6).

(See also Problem **17**.) 'Speculative' short selling of, say, the pound induces interest arbitragers to sell spot sterling. So the interest parity leverages a process that can violently agitate spot rates with very little money changing hands. Official bids for future sterling combat such a contingency in the way that a sharp rise in Bank Rate does: a sharp rise in Bank Rate requires that spot sterling go to a premium in order to sustain the interest parity.

Problems **23–28** lie in the domain of the new classical macroeconomics. Since the principal controlling propositions have already been established, it is useful to kill two birds with one stone now: 'the principal controlling propositions' can be exemplified and thus further clarified; an interesting, quite novel, approach to the theory of economic policy can be limned.

Problem 23

23(a)   Consider the theory of time profiles of prices of non-renewable resources. In such analysis (governed by dynamic-programming paradigms), it is fruitful to work backwards from a stipulated end-point, say date t. For $p_t \uparrow$, p_{t-h} must increase correspondingly – as then must p_{t-2h}, etc.

23(b)   There is *upward* pressure on nominal B interest rates, as the analysis of Choice **23(a)** shows. Assuming, for simplicity, that there is *a* common global real interest rate, the inflation premium imposed in B must increase. In a perfectly-smooth (frictionless) case in which it is announced that a 20% depreciation is to be made effective one year from now, interest rates must rise at once so that holders of B-dollar securities of one-year maturity obtain running-yield compensation for capital loss (measured in foreign units). And the yield curve will float up to satisfy the arbitrage formula modelled on $(1+r_{02})^2 = (1+r_{01})(1+r_{12})$. Neutrality (i.e. invariance of real action) requires that the B inflation rate increase correspondingly – leading to the rather shattering conclusion that neutrality cannot be preserved unless the depreciation process begins *now* – say at an annual rate of 20%, so that, after one year, the rate is 20% below the present level . . . It appears that the correct analysis is considerably more complex than that usually proffered.

23(c)   See a related analysis of announced money-supply changes by
Sheffrin (1983, pp. 84–6.) Assured infinite (!) rates of return
should not be obtainable on the eve of an announced depreciation by acquiring stocks of common goods!

There will *not* be a haemorrhage of reserve assets, including
gold, in the wake of the depreciation-announcement. See the
annotation of choice **23(b)**: nominal rates of return in *B* rise to
offset capital loss from *B*-dollar-denominated holdings.

If(!) wages and prices are imperfectly flexible (so that, *inter
alia*, long-term contracts do not exert persisting effects), there
will be 'real spillovers' like the following. Since *B* prices are
inertial, when depreciation occurs (in a script that we have
seen precludes neutrality in any case), terms of trade will be
misaligned (they will be too favourable); and 'goods markets'
will be in disequilibrium.

*Coda to the Annotation of Problem 23: Prices and Interest Rates
Must Change in Order to Preserve 'Real' Neutrality*

Try a proof by impossibility, consulting Figure (3.5). The exchange
rate, now at *a*, is to be at *b* at date *α*. If the exchange rate falls at once
to *b*, terms of trade change unless prices increase appropriately. If
prices do not change, the exchange rate must remain at *a* if terms of

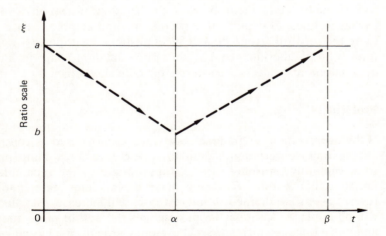

Figure 3.5   Anticipated currency parity changes: to and fro

trade are not to change. But then, the interest parity requires that nominal, and so real, interest rates increase to compensate for expected losses on holdings of 'our' currency over the 0α interval; and neutrality is violated. Etc.

Now consider the properties of the path displayed by Figure (3.5) – stipulating that the authorities announce at the outset that an exchange rate of b is to be validated at date α.

1. Prices start rising with the announcement.
2. Nominal interest rates increase in lock step with prices.
3. The foreign-exchange rate smoothly floats down to b. There is no overshooting: the new exchange rate is approached from above.
4. Nominal money balances increase over the traverse in order to maintain real monetary balances intact.
5. Points 1–4 require that an announcement at date zero that the exchange rate is to be at b at date α concern the *path* of the exchange rate on the $0/\alpha$ interval: a *functional* must be announced.
6. Corresponding paths for prices, interest rates and money supply are to be announced.

In the upshot, neutrality is preserved, so that the terms of trade are constant.

Finally, preservation of *interest parity* requires that interest rates rise virtually simultaneously with the announcement on foreign-exchange rates. But rational expectations, and common sense, require the forward rate to be an efficient estimator of the spot rate in future. So equilibrium requires that price inflation adapt to higher nominal interest rates so that terms of trade stay intact.

Problem 24

If the depreciation programme aborts, wages, governed by contracts anticipating depreciation, continue to increase, preventing prices from smoothly returning to levels appropriate to the rehabilitated initial exchange rate. B's trade balance will deteriorate; and, as reserve assets are drained, B interest rates will increase. 'Stagflation' will be in place. A similar script describes the upshot of an aborted announced plan to increase secular money-growth in a closed economy.

A Much More Elaborate Annotation

We must interpret an unrealized depreciation as a cancelled one; our freedom of action is heavily constrained by the need to obey arbitrage formulae. So we stipulate that the exchange rate is to be taken back up to a according to the path described by Figure (3.5): a is to be attained at date β. The machinery of Problem **23** is operated in reverse. Turning to specific choices:

24(a) At one level, choice **24(a)** is trivially true. At another level, it posits a vital proposition: under rational expectations, if *new* information is obtained, the system will shudder; *anticipated* events will have been discounted, so that however dramatic may be such events, the system's path will be unaffected. Think of a dramatic, but anticipated, change in the tax-code or in monetary policy.

24(b) Assume that the traverse has been smoothly under way when it is suddenly, and unexpectedly, announced that policy has been reversed so that rate a is to be restored. Any real-world scheme exhibits enough inertia for prices to continue to rise after the shock announcement is made. So nominal interest rates will remain locked into the inertial inflation path, so that the exchange rate must overshoot; the exchange rate must attain a from above if interest rates in 'our' economy are to be higher than world rates over the adjustment interval; i.e. higher yields must be offset by foreign-exchange-rate depreciation.

   In the canonical script, described in the preface to exegesis of the specific choices, the system is inertia-free; there is neither stagflation nor overshooting.

24(c) If inflation turns out to be lower than had been expected, so that embedded inflation-premia are excessive, it follows that *ex post* real interest rates are higher than if inflation had been correctly forecast – real interest rates are necessarily implicit and are subject to very large standard errors of estimate when inflation behaviour is volatile. Will inflation fall once inertia is overcome? Yes. Consult Figure 3.5.

The exchange rate must increase over the interval terminating at date ß. So nominal interest rates must fall over the interval. *And* under rational expectations, the inflation-premium component of an interest rate is an efficient estimation of inflation over the life of a credit instrument. The inflation rate falls over the interval. *And* preservation of *neutrality* requires that real interest rates remain the same. Choice **24(c)** is rejected.

Problem 25

25(a) Inertia alone assures that inflation will remain on course at impact, and perhaps for some time afterwards. So terms of trade will fall, *stimulating* aggregate demand.

25(B) Real wages fall because of effects of embedded contracts. An admittedly primitive theory of macro-supply implies that output will increase above trend. And the exchange rate stands below purchasing power parity: real exports will increase, as will import-substitution – so, indeed, the standard of living may fall.

25(c) If expectations are formed *adaptively*, interest rates will rise less rapidly at first but will continue to rise after inflation peaks, leading to a downturn in the real economy. *Aggregate supply is stimulated* by the putatively lower real wage rate(s). (See choice **25(b)**.) . . . This analysis follows the format of Lucas's business cycle theory. Again see Sheffrin (1983).

Problem 26

26(a) This choice is especially interesting. The analysis pivots on whether the change in the growth rate of the liquidity base is unexpected. Initially, demand prices for unindexed securities are not discounted by higher inflation expectations; and banks are excessively liquid. But an expected increase in money-growth exerts *upward* pressure on interest rates – excluding frictions (embodying adaptive expectations and embedded contracts) that lead to virtually predetermined inflation profiles over considerable intervals; and so permit monetary authorities to influence real rates of interest on those intervals.

26(b) It is useful to introduce *Mundell–Fleming theory* at this point. (See Frenkel and Razin, 1987.) Mundell–Fleming theory is a natural extension of rather naive Keynesian modelling to open-economy situations. So it entails a monetary theory of the real rate of interest; and a monetary approach to the real rate of interest easily generates the outcome described by choice **26(b)**, however naively.

26(c) Go back to Problem **25**. Since prices and – especially – wages, are inertial, the short-run effects of the currency depreciation entail lower real wages.

Ergo: **26(D)**: all of the above choices are correct.

Problem 27

27(a) The result described by choice **27(A)** can be reached via two routes. In Mundell–Fleming theory, depressing effects of monetary contraction on aggregate demand cause the currency to appreciate in the short run. As time goes on, our inflation slows, validating the appreciated currency. In the long run, real effects of nominal changes are nil in all proper macroeconomic theories. (Mundell–Fleming theory implies higher real rates of interest in the short run with concomitant depressing effects on the real economy.)

The second azimuth follows implication of the interest parity, requiring that our forward rate go to a discount, since our interest rate is to rise. But the forward rate is to forecast spot rate in future; and under rational expectations the market will not properly expect the spot rate to fall below initial levels in future. So current spot rate must rise.

27(b) The interest rate parity is *inviolate*. An overshooting episode (see choice **27A**) does not imply violation of the interest parity; on the contrary, it is required to maintain interest parity.

27(c) Inflation concerns rising, not high, or higher, prices. Inflation concerns $\dot{p}/p - (dp/dt)/p$ – not p or dp.

Problem 28

28(A) Recall an earlier problem in which an increase in secular monetary growth leads to temporarily lower nominal (and real) interest rates – so that the interest parity mandates that the new, lower exchange rate be approached from below, so that there is no overshooting. Problem **23** shows how the exchange rate can be shepherded downward without overshooting if our interest rates promptly increase.

28(b) See Sargent and Wallace (1976), annotated by Burstein (1986, pp. 91–3). In the real world, monetary changes are never strictly neutral. But adaptation of the economy to monetary shock will surely be at least as successful when the economy knows what hit it than when it does not. At a higher level of abstraction, the point is that real economic magnitudes are conditioned by scarcity, and so entail opportunity costs; while a nominal magnitude can be costlessly floated up or down. Say that an initial state is an equilibrium state. If a merely-nominal control variable is altered, and all other nominal variables are freely adjustable, economic agents can rediscover the initial equilibrium state: nothing has happened to change their preferences; and no real constraint is changed. The real (equilibrium) state of the system will be preserved.

28(c) Consider a *simpliste* version of the quantity theory of money: $\pi = m - \varrho$. If monetary velocity is extremely well behaved, the inflation rate falls. The vignette illustrates how far apart are 'classical' monetary theory and the theory, loosely based on Keynes's *General Theory*, controlling the Phillips Curve. (See especially Friedman, 1968 and Frisch, 1983.) Consolidating this point, go back to Irving Fisher's suggestion that an observed market rate of interest be perceived as entailing a real rate and an inflation premium: anticipation of lower monetary growth, accompanied by lower inflation, must lead to lower market rates of interest. Fisher's idea has been immensely influential; and it lends transparency to monetary theory.

Problem 29

29(b) This choice interestingly illustrates the theory. In a closed system, if the growth rate of monetary liabilities of banks is cut back (perhaps because of slower growth of 'high powered money'), resulting increased demand for substitute products, especially the paper of non-banking financial companies, makes it possible for such companies to extract wider spreads (e.g. to reduce their deposit-rates relative to open-market yields), inducing them to aim at expanded balance sheets – easily achieved. And bank clients will switch to non-monetary bank liabilities (since yields of monetary liabilities will have declined, absolutely and relatively); see Burstein (1986, Chapter 3).

'Euro'-institutions (financial companies) belong to the set of companies not called domestic banks. (*Banks* are now typically defined in terms of the regulatory process imposed on them!) This point is usually carried too far: it is typically stipulated that a British financial house increases its dollar-denominated liabilities only by buying drafts on American banks: i.e. by receiving 'dollar deposits'. This is quite preposterous. Spontaneous dealings on a vast scale o'er the world continuously generate, and erase, obligations to supply dollar (sterling, yen, mark, franc . . .) consideration on demand, or on other terms. An important transaction of this sort finds A committed to supply a quantity of marks capable of buying x pounds on the due date. And there are myriad options-like deals that effectively transform i-dollar into j-dollar liquidity.

Problem 30

30(a) At one level the problem is trivial: to the extent that crude-oil exporters are major 'Euro-dollar' holders, deterioration of their cash flow will impede growth of the stock of Euro-dollar holdings. Obviously!

At another level, the problem is fiendishly difficult. In financial markets the forces that shift demand curves cannot be separated from those shifting supply curves – thus blocking identification of the parameters of supply and demand functions and indeed clouding these concepts as distinct entities.

30(b) The problem merely hints (another pathetic fallacy!) at ways in which response to risk exposure may become internalized so that transformations are accomplished off market. A suggestive analogy concerns ways in which 'leads and lags' in international payments may contribute to volatility of foreign-exchange markets. British importers, owing 'dollars' to American exporters, will hasten to remit if they expect the dollar to appreciate; and will display what Mr Lincoln called 'the slows' if they expect the dollar to fall. In the actual problem, there are rich possibilities for changing parts-sources, plant locations, etc. And, obviously, the cost and indeed availability of cover in financial markets influences the extent to which cover will be internalized – along lines familiar to students of vertical-integration theory. For example, it is very difficult to hedge long-term risks in the financial markets (see McKinnon, 1979).

Problem 31

31(a) See especially Einzig (1970), McKinnon (1979) and Rivera-Batiz and Rivera-Batiz (1985, Chapter 3).

31(b) The substantial extent to which growth of the Euro-currency markets has been a response (often an evasive one) to regulation is clear from the references. Financial 'products' are now bought and sold globally; and there has been quite remarkable innovation of highly sophisticated techniques in data processing, communication, risk shifting, etc. The upshot is an amorphous market structure that cannot be identified in detail, let alone regulated. *Deregulation* is in many ways a misnomer now: there is little to regulate.

31(c) 'Petro-dollars' are funds accumulated, and being accumulated, by petroleum exporters that are intermediated by huge international banking institutions. Petro-dollar accumulation had its heyday when low-absorbing petroleum exporters, accumulating massive sums in the wake of the 1973 and 1979 oil shocks, lacked confidence in their portfolio-management skills.

Bibliographical Note

Mundell–Fleming theory is copiously discussed, and referenced, by Frenkel and Razin (1987).

Problems rooted in rational, or forward-looking, expectations are illuminated by Sheffrin (1983). And Problems **23–28** are parallel to a sometimes quite different discussion by Rivera-Batiz and Rivera-Batiz (1985, Chapter 15).

4 Lecture Four: Theory of Policy in Open Economies, With Applications

In a number of important instances, the lecture is overshadowed by problem annotations. The case method of instruction is prominent in this chapter.

4.1 THEORY OF POLICY IN THE TINBERGEN (1963) MODE

The canonical statical macro policy problem has the following form (eliding 'curvature' requirements and the like for the sake of rapid exposition):

$$\max U(x_1, x_2) \qquad \text{an indirect utility function} \tag{4.1}$$

subject to

$$x_1 = \phi\,(\alpha, \beta) \tag{4.2}$$

$$x_2 = \psi\,(\alpha, \beta) \tag{4.3}$$

National income may be symbolized by x_1; and the increase in foreign-asset holdings by x_2. Controls α and β may be public spending and the exchange rate. The problem is to choose a feasible vector (α, β) so that U () is maximized.

Interpolation

In a fixed foreign-exchange-rate régime, the exchange rate is readily acceptable as a control; but not in a floating-rate régime – at least not until the following 'trick' is performed. The 'trick' requires that 'physical' instruments be distinguished from notional ones. Thus, even if the exchange rate is decreed by Authority, as is the Bank Rate, the levels chosen for both *variables* may emerge from a formulation in which other economic magnitudes are mathematically predetermined, or otherwise parametrized – so that the Authorities' 'physical' control of the Bank Rate masks its mathematical endogeneity. The controlling concept, associated with Tinbergen (1963), is based on an underdetermined mathematical system; excess degrees of freedom are used to select criteria included in the objective function – so that 'physical' controls are transformed into endogenous variables. In the upshot, the criterion is maximized, or minimized, subject to the economic model or its reduced form (in which endogenous variables are described as functions of parameters).

It is easily shown that, in the solution

$$-\psi_\alpha U_2 = \phi_\alpha U_1 \tag{4.4}$$

$$-\psi_\beta U_2 = \phi_\beta U_1 \tag{4.5}$$

The loss resulting from switching a unit of α or β from promotion of X_2 is, in the solution, equal to the gain from the resulting increment in X_1.

4.1.1   An Application at a General Level

Indirectly define a criterion on variables (z, y, ξ), respectively symbolizing the rate of foreign asset accumulation (linked to the trade surplus), gross domestic product and the terms of trade. Variable z affects wealth and subsequent income from services of capital (human and non-human) sited abroad; cf.y'. In a Keynesian mode, y maps into the level of employment as well as availability of goods for present and future consumption. And ξ contributes to the living standard: higher terms of trade permit a unit of exports to exchange for more imported goods. The criterion is to be maximized, subject to the model's reduced form; the upshot is described in Table (4.1)

Remarks about Implications of Table 4.1

Studying variation in ξ, perceived instrumentally, better terms of trade are conventionally perceived to exercise a drag on aggregate output, but to have a positive partial effect on living standards; and

Table 4.1 Partial impacts of instruments on criteria

| Criterion | Instrument | | |
	α	ξ	
z	$(-)$	$(-)$	The signs display the impact of
			the instrument on the criterion
y	$(+)$	$(-)$	(more or less that of a partial
			derivative)
ξ	n.a.	$(+)$	

effects on foreign-asset accumulation are to be negative, since the familiar Marshall–Lerner condition (assumed to hold) assures that effects of exchange-appreciation on the trade balance are negative. As for the parameter, α, indexing the intensity of fiscal policy, the signs follow the standard Keynesian drill.

Stating the Problem More Formally

The criterion is maximized subject to the reduced form of a simple macroeconomic model as follows

$$\max U(z, y, \xi) \tag{4.6}$$

subject to

$$z = z(\alpha, \xi) \tag{4.7}$$

$$y = y(\alpha, \xi) \tag{4.8}$$

The Jacobian matrix (matrix of first-order partial derivatives) is:

$$J = \begin{bmatrix} (-) & (-) \\ (+) & (-) \end{bmatrix} \tag{4.9}$$

Consider the feasible region of the control space, supplying all admissible (α, ξ) combinations. By solving the system comprised of equations (4.7) and (4.8), we can map each (α, ξ) pair into a (z^*, y^*) pair. (We elide the details showing how the optimal feasible pair is discovered.)

The theory of policy, in the Tinbergen mode, boils down to properties of an underdetermined system of simultaneous equations.

Excess degrees of freedom are spent on choices of solution-values of at least some of the variables belonging to the criterion function.

4.1.2   An Application: *Homo Sapiens* vs Nature

Consider the properties of ecological equilibrium on an earth from which the species *homo sapiens* has been banished. An $\dot{x} = f(x)$ format would be quite proper: the motion of the system ($\dot{x}$) is a function of its state (vector x); $0 = f(\bar{x})$ represents an equilibrium state, a rest-point, and is a point of (locally or globally) stable equilibrium if it exerts attractive force so that, in a one-variable case, the upshot is described by Figure 4.1. The techniques and paradigms of physical science work nicely to this point. *Now* introduce *Man* (*homo sapiens*). The upshot is quite shattering. Man, in a supreme display of hubris, uses Nature's laws as a constraint set. Indeed, if utility is collectively discounted, human society might, at date t_0 choose an optimal(!) path calling for ecological ruin at date t_1.

The theory of economic policy entails exercise of *free will*; and so cannot be modelled purely deterministically. (Perhaps the most distinctive human quality is intense self-consciousness). And there is a near-lying corollary to the 'theorem'. Any equilibrium of a human process contains strategic (e.g. game-theoretic) components; 'equilibrium' macroeconomic features of the global economic complex are an outcome of strategic interplay; they cannot be represented by a sort of orrery.

4.1.3   Applications: A Specialized Paradigm; Extensions to Foreign-Asset-Accumulation Programmes – The Japan Problem

A Formal Problem Without Capital Flows

Consider the following simplistic system:

$$\max U(y, \xi) \tag{4.10}$$

subject to

$$y = \phi(A, \xi) \tag{4.11}$$

$$J(y, \xi) = X(\xi) \tag{4.12}$$

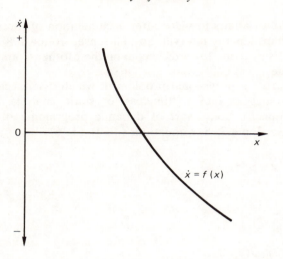

Figure 4.1   A stable differential equation

Public-sector expenditures on goods and services are symbolized by A; y and ξ represent gross domestic product and terms of trade *comme d'habitude*.

A Lagrangean is formed in the usual way. (This is trivial for the mathematically initiated, and too recondite for the uninitiated. So details are omitted.) The upshot boils down to equation (4.13), which can be interpreted so that its gist is accessible to all readers:

$$U_y/U_\xi = J_y/(J_\xi - X_\xi) \tag{4.13}$$

In the solution of a model with clear Keynesian content, the rate of substitution between output and terms of trade (U_y/U_ξ) equals the ratio:

> Rate at which the trade balance
> deteriorates as y increases
> ────────────────────────
> Rate at which the trade balance
> deteriorates as terms of trade improve

The Japan Problem

Recall from Lecture Two that the 'Mother Country' problem concerns a state of affairs in place after accumulation of foreign assets over a perhaps lengthy interval. So in a sense, from a 1988 perspective, Japan is evolving towards becoming the Mother Country of the United States.

We construct a provisional problem in which asset-accumulation strategy is suggested by a 'timeless' or static analysis. The true problem concerns some sort of dynamic programme of the sort limned in Section 4.2. See equations (4.14)–(4.16):

$$U = U(y, X_i, z) \tag{4.14}$$

subject to

$$y = \phi(A, \xi) \tag{4.15}$$

$$z = X(\xi) - J(y, \xi) \tag{4.16}$$

The rate of increase of foreign-asset holdings is represented by z. This problem ignores the cumulant of z, i.e. Z. A properly-dynamical paradigm centres on the cumulant, Z. See Section 4.2

Form the Lagrangean as before. In the upshot of setting partial derivatives equal to zero, equations (4.17) and (4.18) are obtained:

$$U_y + U_z J_y = 0 \tag{4.17}$$

$$U_\xi - U_z (J_\xi - X_\xi) = 0 \tag{4.18}$$

Equation (4.17) shows that, in the solution, the indirect marginal utility of gross domestic product is equal to the indirect marginal utility of foreign-asset accumulation multiplied by the rate at which such accumulation(z) declines (due to import-stimulus) as GDP(y) increases. Equation (4.18) shows that, in the solution, the indirect marginal utility of terms of trade is equal to the indirect marginal utility of foreign-asset accumulation (z) multiplied by the rate at which the trade balance changes with terms of trade . . . These propositions are illustrated by Figures 4.2a–c. Figure (4.2a) shows that the transformation rate between terms of trade and foreign-asset accumulation is equal to the rate of substitution between these variables in the indirect utility function. And Figures 4.2b and 4.2c make equivalent statements about the terms-of-trade/gross domestic product and gross domestic product/foreign asset-accumulation pairs.

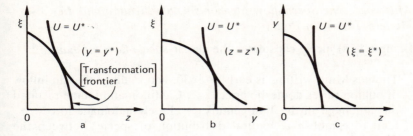

Figure 4.2a, b, c   Figures illustrating transformation relationships in the solution of the Japan Problem

By way of a preliminary interpretive remark, if 'production possibilities' are 'convex' enough *and* if the equivalent of 'free' expansion to scale is precluded (so that, for example, it becomes more difficult, *ceteris paribus*, to expand gross domestic product as it becomes larger), a given rate of asset accumulation may require declining terms of trade as time goes on. A diminishing-returns (or, better, variable-proportions) principle may prevail. Or, more simply, if Japan's income-growth were to be more buoyant than say that of other members of the Group of Ten over an extended interval, and if $\partial J/\partial y$ (i.e. J_y) is 'large', then terms of trade must persistently fall if a given asset-accumulation target-path is to be followed.

Obviously, the implicit dynamic programme is driven by *free will*; the governing theory is that of *choice*. And, of course, identical paradigms describe the other $n-1$ programmes. So *equilibrium cannot* be defined as the rest point of a deterministic $\dot{x} = f(x)$ scheme. And, indeed, any equilibrium must be a saddle point of an n-person game: n programmes must jibe so that no player gains advantage from altering his programme; so coherent a state suggests the sort of persistence belonging to the idea of equilibrium.

The 'Japan Problem' is amenable to common-sensical reflection. As asset accumulation runs ahead of *per capita* consumption, the rate of substitution between these variables (in political–economic/ geopolitical calculation) will increasingly favour consumption – an outcome reinforced by Japan's modest geopolitical pretensions (now). So an informal stability-outcome is easily obtained.

Afterword: The Specie-flow Mechanism, Sterilization and the Modern Theory of Policy

Blaug (1978) nicely capsulates the classic *specie-flow mechanism*:

> Thomas Mun, writing as early as 1630, had realized that an inflow of bullion raises domestic prices . . . Cantillon and Hume restated this argument in the 18th century . . . Purely automatic forces . . . tend to establish a 'natural distribution of specie' between the trading countries of the world . . . [E]xternal trade and gold are akin to water in two connected vessels that is constantly seeking a common level.

> Blaug (1978, p. 13)

The contrast with mercantilist thought is complete: there is simply no room for asset-accumulation policy in the classical paradigm, although Thornton and Mill clearly established the lineaments of the Bank Rate régime that came to the fore in the latter half of the 19th century: Bank Rate was manipulated to govern short-term capital flows (see Sayers, 1957). (The flows concerned exchanges of *devisen* and gold for securities.) So, in fact, classical and neoclassical economics contained conflicting strands of thought: the mechanistic Humean mechanism and the purposive control mechanism (Bank Rate) first perceived by Henry Thornton and elaborated on by J. S. Mill.

Keynes (1930, II) explains the *sterilization* episodes of the 1920s (finding France and the United States absorbing gold *and* shutting off inflationary consequences – through open-market sales of securities by the central bank, for example – with some asperity. The United States and France did not obey the rules of the specie-flow mechanism. But proper *mechanisms* do not depend on the Virtue of the particles putatively subject to their Laws! The moral-philosophical content of the correct analysis is ineradicable.

Keynes (1930, II) makes an important point that exercises powerful influence on his Bancor scheme, proposed for the post-war régime that in fact was shaped by the American (Harry Dexter White *et al.*) plan – i.e. the Bretton Woods system. Trade-imbalance, sustained over time, operates asymmetrically: sterilized specie inflows can be sustained indefinitely, but specie/reserve-asset outflows must be corrected if Ruin is to be averted. The burden of adjustment tends to be borne, for much the most part, by economies in external deficit; and indeed the IMF drill, calling for fiscal contraction, currency depreciation, etc. perfectly embodies the response-pattern Keynes deplored. The upshot is often characterized as a 'deflationary bias' of the adjustment mechanism – a locution that is less acceptable now that the Phillips Curve is discredited (i.e. the idea that there is a well-defined trade-off between real growth and inflation is discredited.)

Not that the general idea of a 'natural distribution of specie' must be totally abandoned: games have solutions! But the parametric format of the proper problem is very different from that of the mechanistic one: Nature controls transformation possibilities, but not the interaction of the players' strategic planning.

(Keynes's admiration of Silvio Gesell's stamped-money scheme, intended to discourage hoarding, is a precursor of his proposal to tax accumulations that are residues of persistent trade surpluses. See Keynes, 1936. pp. 353ff.)

4.2 DYNAMIC THEORY OF POLICY

4.2.1 Sketch of an Heuristic Argument

The problem is one in economic navigation. The ship has been blown off course; indeed it may now be desirable to sail for a different port. And a nice point concerning geometry is near-lying: it is especially inappropriate in navigational problems to confine one's self to plane geometry; the geometry of the surface of a sphere is so obviously pertinent. A rather compelling consideration is this. It is quite preposterous that a variable that has escaped from the attractive force of an equilibrium state should go to 'infinity' – as happens on the plane; on a sphere much more plausible disequilibrium motions can be modelled.

It is highly plausible that a loss function should describe consequences of being off course; and that the costs of regaining the 'equilibrium path' should be modelled in the way production costs are modelled. Figure 4.3 facilitates amplification of these remarks. A simple transformation of coordinates assigns the vector $(0, 0)$ to the 'equilibrium' or target values of consumption *per capita* and of foreign assets cum gold; variables ζ and v are accordingly *deviations* of actual and targeted positions – and can assume negative, as well as positive, values.

We require a loss function so that points in (v, ζ) space can be

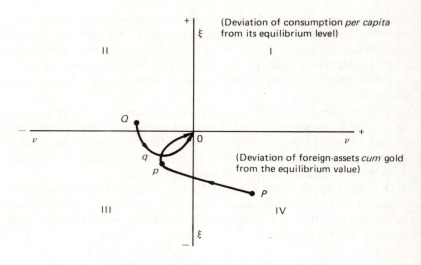

Figure 4.3   Dynamic adjustments in four quadrants

mapped into Loss (very crudely, disutility). But there is a rub. *Time* does not appear explicitly in a phase diagram like Figure (4.3). *And* total loss suffered on an off-course ('disequilibrium') interval depends not only on where one has been but also on how long one has been off · course: recovery may be attained through an excruciatingly painful *wrench* of the economy or by a gentle process of rehabilitation, accompanied by rest and recreation so to speak. Section 4.2.2 is able to be more explicit on this point.

Two Rehabilitatory Episodes

Starting at *P* (lying in Quadrant IV in Figure 4.3) the foreign-asset position is 'over full' but living standards are below their targeted (tacitly secularly feasible) norm. Look at the problem from the Government's standpoint, thus noting such comparatively recent developments as 'the economic theory of government' and public-choice theory: sometimes the most significant tussle is between the perceived self-interest of public 'servants' and the public interest as it may be perceived by the Great Engineer in the Sky. The next general election hinges on prompt recovery of living standards. And the mass of voters is aware of the foreign-asset position only when its insufficiency leads to harsh measures; furthermore, ample lines of central-bank swap credit are available, especially since our liquidity has been so ample for some time. So, as happened in Israel in Mr Begin's time, exchange controls might be released not long before the Election. Or the banks may be flooded with liquidity, leading to a massive expansion of domestic credit (see Lecture Nine), sucking in imports. Or taxes may be cut, perhaps accompanied by sharply increased public spending. There is time to correct resulting insufficiency of foreign-assets, starting at phase-point p; many economists would describe the path from p to $(0,0)$ as one along which fiscal policy is expansive and Bank Rate increases, perhaps substantially.

Of course, unalloyed concern for the Commonweal may map into the path from P to $(0, 0)$ just discussed.

Starting at Q (lying in Quadrant II in Figure 4.3), one readily constructs scenarios evoking the salad days of the gold standard, say from 1870 to 1914. (See Sayers, 1957 and Viner, 1937 among many distinguished discussions.) And the rôle of *time* is easily explained. At Q the reserve position is below par. And living standards are slightly above par: a consumption boom may have drained foreign reserves. The loss function is asymmetrical: typically thin reserve ratios make sustained reserve-outflow disastrously infeasible (Figure 4.3 displays reserve *stocks*); sub-par foreign-reserve holdings may threaten the viability of the state – then otherwise minor adverse developments may cause collapse; one is put in mind of one of the sounder defences of the mercantilist mind set. So time is of the essence! Bank rate is hiked dramatically; and bank liquidity may be rapidly drained off; and taxes may be sharply increased while public-sector expenditures are slashed. These draconian measures lead to a sharp contraction in consumption per head and, doubtless, in employment. (Since the real world 'policy space' is n-dimensional, the analysis is rigorously justifiable only if levels of employment – and, indeed, levels of all the variables not displayed in Figure 4.3 – are unchanged for the analysis.) However, if correction is accomplished rapidly, total loss over the correction-interval may be quite moderate – keeping in mind that deficiency in the foreign-reserve position so massively affects the loss function that policy-choice is very severely restricted.

Phase-point q represents a turning point (non-mathematically; from a mathematical point of view it may well be at a discontinuity). The foreign-asset position is sufficiently restored, and global confidence has been enough reestablished, so that, say, more expansionary fiscal policy becomes feasible.

Concluding Observations

1. Stability analysis looks like a red herring here. It seems inconceivable that the economic-policy authorities will do the equivalent to sailing from Spain to America when they mean to sail to Djibouti – although, on the sphere, they may well end up at Djibouti anyhow. Surely built-in corrective mechanisms (one thinks of retro-rocket systems of space-ships), are available. Of course, possibilities for policy-inefficiency are but drawings from an infinite world of negation.

2. The trade-off nexus is seriously distorted by a schema in which quantities are not *dated*. Thus an apparent trade-off between consumption and asset accumulation may well be one between consumption now and (more) consumption later.

3. For the sake of simplicity, targets have been defined as points, (x^*), in policy space. Properly, targets are defined as time-paths, not points (in finite spaces).

4. To repeat, purely mechanical models of the $\dot{x} = f(x)$ type must be viewed very sceptically indeed. Policy problems are *not* deterministic.

5. Again by way of probing more penetratingly into the meaning of stability analysis, shocks, blowing the economy off course, generate the equivalent to new sets of initial conditions – leading to reformulation of targets. Prolonged, severe drought may so undermine the agricultural economy that it becomes optimal to plan to industrialize more rapidly and widely.

6. In Lecture Five, the general ideas explored here will be reified in the context of admittedly rather simplistic, quite Keynesian models. Operational techniques will be better defined.

4.2.2 A More Rigorous Dynamic Analysis

The 'rigour' of the following material is to some extent specious: troublesome 'time inconsistency' problems are finessed. See Kydland and Prescott (1977); and Buiter (1980).

The 17th Century (John Bernoulli) Origins of the Analysis (See Allen, 1938, pp. 424ff.)

We alluded to the brachistochrone problem of John Bernoulli in Lecture Three. Indeed refer now to Figure 3.1. And let x represent an economy's foreign asset/gold position. The 'loss function' is particularly simple: elapsed time is to be minimized subject to the fixed end-points and the roughly parabolic properties of gravitational influence. Even this simplistic formulation contains an economically interesting property: the accumulation-path *overshoots*: asset-accumulation *exceeds* its target value on the optimal path leading to final achievement of the target value.

A Sketch of an Optimal Control Treatment of the Canonical Dynamic Problem

In words, a loss function is defined on all relevant states of the system; but loss is independent of calendar date or of the process's history. That is to say, a vector δ° of deviations from target values maps into a rate at which Loss is being generated, L°, invariantly against calendar date and how the system got to state δ°. The problem is to choose a path for vector δ that minimizes the integral (a limit sum), $\int f(t)dt$, where $f(t)$ defines the 'rate of loss' at instant $t = \tau$. So a *curve* is to be selected; a time-path is to be selected, from the set of admissible paths. Instead of selecting points, we select curves (containing infinities of points). In the general case, the time-interval on which correction is to occur is itself an endogenous variable: advantages of prompter correction are traded off against the more severe pain that may be incurred in accepting a more severe treatment – the terms of trade being defined by the structure of the model, so that the proper dynamic problem is isomorphic with the static one in that a criterion (think of utility) is maximized, or minimized, subject to the structure of the underlying model.

In optimal-control theory, variables are dichotomized as *state* variables and *control* variables. And 'the movement of state variables is governed by first order differential equations' (Kamien and Schwartz, 1981, p. 111). As for controls,

> The control u influences the objective, both directly (through its own value) and indirectly through its impact on the evolution of the state variable x.
>
> Kamien and Schwartz (1981, p. 112)

Continuing discussion of the isomorphism of the canonical statical and dynamical problems, the equivalent to the Lagrangean of the statical problem is a *Hamiltonian*. And the optimal-control problem generates multipliers like the Lagrange multipliers; the multipliers measure the contributions to the value of the solution of marginal relaxations of the constraints.

A Stylized Economic Example

Consider the following problem, drawn from a large population of more-or-less Keynesian schemes:

$$\int f(v, \theta)dt \tag{4.19}$$

subject to

$$\dot{v} = \dot{v}\,(R, G) \tag{4.20}$$

$$\dot{\theta} = \dot{\theta}\,(R, G) \tag{4.21}$$

(Other constraints are suppressed. And the controls, R and G, do not appear in the objective function of equation (4.19).)

Deviations from target values for gross domestic product and terms-of-trade values are denominated v and θ. The controls are public-sector expenditure (G) and Bank Rate (R). Equations (4.20) and (4.21) are differential equations, supplying the laws of motion of the state variables as functions of the control-levels; equations (4.20) and (4.21) constrain the problem.

We are to discover *paths* for the controls (G and R) that minimize the loss function. It is obvious that the proper paradigm excludes *assignment* of controls to state variables; and indeed common sense informs us that it must be inefficient to specialize so intrinsically general a problem.

A Better Specified Economic Example

Readers of a mathematical bent will benefit from a more concrete illustration, supplying a sense of the operational follow-up of the general paradigm; and clarifying the paradigm's properties. A production-planning problem, developed by Kamien and Schwartz (1981, pp. 137–8), is converted into a trade-balance-planning problem, leading to a target-level for foreign-asset holdings. Along 'neo-classical' lines, exporting is perceived to incur loss, made up for by the utility of the imports obtained for our exports; a more positive trade balance associates with *cost*. And foreign-asset holdings (tacitly assumed to take barren forms like gold, and so to conform to Adam Smith's *dead stock* idea) are to entail an inventory-holding cost. For the convenience of readers referring back to Kamien and Schwartz (an excellent idea!), their notation is preserved: $x(t)$ is the foreign-asset (inventory) level; $u(t)$ is the flow-rate of the trade-account (the production rate).

$$\int_0^T (c_1 u^2 + c_2 x) dt \qquad (4.22)$$

subject to

$$\dot{x}(t) = u(t); x(0) = 0; x(T) = B; u(t) \geqslant 0 \qquad (4.23)$$

Foreign-asset accumulation, starting from scratch, is to attain level B by T. The equivalent to interest-and-handling costs of inventory holding is c_2 – so that $c_2 x$ has the dimension of a flow; the equivalent to production cost – *i.e.* the rate at which cost is incurred in accumulating foreign assets (inventory) is, for our purposes, precariously stated as $c_1 u^2$.

Now form the Hamiltonian:

$$H = c_1 u^2 + c_2 x + u \qquad (4.24)$$

$$\partial H / \partial u = 2c_1 u + \lambda = 0 \qquad (4.25)$$

$$\lambda = -\partial H / \partial x = -c_2 \qquad (4.26)$$

The solution of this simplified problem is reached quite easily. Thus λ is obtained by integrating equation (4.26); cf. $\lambda(t) = -c_2 t + a$ *constant of integration*. Substitute this value for λ into equation (4.25), obtaining a solution for $u(t)$. Substitute for u in equation (4.23). Then integrate; and use the boundary conditions to obtain the two constants of integration. We obtain:

$$x(t) = c_2 t(t-T)/4c_1 + Bt/T \qquad (4.27)$$

$$u(t) = c_2(2t-T)/4c_1 + B/T \qquad (4.28)$$

$$\lambda(t) = c_2 T/2 - 2c_1 B/T - c_2 t \qquad \text{(so the price of the constraint falls over time)} \quad (4.29)$$

(The problem set, immediately following, will both solidify and deepen understanding of the analysis of the lecture, while communicating better with what may be standard treatments of open-economy dynamic-policy theory.)

An Annotated Problem Set For Lecture Four

PROBLEMS

Problems **32**, **33** and **34** are based on the following scheme, developed in Lecture Four:

$$\max U = U(y,z,\xi) \quad z = X - J \qquad (4.30)$$
$$\xi = \text{terms of trade (mediated by the exchange rate)}$$

subject to

$$y = y(\alpha,\tau,\xi) \qquad (4.31)$$
$$\alpha = \text{public-sector expenditure}$$
$$z = z(\alpha,\tau,\xi) \quad \tau = \text{tax-severity index} \qquad (4.32)$$

32. Take $\xi = \xi^*$ and $\tau = \tau^*$ so that the available control is α. Then it is:

- **(a)** possible to attain the selected position (y^*, z^*) by varying α;
- **(B)** possible to attain y^*, accepting the emergent value for z by varying α;
- **(c)** not possible to attain z^*, accepting the emergent value for y, by varying α;
- **(d)** all of the above choices are correct;
- **(e)** none of the above choices is correct.

33. Choose the correct statement:

- **(A)** variation of $\xi - \alpha$ and τ fixed – pushes y and z in the same direction;
- **(b)** variation of $\alpha - \xi$ and τ fixed – pushes y and z in the same direction;

89

(c) if α, ξ and τ are free to vary, y and z must be pushed in the same direction;

34. Choose the correct statement:

(a) if the tax rate is cut, capital inflow increases;
(B) if government spending is cut, capital outflow increases;
(c) if ξ is cut, the standard of living will rise since $\partial \bar{y}/\partial \xi = (+)$;
(d) all of the above choices are correct;
(e) none of the above choices is correct.

35. Choose the correct statement:

(a) the text emphasizes that fiscal policy should be assigned exclusive responsibility for a dynamic reserve-accumulation programme, while monetary policy ought to be assigned to inflation fighting;
(B) 'assignment' of cash balances to transactions, precautionary and store-of-value rôles is invalid in the way that the concept of exclusive target assignment is invalid;
(c) the assignment problem pertains to equilibrium states, but not to the dynamics of disequilibrium states;
(d) all of the above choices are correct;
(e) none of the above choices is correct.

36. Choose the correct statement:

(a) at P in Figure 4.4, GDP(y) is maximized;
(b) if government spending is increased, both curves shift rightward;
(c) the most effective way to bring about currency appreciation is to make fiscal policy more expansive – in contrast with the 'full employment' case;
(d) all of the above choices are correct;
(E) none of the above choices is correct.

37. (This problem is also controlled by Figure 4.4.) If the target value for z (to be interpreted as 'change in foreign assets') increases:

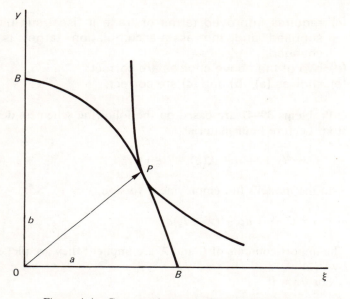

Figure 4.4   Construction controlling Problem 36

1. In the proper problem, the objective function contains $Z_t = \int z\,(t)\,dt$ as an argument.
2. The vector (a, b) yields more 'z' than does $\overrightarrow{OP}$.
3. We must know the solution in advance to deploy the figure: the z value parametric for the indifference map in this space is that yielded at P. Figure 4.4. is merely illustrative.

    (a) the pay-off described by $U(\cdot)$ increases because of changes in each of y, ξ and z;
    (b) consumption may fall despite increased Gross Domestic Product;
    (c) as time elapses, worse terms of trade may have to be accepted to sustain a given trade surplus;
    (D) two of the above choices are correct;
    (e) choices **(a)**, **(b)** and **(c)** are correct.

38. The solution of the problem controlling Problems **36** and **37**:

    (A) entails growth of foreign assets if $\bar{z}$ is positive;
    (b) must be efficient relative to the proper dynamic problem, not displayed here;

(c) requires improved terms of trade if fiscal stimulus is supplied and the asset-accumulation target is unchanged;
(d) two of the above choices are correct;
(e) choices **(a)**, **(b)** and **(c)** are correct.

Problems **39–41** are based on the following schemes, derived from Lecture Four material:

$$y = C(y,\tau) + \alpha + X(\xi) - J(\xi,y) \tag{4.33}$$

In the model's full-employment version, $y = y^*$. So:

$$0 = C_\tau d\tau + d\alpha + (X_\xi - J_\xi)d\xi \tag{4.34}$$

The import-contents of C and X are implicit; they are picked up by 'J'.
For $d\tau = 0$,

$$(-)d\alpha = (+)d\xi; \; d\xi/d\alpha = (-) \tag{4.35}$$

For $d\xi = (-)$, tax-intensity must increase. And living standards fall as the trade account improves. Indeed, for a given negative change in terms of trade, the more elastic is demand for our exports, the more living standards must fall.
In the less-than-full employment version:

$$(1-C_y+J_y)dy = d\alpha + C_\tau d\tau + (X_\xi - J_\xi)d\xi \tag{4.36}$$

$$dy/d\alpha_{d\tau=d\xi=0} = 1/(1-C_y+J_y) \tag{4.37}$$

The foreign balance deteriorates: imports increase with income. So, if wealth is to be kept intact and stimulus to output sustained, it may be necessary to depreciate the currency when autonomous spending increases.
Now consider currency depreciation $[d(\xi) = (-)]$. The upshot is the same as in the scenario just examined. Living standards may fall if the increase in exports exceeds $(dy + dJ)$, noting that imports may *fall*.
The reader should manipulate the scheme further: e.g. consider combinations entailing changes in 'tax-intensity'.

The analysis explains consumer-goods booms following tax-cuts. Thus, if American trade deficits are to shrink, or be replaced by surpluses in a reformed global equilibrium, American living standards may fall: the United States would then be stimulated in the way that defeated powers are by reparations burdens!

39. In the *full-employment* version of the model, if our currency is depreciated $[d\xi = (-)]$:

    (A) living standards fall;
    (b) foreign-asset accumulation falls;
    (c) living standards increase more if demand for our exports is price elastic;
    (d) all of the above choices are correct;
    (e) none of the above choices is correct.

40. Which of the following are correct implications of the model?:

    (a) persistent American trade deficits in recent years have been at the expense of American living standards;
    (b) a process in which the American trade account turns positive and the Japanese one negative resembles the one governing successful French discharge of the reparations burden imposed by Prussia in 1870;
    (c) in the *less-than-full-employment* version of the model, if wealth is to be kept intact while fiscal policy stimulus is sustained, it may be necessary to depreciate the currency;
    (d) in the *less-than-full-employment* version of the model, fiscal stimulus, accompanied by currency depreciation, may lead to higher living standards in the long run;
    (E) three of the above choices are correct.

41. Choose the correct statement:

    (a) in the *full-employment* version of the model, $d\tau/d\xi = (-)$;
    (b) in the *less-than-full-employment* version of the model $dy/d\alpha = 0$ unless, at the same time, $d\tau = 0$;
    (c) fiscal contraction, accompanied by currency deprecia-

tion, may lead to higher living standards in the long run;
  (D) two of the above choices are correct;
  (e) none of the above choices is correct.

42. Choose the correct statement:

  (A) if we wish to increase our holdings of foreign assets, valued in a foreign measure, by a given amount, the process will be 'cheaper' if demand for our exports and our demand for imports are elastic;
  (b) the New York stock market receives stimulus if the US dollar is falling and elasticities of expectation are strongly positive;
  (c) the chief aim of the crawling peg is to encourage speculative activity, noting that speculation is normally stabilizing;
  (d) two of the above choices are correct;
  (e) choices **(a)**, **(b)** and **(c)** are correct.

43. If the target value for the rate at which foreign assets are being accumulated is reduced:

  (a) consumption may increase even if GDP decreases;
  (b) as time goes on, improving terms of trade may be consistent with the new target;
  (c) the pay-off $[U(\cdot)]$ in the model prefacing Problems **39–41** is unaffected, since it responds only to current consumption;
  (D) two of the above choices are correct;
  (e) none of the above choices is correct.

Problems **44** and **45** are linked to the following application of Lecture Four's précis of the theory of open-economy policy dynamics.

As for *assignment* of instruments to targets, distinguish properties of efficient assignment of instruments to equilibrium-value targets from efficient assignments in navigational problems in which indeed an inefficient assignment may direct the ship *away* from port. (Figure 4.4, controlling Problem **36**, illustrates the 'static' case.) But the statical and dynamical paradigms are linked. Thus consider all instrument-paths, $[f(t)]$ permitting the economy to regain the targeted constellation x^*. The path $f^*(t)$ maximizes the functional $U = h\{t\}$.

The notion that, in the general case, instruments should be assigned to pieces of problems – that, for example, the fiscal instrument should be assigned to internal balance and the monetary instrument to external balance – is analytically improper. The proper problem requires choice of a time-path of a set of instruments that maps into a time-path of targeted variables. 'Corner solutions' will be rare: *how* can it be proper to ignore effects of interest rates on the internal balance; or of fiscal policy on the external balance? Optimal feasible solutions generally call for 'mixed' strategies.

Returning to the proper dynamical problem, once initial conditions (here properties of the initial displacement) are specified, the corresponding optimal control problem entails fixed endpoints in the phase space; together with freedom of choice of the time interval over which the correction is to evolve; in general, more rapid correction entails costs.

The more or less conventional dynamical theory of openeconomy policy, however flawed, is to be explained.

The targeted values for, say, the growth rate of GDP and the proportion borne by the trade deficit to GDP associate with a counterpart control path; controls may be 'the' interest rate and the tax/spending policy of the public sector (fiscal policy). Now say that the economy has been blown off course; and is to be put back on course by manipulation of the controls. It is useful to transform variables so that the origin, in control space, represents normal values of the controls and (r, a) deviations of the monetary and fiscal controls from that norm. Of course, the transformed control variables can assume negative values.

Next a taxonomy is constructed. If the economy is off target, aggregate demand may be overheated or cooled off; the trade balance may be more positive, or more negative, than its targeted position. Possible outcomes are described by the vectors

$(+,+)$ (1)
$(-,+)$ (2)
$(+,-)$ (3)
$(-,-)$ (4)

A single illustration illuminates the schema. In State 2 $(-,+)$ the economy is cooled off below targeted temperature and the trade balance is too positive.

Typically flawed dynamic paradigms assign each control to one target variable; optimal assignment is said to be determined by relative strengths of impacts of instruments on targets. If fiscal policy is assigned to internal balance, then, in the State 1 $(+,+)$ case, fiscal policy becomes contractive so that the internal economy will cool off. And there is a positive direct effect on the trade balance. (In the conventional model, interest rates are stipulated to be controlled.) Assuming that fiscal actions exert greater force on internal than on external states, the upshot, so far, is described in the following way:

$$\downarrow, \uparrow$$
$$. \quad (+,+)$$

And monetary policy will be relaxed (say, Bank Rate is cut) in order to discourage capital inflow; and *expansive* effects on aggregate demand, partially offsetting those of fiscal contraction, will encourage imports.

Some remarks on Bank Rate and capital (out)inflow are called for at this point. The lecture shows that *terms of trade* comprise a criterion for an indirect utility function; and, under floating rates, are instrumental *via* the exchange rates. The problem set concerns fixed-rate régimes in which price behaviour affects terms of trade and in which the immediate criterion for monetary authorities concerns *foreign assets*. So far we have imitated behaviour of the *ante-bellum* gold standard under which British Bank Rate was sensitized to the Bank of England's reserve position. (See Sayers, 1957.) Here monetary policy is defined by a Bank Rate mode; and trade-balance effects of monetary actions are not prominent in the immediate field of vision of the Authorities: effects of monetary policy on the trade balance are mediated by effects on aggregate demand for goods and services, effects weaker than those of concomitant fiscal policy pushing in the opposite direction; the state of the trade balance stands proxy for change in the net foreign asset position (cf. capital inflow).

(In a monetary-aggregate mode of monetary policy, effects on prices and the trade account of changes in monetary growth are emphasized. But monetarists readily concede that such effects are subject to complex, erratic, long lags. The Bank Rate mode is much more plausible here.)

The effects of a cut in Bank Rate are as follows:

↑ ↓
(+,+)

Lock in the stipulation that fiscal policy has relatively greater impact on internal balance and monetary policy on external balance; and that fiscal policy is targeted on the internal and monetary policy on the external balance; and go on to assess the remaining categories of the taxonomy. But we first insert an interpolation concerning a necessary revision of the accounting scheme.

An Interpolation Concerning a Revision of the Accounting Scheme

It is no longer possible to elide perplexes based on *official transactions*. Thus *A*'s trade balance may be *nil*. But massive sales of *A* government debt held by foreigners may occur, proceeds being directed towards foreign currencies, so that *A*'s central bank, defending the *A*-dollar, must reduce its foreign assets and gold *pari passu*. The asset sales by *A*'s central bank are enregistered in the same column as capital inflow proper, so that substantial capital outflow is offset by reductions in official assets; and is quite consistent with a nil *A* trade balance. To repeat, reserve/foreign asset flows are critical for the dynamic paradigm. (A negative trade balance may discourage capital inflow, so that Bank Rate must be hiked in order to attract reluctant foreign capital before the Bank is drained of its gold/hard currency reserves.) Finally the time scale of the paradigm is contracted. Fragile central-bank reserve-positions may collapse long before trade imbalance can be corrected; reserve outflow often must be staunched within weeks, sometimes days.

The Paradigm Completed: The Remaining Possible States

↑ ↓	↑ ↓	
(−,+)	(−,+)	(2)
↓ ↑	↓ ↑	
(+,−)	(+,−)	(3)
↑ ↓	↓ ↑	
(−,−)	(−,−)	(4)

Fiscal-policy   Monetary policy

Common sense confirms the arrows' implications: when instruments are exclusively assigned to the targets they most affect, convergence is promoted, however inefficiently. Now examine effects of an assignment reversal.

The Results of an Assignment Reversal

$$\overset{\uparrow\ \ \downarrow}{(+,+)} \qquad \overset{\downarrow\ \ \uparrow}{(+,+)} \qquad (1)$$ An unstable outcome (unstable=non convergent)

$$\overset{\uparrow\ \ \downarrow}{(-,+)} \qquad \overset{\uparrow\ \ \downarrow}{(-,+)} \qquad (2)$$ A stable outcome (stable=convergent)

$$\overset{\downarrow\ \ \uparrow}{(+,-)} \qquad \overset{\downarrow\ \ \uparrow}{(+,-)} \qquad (3)$$ A stable outcome

$$\overset{\downarrow\ \ \uparrow}{(-,-)} \qquad \overset{\uparrow\ \ \downarrow}{(-,-)} \qquad (4)$$ An unstable outcome

The outcome of assignment-reversal is described by the phase diagram in Figure 4.5.

The system's phase state must be eventually sent into an 'unstable' quadrant. The flawed control system leads to non-convergence. Of course, save for irrefragible blockheadedness, the scheme will be revised as its unsoundness becomes evident.

44. If monetary policy operates more powerfully on external than on internal balance, and vice versa for fiscal policy:

   (a) the instruction, 'interest rate policy is to promote external balance and fiscal policy internal balance', works except in the $(+,-)$ case;

   (B) the instruction, 'interest rate policy is to promote internal balance and fiscal policy external balance', leads to non-convergence;

   (c) in the $(+,+)$ state, the instruction of choice **(b)** leads to net stimulus to aggregate demand and to gold outflow;

   (d) all of the above choices are correct;

   (e) none of the above choices is correct.

45. Choose the correct statement:

   (a) many economists, following Mundell, suggest the assignment rule, 'give each target to the authority whose

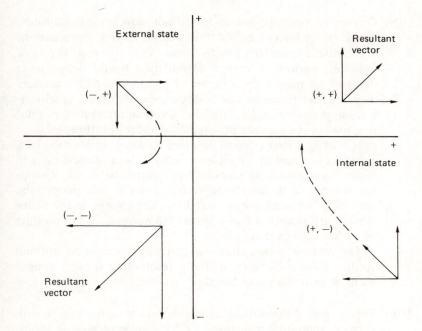

External state

Resultant vector

$(-, +)$

$(+, +)$

$-$ $+$

Internal state

$(-, -)$

$(+, -)$

Resultant vector

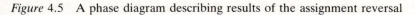

Figure 4.5   A phase diagram describing results of the assignment reversal

instrument has the relatively greater influence on it';

(b) the author argues that correct assignment rules do not assign instruments exclusively to targets, but instead deploy 'mixed strategies';

(c) the *immediate* outcome of the wrong instruction in the $(+,-)$ case is for the economy to cool off and foreign-asset leakage to reverse itself or at least to dry up;

(D) all of the above choices are correct;

(e) none of the above choices is correct.

FURTHER ANNOTATIONS

Problem 35

35(a) This choice is false of course, as has been elaborately demonstrated.

35(b) Obviously, portfolio managers do not stow their certificates, notes, etc. in boxes labelled 'transactions motive', 'precautionary motive', 'speculative motive', etc.! One observes, say, *cash balances*, period. A correct formulation would define, say, demand for money on a vector of parameters β. Parameters measure such things as availability of bridge finance, synchronization of payments and receipts, levels of interest rates relative to expectations about, say, short rates in future, etc.

It is at best imprecise to describe a change in planned cash balances incident to a shift in expectations of interest rates in future as a change in planned 'speculative balances'. Complementarity is obviously pervasive: even if one adopts the simplistic 'separate boxes' paradigm, any change in the quantity of cash stored in Box i affects the marginal value product of cash stored in Box j. Etc.

The lecture shows that the correctly formulated optimal control format eschews anything resembling explicit assignment of instruments to targets.

35(c) False! Indeed the more challenging aspect of the theory concerns navigational principles, i.e. principles governing choice of the optimal path from a displaced initial state of the system to the target path. A loss function is defined on each state of the system. Each correction-path is associated with an integral measuring total loss on the adjustment interval. Etc.

Problem 36

The problem is obviously closely based on the lecture.

36(a) The criterion includes terms of trade as well as GDP. Thus, for $y = y^*$, better terms of trade permit higher levels of consumption. Or, if $y^{**} > y^*$ associates with substantially lower terms of trade, living standards may fall if the initial foreign-asset accumulation target is sustained.

36(b) In the theory of economic choice transformation-functions are sharply separated from utility functions. Preferences are independent of transformation-possibilities.

36(c) If fiscal policy becomes more stimulatory, worse terms of trade must be accepted if the rate at which foreign assets are being acquired is to stay intact.

Problem 37

37(a) *Trade-offs* are intrinsic to any problem concerning maximization subject to constraint. Trade-offs are incident to the *closure* imposed on any proper problem in economic calculus.

37(b) This result is especially important. In general, more rapid accumulation of foreign assets requires that absorption by consumption, investment and public-sector expenditure on goods and services decrease, at least relatively. The possibility that living standards will improve less rapidly, or decline, becomes quite obvious.

37(c) If our growth rate exceeds the global one, there will be continuous pressure against the foreign-asset-accumulation target: our demand for imports is then more buoyant than others' demand for imports. The terms of trade may decline over time.

Problem 38

38(A) The choice (correct of course) emphasizes that the evolution of economic variables should often be portrayed in a setting of *n*-person game theory – not as an outcome *determined* by a set of initial conditions plugged into a 'natural' differential-equation system. The evolution of economic data reflects exercise of will: our 'Japan Problem' supplies an example: the path of accumulation of foreign assets by the Japanese economy is not simply a working-out of Nature's laws, however complex such laws may be; rather it is established by *motivation* – subject to 'technological' constraint.

This book does not develop the dynamic programming techniques required for correct analysis of paths 'established by motivation' and subject to technological constraint.

38(c) See choice **37(c)**.

Problem 42

42(a) High elasticity implies that a small change in terms of trade (say a small depreciation of our currency) leads to a large increase in the trade balance. Foreigners must sell assets in order to finance their trade deficit with us; we acquire these assets.

42(b) If elasticities of expectation are strongly positive, anticipation of capital loss offsets lures supplied by running yield and prospects of exchange-rate appreciation.

42(c) The 'speculation is normally stabilizing' remark trails a red herring. As for the *crawling peg*, see Williamson (1981) and Blejer and Leiderman (1981). Rivera-Batiz and Rivera-Batiz (1985, pp. 545–7) supply a useful précis. The aim of a crawling-peg system is to weaken the thrust of speculation by making it easier to forecast the path of exchange rates. But the following *caveat* applies. Recalling vast forward sales by 'speculators' of currencies propped up by central-bank support operations in the Bretton Woods régime, support operations in which central banks look programmed to let the air out of the j-dollar balloon slowly over a fairly-long interval offer the same sort of lure to 'speculators' as did the more-simplistic Bretton Woods prodecure. (I am indebted to Mr Joel Polan in this connection.)

Problem 43

This problem comprises a reprise of lecture material covered by Problems **36–38** and illustrated by Figure 4.4.

5 Lecture Five: Some Typically Keynesian Exercises in Open-economy Modelling

5.1 PRELIMINARY REMARKS

In classical or neoclassical models of the open economy, flows of goods and funds across frontiers are modulated by terms-of-trade effects and by differences in nominal and real interest rates. There is surely no formal classical treatment of effects of changes in Economy E's aggregate income and output on its balance of payments. The burden of adjustment is borne by prices, not quantities. Purely Keynesian models invert the analysis: the adjustment-burden is borne by changes in aggregate income and output: price-adjustment may even be ignored.

Interpolation

Recall from Lecture Two that Keynes (1936) pointed out that small open economies should not be modelled along what came to be known as Keynesian lines! Wage flexibility permits an indefinite amount of labour to be absorbed by the export sector and by import substitution – albeit perhaps at immiserating wages. So the economies modelled in Lecture Five must be large enough for the elasticity of demand for the jth economy's exports to be bounded.

* * *

A number of Keynesian schemae are developed, extending the policy-theoretic material of Lecture Four and introducing quite serious, if ageing, stability analysis. This Lecture's concluding segment exemplifies the Keynesian/neoclassical synthesis that still exercises influence via 'ISLM' and its extensions.

5.2   AN ESPECIALLY CRUDE KEYNESIAN MODEL AND ITS MATRIX EXTENSIONS

On the plane of economic theory, regional and 'international' modelling are not distinguishable. And regional multipliers are notably small; leakages are notably large; think of Metropolitan Toronto and the *large* import content of its bill of final goods. These remarks are picked up in the continuing discussion of equations (5.1) and (5.2) below.

The crude model, spanned by equations (5.1) and (5.2), is sometimes taken very seriously; it is said that economic growth may be keyed quite strictly to exports – cf. export-led growth.

$$y = A + f(y, r) + X^\circ - J(y) \tag{5.1}$$

$$X^\circ = J(y) \tag{5.2}$$

Capital flows are excluded from the recursive system. Solve equation (5.2) for $\bar{y}$: $X^\circ = \int_0^{\bar{y}} [1/J'(y)]dy$. The solution value of $\bar{y}$ is thus indirectly revealed. For a linear import/income relation – say for a propensity to import of $\alpha - \bar{y} = (1/\alpha)X^\circ$. The multiplier on exports is valued at $(1/J'(y))$; the 'investment multiplier – the multiplier on autonomous expenditure – is *nil*. (The solution value for r (i.e. $\bar{r}$) is obtained by simply plugging $\bar{y}$ into equation (5.1).)

Some sense of relative magnitudes in a small open economy (including a metropolitan area) is supplied by the following hypothetically quantified version of equation (5.1). See equation (5.3).

$$440 = 40 + 400 + 800 - 800 \tag{5.3}$$

The value of finished goods is 1,240. The import content of this bill is about 67 cents in the dollar (67 pence in the pound). And, pro rata, exporting supplies two thirds of the economy's jobs.

The upshot of this analysis of very open economies for tariff policy is quite substantial, and has often been cited by the late Harry Johnson and others in connection with obstacles to third-world development. A 10% *ad valorem* tariff on the exports of the above economy amounts to about a 30% *ad valorem* tariff on *value added* by the economy.

A Matrix Extension of the Analysis

Notational conventions are established quite easily.

$a_i y_i$ = importation by the ith economy
$a_{12} y_2$ = the second economy's imports from the first (the first's exports to the second); a_{12} is the propensity of the second economy to import from the first

(In a fuller analysis, the impact of terms of trade on the a_{ij} terms would be probed.)

The system of equations of equation (5.4) is merely an n-economy version of equation (5.2), i.e. the requirement that trade balances be nil (in aggregate; it is *not* required that trade flows between any two nodes be balanced). The canonical form of equation (5.4) is $Ay = 0$. And an interesting conflation of mathematics and economics becomes immediately important.

> If $Ax = 0$ is a system of m homogeneous equations in n variables where A is a given matrix of order $m \times n$ and rank r, then the condition for a non-zero solution of x is that $r < n$ . . . If $m = n$ [as in equation (5.4)], there is a solution if A is singular.
>
> Allen (1963, p. 455)

> The matrix A of order $m \times n$ has rank r if at least one of the sub-matrices of order $r \times r$ has a non-zero determinant and if all square sub-matrices of higher order have zero determinants.
>
> Allen (1963, p. 437)

Economic reasoning establishes that the determinant of A is zero; and that a $(n\text{-}1) \times (n\text{-}1)$ sub-matrix has a non-zero determinant. Thus, if n-1 trade balances are nil, the nth must be nil: the construction possesses a zero-sum property. And further mathematical analysis establishes that the system of equation (5.4) can be solved to a factor of proportionality. 'When $r < n$, there are "surplus" variables which cause no trouble, once they are assigned arbitrary values and the r selected variables found in terms of them' (Allen, 1963, p. 459). Here there is *one* surplus value; we may normalize on say y_1, that is solve for $(\bar{y}_i/y_1^0)$. And it is easy to establish that, for a positive change in a propensity to import from the ith economy, *ceteris paribus*, $d\bar{y}_i > 0$;

and that, indeed, there is no other source for a positive change in $\bar{y}_i$. The matrix-based problem is isomorphic to the simplistic single-economy treatment of equations (5.1) and (5.2):

$$a_1 y_1 - a_{12} y_2 - \ldots - a_{1_n} y_n = 0$$

$$-a_{21} y_1 + a_2 y_2 - \ldots - a_{2n} y_n = 0 \tag{5.4}$$

$$\ldots \ldots \ldots \ldots \ldots$$

$$-a_{n1} y_1 - a_{n2} y_2 - \ldots + a_n y_n = 0$$

5.3   A MORE INTERESTING MODEL WITH A KEYNESIAN COMPLEXION

This model, spanned by equations (5.5) and (5.6), also requires nil trade balances, thus eliding capital flows. (Of course, in a longer run, trade imbalances are quite constrained – admittedly short of the severe constraint of the model under study.)

$$y = A + f(y) + X(\alpha, \xi) - J(y, \xi) \tag{5.5}$$

$$X(\ ) = J(\ ) \tag{5.6}$$

(Terms of trade and preference for our exports are symbolized by ξ and α.)

The model is recursive. Substitute equation (5.6) into equation (5.5) so that we solve for $\bar{y} = A + f(y)$. There results the *closed system* multiplier. After plugging $\bar{y}$ into equation (5.6), 'equilibrium' terms of trade are discovered.

The embedded policy-choice problem is easy to perceive. The system's reduced form, mapping solution sets of endogenous variables from parameter-value sets, displays feasible $(A, \bar{\xi})$ combinations. Stimulus to aggregate demand supplied by more expansive fiscal policy must be accompanied by worse terms of trade so that stimulus to imports from higher income is offset by the negative effect on imports and positive effect on exports of lower terms of trade.

Generalization to Explicit Treatment of n Economies

The generalization of the model leads to a quite intriguing game-theoretic interpretation.

$$X^1(\xi;\gamma) = J^1(\xi;\gamma)$$

. . . . (5.7)

$$X^n(\xi;\gamma) = J^n(\xi,\gamma)$$

vector $\xi = (\xi_1, \ldots, \xi_n)$

vector $\gamma = (A_1, \ldots, A_n)$

For $\gamma = \gamma^*$, the vector of controls (each player having one control), a solution vector $(1,\bar{\bar{\xi}}_2, \ldots \bar{\bar{\xi}}_n)$ emerges – normalizing on ξ_1 after noting that there cannot be more than n-1 independent equations in the n-equation (5.7) system: since the nth trade-account surplus equals the sum of the other n-1 trade deficits, satisfaction of n-1 equations implies satisfaction of the nth. (It is best to elide the 'law of one price' whenever possible – a 'law' that is both absurd as a practical matter and powerful in its impact on putative outcomes.)

In a Cournot–Nash format, where the controls are γ, for $(A_2^*, \ldots, A_n^*)$, the first economy solves for $\bar{A}_1$ (so that, indeed, 'controls' become endogenous) relative to terms of trade emerging from any choice for A_1. Similarly for the second economy. Etc. Equilibrium requires that each element of γ be optimal relative to the other elements (e.g. $(A_2, \ldots, A_n)$.) Or, more satisfactorily, we may search for a non-empty core of a problem – i. e. for a set of imputations (pay-offs registered on the players' 'utility' functions) possessing a sort of inner stability in that it is in the interest of no player to join a new coalition.

The players do not cooperate. And cooperation would improve the outcome. Why is the game non-cooperative? In some ways that is the central Keynesian query. *Why* cannot the players discover the core of the *true* collective problem? Why do they operate in a restricted choice space?

(Problems **39–41**, attached to Lecture Four, are conceived and annotated in a Keynesian mode. They are profitably reviewed at this point.)

5.4 A TWO-ECONOMY PROBLEM IN A KEYNESIAN MODE: 'THE CANADA/UNITED STATES PROBLEM'

The following stylized data are suggestive for the Canada/United States economic nexus. The data are schematically displayed as follows

	United States	Canada
Income	1,000	100
Autonomous expenditure	1,200	120
Policy-switch variable (initially *nil*)	a_1	a_2
Sensitivity to interest rates(s)	$-0.3r$	$-0.03r$
Sensitivity of J_i to the foreign-exchange-rate index	-0.2ξ	$+0.3\xi$

Remarks

Initial solution values for the indices are $(\bar{\xi}, \bar{r}) = (0, 666)$. The systemic determinant is 0.033. And the foreign-exchange-rate index measures the amount of American currency purchased by a unit of Canadian currency.

Equations (5.8) – (5.11) model the system:

US $\qquad\qquad 1,000 = 1,200 + 0.1\xi - 0.3r + a_1 \qquad\qquad$ (5.8)

Canada $\qquad\quad 100 = \qquad 120 - 0.1\xi - 0.03r + a_2 \qquad\quad$ (5.9)

US $\qquad\qquad 0.3dr - 0.1d\xi = da_1 \qquad\qquad\qquad$ (5.10)

Canada $\qquad 0.03dr + 0.1d\xi = da_2 \qquad\qquad\qquad$ (5.11)

Exercise One $\quad da_1 = 0; \; da_2 = 10$

There is no switch in American policy; Canadian public expenditure increases by 10 units. In the new solution: the foreign-exchange-rate *index* increases by 90.1 from an initial nil value; the real interest rate index increases by 30.3 units – in ratio form, the increase is 30.3/666.

Exercise Two $\quad da_1 = 100; \; da_2 = 0$

The effect on the exchange-rate index is:

$$\begin{bmatrix} 0.3 & 100 \\ 0.03 & 0 \end{bmatrix} / (0.033) = -90.1 \qquad\qquad (5.12)$$

A 100 unit increase in American public spending has the same effect on the foreign-exchange-rate index as a 10 unit increase in Canadian public spending, allowing for sign. This outcome is easily explained in the following way. American and Canadian imports (exports) are to change by the same absolute amount; and Canadian imports from the United States (in this two-economy model) are ten times larger, relative to Canadian income, than American imports, relative to American income.

The 100 unit increase in American public spending leads to a 303 unit increase in the (real) interest rate index. A dollar of public expenditure has the same effect on the common real interest rate, no matter who spends it. The absolute value of the American public-spending change is ten times that of the Canadian one – while relative changes are the same.

Implications for Canadian Policy (Carrying Implications for Small-open-economy Policy en général)

The problem is controlled by a tacit stipulation that Canadian monetary policy cannot influence real interest rates; nor, indeed, does it preclude the attractive stipulation that the Federal Reserve cannot do so either! As for fiscal policy, interest rates relevant for Canadians are more influenced by American than by Canadian fiscal policy – assuming, reasonably enough, that changes in American fiscal magnitudes are apt to be much larger, absolutely, than changes in Canadian fiscal magnitudes. But changes in Canadian fiscal policy get multiplied up, so to speak, by the massive importance of foreign trade in the Canadian income accounts: Canadian fiscal policy has relatively more impact on exchange rates than does American fiscal policy: the American economy is less open.

Concluding Remarks

1. Lecture Three shows how the Bank of Canada can influence exchange rates through its control over a number of nominal short-term interest rates at Toronto or Montreal – and of course its monetary-base growth-rate policies inevitably affect nominal exchange rates (and, transitionally, real exchange rates).

   Interestingly, reconciliation of higher nominal rates at Toronto than at New York, or London, requires that Canadian inflation be correspondingly higher – once the markets adapt to the policy format.

2. In a nexus comprised of fairly large open economies, the analysis

of Section 5.4 has game-theoretic ramifications: one then searches for saddlepoints of fiscal-policy games, in ways that are especially prominent for *tax*-policy, a point made especially saliently by Charles Tiebout (1956).

5.5 DYNAMIC STABILITY OF KEYNESIAN OPEN-ECONOMY SCHEMES

Relying on Metzler (1942, p. 100ff), we are to study some problems in the dynamic stability of rather simplistic Keynesian systems. This sort of stability analysis contains a deep flaw, not truly exposed until the rational-expectations literature took hold. (The stagnation of macroeconomic theory inspired by Keynes's work is displayed by the fact that a 1942 article well represents its *genre* in 1988 – even allowing for Professor Metzler's genius.) In a régime of rational expectations, policy-makers continuously reassess their actions in the light of continuous observation of the data they seek to influence – twisting the seminal work of Lucas (1976) which concerned the *public*'s integration of the authorities' programmes; see Sheffrin (1983) for a lucid précis of Lucas's analysis. If it becomes apparent that the initial programme will cause the economy to plunge beyond targeted positions, control-programmes will be reprogrammed: tax-/expenditure-policies, interest-rate targets, etc. will be altered. Once again, deterministic modelling (i.e. modelling dominated by Nature even though Nature may behave stochastically) must make way for exercise of free will by agents who incorporate Nature into their programmes by the hubristic device of including her influence in constraint sets.

Finally, the inevitably massive specification errors of models that are so simple are not seriously probed – as they surely should have been by many policy-makers who, over the years, have taken simplistic Keynesian modelling very seriously indeed.

Consider the system comprising equations (5.13)–(5.16)

$$C_t = f^1(Y_{t-1}) + f^2(Y_{t-1}) \tag{5.13}$$

$$I_t = f^3(Y_{t-1}) + g^2(Y'_{t-1}) - f^2(Y_{t-1}) \tag{5.14}$$

$$C'_t = g^1(Y'_{t-1}) + g^2(Y'_{t-1}) \tag{5.15}$$

$$I'_t = g^3(Y'_{t-1}) + f^2(Y_{t-1}) - g^2(Y'_{t-1}) \tag{5.16}$$

It is more plausible to write the domestic investment functions as $F^i(Y_{t-1} - Y_{t-2})$. Then the solutions are richer, but more difficult to obtain. The analysis is merely suggestive in any case.

Consumption is the sum of consumption of domestic goods and imports – functionally dependent on income lagged one period. Investment is 'divided between net increases in producers' stocks by domestic manufacturers and increases in foreign claims arising from favourable trade balances' (Metzler, 1942, p. 99).

Plugging the values for consumption and investment called for by equations (5.13)–(5.16) into the accounting identities defining aggregate income:

$$Y_t = f^1(Y_{t-1}) + f^3(Y_{t-1}) + g^3(Y'_{t-1}) \tag{5.17}$$

$$Y'_t = g^1(Y'_{t-1}) + g^3(Y'_{t-1}) + f^2(Y_{t-1}) \tag{5.18}$$

Assume that equations (5.17) and (5.18) have the particular solution $(\bar{Y}, \bar{Y}')$. Then take linear approximations in the neighbourhood of the solution by expanding the functions by Taylor's series, neglecting all but first-order terms. Define $\partial f^1/\partial Y$ as c; and $\partial g^1/\partial Y'$ as c'. And the gradients for importation and investment are (m, m') and (v, v'). Equations (5.17) and (5.18) describe the upshot (where $Y_t - \bar{Y}_t = y_t$):

$$y_t = (c + v)y_{t-1} + m'y'_{t-1} \tag{5.19}$$

$$y'_t = (c' + v')y'_{t-1} + my_{t-1} \tag{5.20}$$

The stability condition for an economy in isolation is $c + v < 1$.

Where λ_1 and λ_2 are roots of the quadratic equation (5.21) and where (A, B, C, D) are constants determined by initial conditions, the general solution of the linearized system is supplied by equations (5.22) and (5.23):

$$DET \begin{bmatrix} (c+v) - \lambda & m' \\ m & (c'+v'-\lambda) \end{bmatrix} = 0 \tag{5.21}$$

$$Y_t = \bar{Y} + A\lambda_1^t + B\lambda_2^t \tag{5.22}$$

$$Y'_t = \bar{Y}' + C\lambda_1^t + D\lambda_2^t \tag{5.23}$$

In less primitive modelling of this sort, $\bar{Y}$ becomes a benchmark path such as $Y_o e^{pt}$. The *genre* was quite fully developed by Samuelson and Hicks, *inter alios*.

Systemic stability requires that the remainder parts of equations (5.22) and (5.23) approach zero as t becomes large,[1] a condition that is fulfilled if the absolute values of eigenvalues λ_1 and λ_2 are less than unity. The necessary and sufficient conditions for this to be true are:

$$c + v + c' + v' < 1 + (c+v)(c'+v') - mm' < 2 \qquad (5.24)$$

The following inferences are extracted from inequalities (5.24).

The $c + v + c' + v' < 2$ condition shows that at least one of the economies must be stable in isolation.

Supposing that the second economy is stable in isolation, and writing $c' + v' = \sigma < 1$, the stability condition boils down to:

$$(c+v) + mm'/(1-\sigma) < 1 \qquad (5.25)$$

It follows from inequality (5.25) that 'if both economies are stable when isolated, the world economy will likewise be stable' (Metzler, 1942, p. 102).

It also follows from (5.25) that 'if both economies are unstable when isolated, the world economy will likewise be unstable' (Metzler, 1942, p. 103).

It follows from (5.25) that 'an economy which would be unstable when left to itself may be perfectly stable in a two-economy world because of the dampening influence of low propensities in the other economy' (Metzler, 1942, p. 103). Thus the first economy's total propensity to spend may exceed unity; it is unstable in isolation. But its propensity to spend on *home* goods may be quite small; and the propensity to import of the second (stable) economy may be 'small'. So the product, (mm'), may approach zero.

5.6 INTRODUCTION OF CAPITAL FLOWS INTO ESSENTIALLY KEYNESIAN SYSTEMS: METZLER'S MODEL

See Lecture Four, especially its problems and their annotations, for related material.

The following material, based on 1955 lectures by Professor Lloyd Metzler, revises my 1963 précis – see Burstein (1963, pp. 799–804). The material is indeed dated; but ISLM is still popular and has even more ancient origins. Metzler's schema is related to Hicks's (ISLM), and also has roots in Keynes (1930, I, Chapter 13, Section 4).

Metzler's schema is a modified Keynesian system encompassing effects of terms of trade and interest-rate differentials. Employment levels are parametric for the problem; there may be 'full employment' – whatever that means.

The model, deploying a common unit of account, conforms better to fixed-rate than to floating-rate postulations. It contains two simple 'shmoo' economies. Shmoos are all-purpose goods; aggregation is quite complete. Nor is that all: public sectors are neglected for the sake of simplicity.

Equations (5.26) and (5.27) define positive or negative excess of planned saving over planned investment, measured in shmoos, in Economies A and B. Interest rates and price levels are symbolized by r_a, r_b, p_a, and p_b:

$$(S-I)^a = f(r_a, r_b, p_a, p_b) \tag{5.26}$$

$$(S-I)^b = F(r_a, r_b, p_a, p_b) \tag{5.27}$$

Equation (5.28), as well as equations (5.26) and (5.27), are zero-order homogeneous in the price levels: only the ratio p_a/p_b can be determined. And shmoos are identical, except that A shmoos may be stamped with the Stars and Stripes and B shmoos with Union Jacks; there is patriotic shmoo illusion.

I^a and I^b are planned rates of absorption of goods for investment purposes; S^a and S^b are planned differences between sales receipts and expenditures on consumption goods, always measuring in shmoos. Factor income earned abroad, y', is neglected.

Turn to equations (5.28) and (5.29):

$$(X-J)^a = g(r_a, r_b, p_a, p_b) \tag{5.28}$$

$$(X-J)^a = - (X-J)^b \tag{5.29}$$

Economy A's real trade surplus, positive or negative, is measured by $(X-J)^a$.

Equation (5.30) requires that production plans of A producers be precisely fulfilled by absorption (demand) outcomes:

$$(X^a - J^a) = S^a - I^a; X^a + I^a = S^a + J^a \qquad (5.30)$$

Equation (5.30) is verified by Equations (5.31) and (5.32) – noting that $S = y - C$:

$$y = C + I + X - J \qquad (5.31)$$

$$S - I = X - J \qquad (5.32)$$

The right-hand side of equation (5.31) defines absorption; and the left-hand side domestic production (GDP); see Lecture Two.

Now assign a common arbitrary value to $(X-J)^a$ and $(S-I)^a$; and assign that value's 'negative' (cf. $(-1)(x)$) to $(X-J)^b$ and $(S-I)^b$. Domestic production is to be absorbed in both economies; and the excess of saving over investment in A will be equal to the excess of investment over saving in B. It becomes possible to solve the system comprised of equations (5.26)–(5.28) for the solution vector $(\bar{r}_a, \bar{r}_b, \bar{\pi})$, where $\bar{\pi}$ denotes the solution value for p_a/p_b.

Assume that $(\bar{r}_b - \bar{r}_a)$ is positive for $(X-J)^a = 0$: in a sense the 'natural rate of interest' is higher in B than in A. The algebraic value of $(r_b - r_a)$ should decrease as $(X-J)^a$ is stipulated to increase: more positive values of $(S - I)^a$ – i.e. more positive values of $(I - S)^b$ – map into higher values for r_a and lower ones for r_b. If domestic interest rates dominate in savings and investment plans, the upshot is Figure (5.1).

The BB curve is a locus of pairs of A trade-account surpluses (B trade-account deficits) and interest-rate differentials consistent with absorption equalling production in both economies. (The interest-rate differentials associate with particular solution values for interest rates in both economies.)

Equation (5.33) concerns capital outflow:

$$\varkappa = h\,(r_b - r_a) \qquad (5.33)$$

Capital outflow ($\varkappa$) measures the rate of excess of A agent purchases of B securities over B agent purchases of A securities. To repeat, income earned by sales of factor services abroad (y') is largely elided. Such income, and transfers of it through dividend and interest pay-

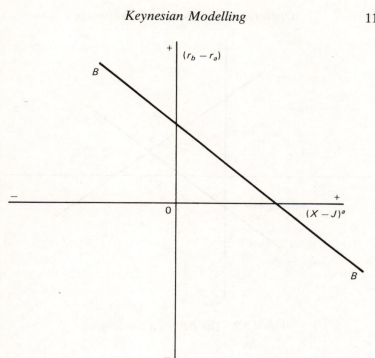

Figure 5.1   The *BB* curve

ments, are buried in the capital account; transfers, on net, are to be in favour of *B*. And $h'(r_b - r_a) > 0$.

The $\varkappa/\varkappa$ curve (see Figure 5.2) associates planned capital outflow (from *A* to *B*) with interest-rate differentials $(r_b - r_a)$. So net capital outflow – always measured in shmoos – from *B* to *A* is registered by a negative number.

Consider properties of Point *P* in Figure 5.2, the intersection of the *BB* and $\varkappa/\varkappa$ curves. Equation (5.34) holds at *P*:

$$\varkappa = (X-J)^a \tag{5.34}$$

Capital outflow equals the trade surplus. At *P*, and only at *P*, planned capital outflow (inflow) equals the actual financial surplus (deficit); and production equals absorption in both economies. (See Lecture Two.)

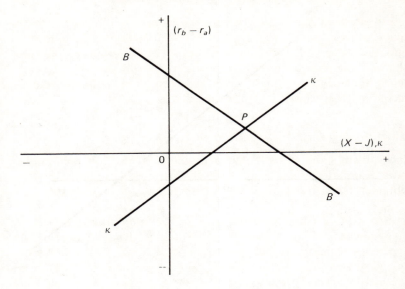

Figure 5.2　The $BB - \varkappa/\varkappa$ construction

Money is now to be explicitly injected into the system. Anticipating Lecture Eight, a gold standard is modelled. Consider Equations (5.35)–(5.38):

$$\phi(\Gamma_a) = \psi(p_a, p_b, \bar{r}_a, \bar{r}_b) \tag{5.35}$$

$$\Phi(\Gamma_b) = L(p_a, p_b, \bar{r}_a, \bar{r}_b) \tag{5.36}$$

$$p_a = (\bar{\pi})p_b \tag{5.37}$$

$$\Gamma_a + \Gamma_b = G^{\circ} \tag{5.38}$$

Functions ϕ and Φ show how supplies of money in the two economies depend on gold holdings Γ_a and Γ_b. Functions ψ and L are liquidity preference functions defining demand for money. And price levels are stated in a common unit of account. The public are not permitted to hold gold in either economy. And, finally, equation (5.38) requires that aggregate gold holdings equal the global gold stock! (Non-monetary uses of gold are neglected here, but not in Lecture Eight.)

Equations (5.35)–(5.38) comprise a system of four equations in the unknowns $(p_a, p_b, \Gamma_a, \Gamma_b)$. Equilibrium distribution of the gold stock and the price levels becomes determined. But this 'equilibrium' shares the following unsatisfactory feature with proper ISLM systems: the solution values are in ceaseless flux as the economies, including their capital stocks, evolve.

Two Problems in Comparative Statics

In Problem 1 the global gold-stock increases. In Problem 2 one or both of functions f and F shift. Results are strikingly similar to those obtained by Keynes in Chapter 13, Section 4, of the *Treatise*.

1. *The Global Gold Stock Increases* The solution of the BB–$\varkappa/\varkappa$ system is invariant against the level of the global gold-stock. There are no real-balance effects (see Burstein, 1986, Chapter 9); relative prices must be invariant against the global gold-stock. So, since liquidity preferences are given, prices rise in the same proportion in both economies; and the distribution of (shares in) the global gold-stock are unchanged in the new solution; for a careful proof, see Burstein (1963, p. 835, Note A).

   Adjustment processes may be quite active. If the initial gold-stock increase occurs in B, B prices will rise relative to A prices on impact – surely in the classic script. And B interest rates may fall on impact: see J. S. Mill's prescient discussion, ably annotated by Cagan (1972) and Friedman and Schwartz (1982, Ch. 10). The adjustment process, leading to unchanged interest rates, exemplifies again (!) that, in a proper analysis, changes in money growth may affect interest rates (especially nominal ones), but that money-stock levels should not affect interest rates.

2. *Shifts in Functions f and F* Say that $(S-I)^a$ increases relative to any pair (r_a^*, r_b^*); the BB curve shifts rightward. A's trade surplus must now be greater, relative to (r_a^*, r_b^*) if the greater excess of planned saving over planned investment is to be offset. The equilibrium value of π, $\bar{\pi}$, must fall. And real capital outflow from A to B must increase correspondingly; the interest-rate differential must increase. And, since B must sustain a less 'favourable' trade balance – since its import 'drain' must increase – B's excess of investment over saving must increase: interest rates fall in both economies, the decline in A exceeding that in B.

In the new solution the proportion of the global gold-stock held in *B* may increase: *A*'s demand for money has decreased more than *B*'s. In any case, parametric shifts anywhere impose need for adjustment everywhere. The world becomes a big (un)happy family.

An Annotated Problem Set For Lecture Five

PROBLEMS

46. (See Section 5.4.) Choose the correct statement:

- **(a)** increased American public spending causes equilibrium American and Canadian incomes to increase (see the left-hand sides of equations (5.8) and (5.9));
- **(b)** an increase in Canadian public spending affects Canadian interest rates but not the much larger American economy;
- **(C)** labelling American public spending G, $d\xi/dG < 0$;
- **(d)** all of the above choices are correct;
- **(e)** none of the above choices is correct.

47. (See Section 5.4.) Choose the correct statement:

- **(A)** a 5% increase in American public spending affects Canadian interest rates more than a 10% increase in Canadian public spending;
- **(b)** if the Canadian propensity to import exceeds the American one, a dollar increase in Canadian public spending affects interest rates more than a dollar increase in American public spending;
- **(c)** a 10% increase in Canadian public spending affects the exchange rate more than a 10% increase in American public expenditure;
- **(d)** all of the above choices are correct;
- **(e)** none of the above choices is correct.

48. (See Section 5.4.) Choose the correct statement:

- **(A)** if Canada increases its public spending – American fiscal policy the same – the Canadian dollar will appreciate;

119

(b) the United States will export less to Canada if the US cuts public spending;

(c) the problem requires balanced trade between the United States and Canada;

(d) all of the above choices are correct;

(e) none of the above choices is correct.

49. (See Section 5.4.) Choose the correct statement:

(a) an increase in the American public-sector borrowing-requirement affects Canadian interest rates;

(b) Canadian fiscal-policy has relatively less impact on the Canadian dollar than on interest rates;

(c) Canadian fiscal-policy affects the foreign-exchange value of the American dollar;

(D) two of the above choices are correct;

(e) none of the above choices is correct.

50. (See Section 5.4 and Lecture Five.) Consider the interaction of Economies *A* and *B*, comprising a global economy. The larger economy, *A*, slumps. It follows that:

(A) floating rates mitigate negative impact on *B* (under conventional trade-based reasoning);

(b) if expectations are formed rationally, mitigating effects of floating rates are still greater;

(c) if *A*'s fiscal policy become more expansive, responding to the slump, effects on *B* will be exacerbated;

(d) two of the above choices are correct;

(e) choices **(a)**, **(b)** and **(c)** are correct.

51. (See Section 5.2.) Choose the correct statement relative to equations (5.1) and (5.2):

(a) the multiplier on *A* is nil;

(b) $dX = (+)$ leads to increased output;

(c) external events dominate our income and employment levels;

(d) two of the above choices are correct;

(E) choices **(a)**, **(b)** and **(c)** are correct.

52. (See Section 5.3: equations (5.5) and (5.6).) Choose the correct statement relative to the model:

(A) a positive change in demand for exports does not affect the level of equilibrium output;

(b) an increase in 'α' leads to depreciation of the currency;

(c) the multiplier on A is substantially lower than in a closed economy;

(d) two of the above choices are correct;

(e) none of the above choices is correct.

Problems **53–56** are based on a reinterpretation of Problems **39–41**. The reinterpretation is pitched up to a high level of abstraction and anticipates Lecture Seven.

Concepts

The After-tax Rate of Return   The before-tax rate of return, Π, is a function of the proportion of GDP devoted to investment: $\Pi = f(i)$. The after-tax rate of return is $\Pi - \tau$, where τ, is a proportional tax rate – or, better, a net transfer rate (cf. transfers *to* the public). So the differential of the after-tax rate of return, relative to $i = i^*$, is $d(\Pi - \tau) = -d\tau$.

The After-tax Cost of Capital   The after-tax cost of capital, r', is defined as $r - \tau$. So, for $r = r^*$, r′ increases if the tax rate is cut: $dr' = -d\tau$.

Open-economy Relations

Risk-adjusted interest elasticities of capital-flows are 'high'. If we try $r' = (r - \tau) = (r - \tau)^*$, then for $dr' = d(r'^*) = 0$, $dr = d\tau$. And, for $r = r^*$, $dr' = -d\tau$. ('τ' refers to Economy E's tax rate.) The $r = r^*/dr' = -d\tau$ case pertains if relevant taxes follow residence and if capital deployed in Economy E is predominantly owned by non-residents. Then tax-policy may mostly affect capital E residents deploy abroad; and, if E is small enough, effects on external costs of capital may be negligible – so that E residents are trapped, unless they move; and E authorities' influence on after-tax cost of capital in E is confined to the perhaps paltry E resident capital deployed in E. See Lecture Seven.

Modelling investment as a function of the after-tax rate of interest (cost of capital), r', it follows that the direct effect of a tax cut on investment in an open economy may be *nil*. (Internally generated corporate funds are invested relative to opportunity-cost calculations, calculations admittedly distorted by most tax codes.) But *effort* is tied to the tax rate so that we may write $y = y(\tau)$. Saving may be stimulated indirectly by a tax-cut via increased output, implying an upward shift in the curve plotting wealth over time (cf. $S = S(W, \tau)$). (Fisher–Knight–Friedman capital theory implies perpetual growth, the growth rate depending on interaction of the twin forces of thrift and productivity.) Still it is at least plausible that a tax-cut should lead to an increased external finance requirement, accompanied 1:1 by a more negative trade account (see Lecture Two). The process is sustainable if the stimulus to gross domestic product is sufficient to stabilize the foreign asset/GDP ratio.

Remark

The analysis has *not* been based on changes in public-sector borrowing requirements. We have tacitly assumed, along new-classical macroeconomic lines, that real economic equilibrium is roughly (*very* roughly; see Burstein, 1986, Chapter 8) invariant against the finance mode (cf. taxation vs domestic borrowing) for public-sector spending. A shift to bond finance thus induces additional saving, equal to displaced revenues, so that families can maintain intact their shares of the jth economy's net real wealth.

This analysis will be substantially extended by Lecture Seven.

The analysis elides effects on interest rates and capital flows of shifts or fluctuations in foreign-exchange-rate expectations, related in part to inflation-expectations. This elision is serious: outcomes are skewed by effects of 'speculation' in foreign-exchange markets.

53. According to the theory, if the jth highly-open economy cuts its tax-rate (τ):

(a) its after-tax interest-rate falls *pari passu* with the tax-cut;
(b) its after-tax rate of return also falls in equilibrium;
(c) Π, determined by $f(i)$, falls;
(d) all of the above choices are correct;
(E) none of the above choices is correct.

54. According to the theory, which of the following is(are) an effect(s) of a tax-increase in the jth economy?:

(a) higher before-tax inflation-adjusted interest rates;
(b) reduced capital inflow;
(c) a lower value in equilibrium of $\Pi = f(i)$;
(D) two of the above choices are correct;
(e) none of the above choices is correct.

55. According to the theory, which of the following are stimuli generated by a tax-cut in the jth economy?:

(a) the effect on the after-tax cost of capital – especially if 'r' is given for the problem;
(B) the effect on effort, surely if the tax-cut is temporary;
(c) the stimulus imparted to capital outflow from the jth economy;
(d) all of the above choices are correct;
(e) none of the above choices is correct.

56. According to the theory:

(a) the most important channel of tax-policy influence on interest rates concerns the public-sector borrowing requirement;
(b) effects of tax changes on GDP_j are approximately the same as those on GNP_j;
(c) recent substantial foreign acquisitions of American-sited industrial capital are a predictably pernicious effect of the 'Reagan' tax cuts;
(d) all of the above choices are correct;
(E) none of the above choices is correct.

SELECTIVE ANNOTATIONS

Problem 48

The model's algebra generates choice **(A)** without doubt. Supplying intuition for this result, assume that the import content of public expenditure is nil (!). Then, obviously, private-sector Canadian demand for Canadian goods, plus American absorption of Canadian goods, is required to fall.

Problem 50

This problem is considerably illuminated by Lecture Six. If the American economy slumps, there will clearly be depressing effects on the Canadian economy (!). But these 'depressing effects' are mitigated by floating rates: then the American dollar will – to the extent that trade events dominate – tend to appreciate, supplying some stimulus to Canadian exports. (The analysis has a strongly Keynesian tonal centre.) Finally, *rational expectations* diminishes the 'stabilizing' contribution of a floating-rate régime: recognition that the Canadian dollar depreciates when the American economy slumps and appreciates when the American economy surges (counterfactually denying influences of investment-market forces on currency-rate movements; cf. Lecture Six) leads to 'speculative' support of the Canadian dollar during American slumps and to 'speculative' selling of the American dollar during American booms.

Problem 52

The problem's choices are usefully assessed by simple algebraic manipulation. In connection with choice **(A)**, note that output levels are *given* for the problem, an assumption that is more attractive in the light of Lecture Seven.

Notes and References

1. The concept of asymptotic stability is appropriate to physical, but not to economic, systems. The parameters of economic systems are thus in ceaseless flux; and policy-intervention ceaselessly revises programmes relative to ceaselessly-changing objectives.

6 Lecture Six: Exchange-rate and Liquidity Régimes

6.1 PRELIMINARY REMARKS

The space of Lecture Six is largely spanned by Friedman's (1953b) study. Until recently the controlling topics of open-economy monetary economics concerned fixed-versus-flexible-rate régimes, properties of international liquidity and debate over alternative liquidity régimes, especially that over the Bretton Woods institutions. Adjustment mechanisms are closely studied, especially by way of contrasting properties of fixed and floating rate régimes. Other standard topics – represented in the problem set and its annotations – include reprises of small-open-economy properties and Keynesian adjustment mechanisms and fresh studies of optimal-currency-zone criteria, the 'Dutch disease', 'stagflation', the Marshall–Lerner condition, the Laursen–Metzler effect and Domestic Credit Expansion (DCE).

The problems and their annotations carry much of the chapter's weight: so varied a set of topics mandates a case method of instruction. And the lengthy chapter does no more than supply some economic logic; the reader's remaining research programme is formidable. (See Krueger, 1983, for a survey; and Meade's magisterial treatise, 1951.)

Some of Lecture Six's material is dated: the lecture covers *traditional* topics. But, along with Lectures Seven – Ten, it offers some innovatory material as well.

6.2 FIXED EXCHANGE RATES: DYNAMICS OF THE SPECIE-FLOW MECHANISM

6.2.1 Mechanics

(See Lecture Four, Section 4.1.3.)

The mechanics of the standard analysis are quite formal, as Figure

125

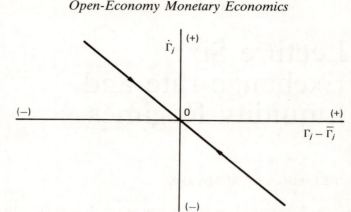

Figure 6.1　The controlling phase diagram

Negative gold stock positions imply that the economy's borrowed gold exceeds its actual stock. An economy whose gold stock is negative is *short* gold.

(6.1) makes clear. Gold positions are measured by Γ; and indeed other official-reserve categories are ignored. The vector $\bar{\Gamma}$ defines equilibrium gold positions, along lines developed in Lecture Eight; at the origin of Figure (6.1) actual and equilibrium gold holdings of the jth economy are identical. (The set-up is not rigorous: the process is controlled by a system of *simultaneous* differential equations; motions in the space of Figure 6.1 are apt to be more complex than the diagram suggests.) Figure 6.1 describes a stable sub-system.

Before explaining the generation of Figure (6.1), we need to display its algebraic underpinnings:

$$\dot{\Gamma}_j = f^j(\Gamma_j - \bar{\Gamma}_j); f'() < 0; f(0) = 0 \tag{6.1}$$

And equation (6.2) limns *systemic* action:

$$\dot{\Gamma} = \phi(\Gamma - \bar{\Gamma}); \phi(0) = 0 \tag{6.2}$$

The underlying economic processes are especially simple: excess liquidity leads to purchase of foreign assets and goods. (Again see Lecture Four, Section 4.1.3; and Lecture Nine establishes the coincidence of the upshot with that of monetary approaches to exchange-rate fluctuation and balances of payments.) Thus equations (6.3) and (6.4), where z represents asset purchases and q the trade balance:

$$z = \psi(\Gamma - \bar{\Gamma}); \psi'() > 0 \qquad (6.3)$$

$$q = h\,(\Gamma - \bar{\Gamma}); h'() < 0 \qquad (6.4)$$

Equation (6.1) follows as a matter of course. (See Lecture Eight and Barsky and Summers, 1988, pp. 528–50, for the importance of substitution between monetary and non-monetary gold.)

Remarks on Price Behaviour and the Nature of Excess Demand

It is tacitly stipulated that price velocity (inflation) is an increasing function of $(\Gamma - \bar{\Gamma})$ – subject to variable lags. Prices thus accelerate when there is excess liquidity.

Inflation need not reflect excess demand; real economic equilibrium is consistent with *any* steady rate of inflation (see Burstein, 1986, Chapter 7). But excess demand in 'goods markets' causes prices to accelerate (i.e. it causes inflation to increase); disequilibrium accelerates prices.

The analysis of Section 6.2.1 focuses on excess supply (demand) of money as a source of excess demand (supply) for goods. Economic crises were in fact provoked by widespread attempts to convert securities into cash – 'conversion' encompassing refusals to renew credit; excess supply of securities mapped into excess demand for money. And the consequences were often dire. Debtors, unable to obtain specie or notes (limited by a harsh fiduciary-issue constraint under the 1844 Bank Charter Act) went under; chains of bankruptcies disorganized goods markets – so that the indirect effects of excess supply of securities often encompassed *gluts* – i.e. excess supplies of goods and labour. Indeed this scenario is the basis of Friedman and Schwartz's (1963) hypothesis that the American Crash (1930–3) was primarily the consequence of the failure of the Federal Reserve to supply cash to mollify exigent creditors, including bank-depositors. (Also see Lecture Two.)

6.2.2 Economics

The mechanics of Section 6.2.1. do not accurately track real-world processes, past or present. Thus say that infusions of gold and silver cause prices to rise in economies $(1, 2, \ldots, m)$. This supplies stimulus to incomes and prices in economies $(m+1, \ldots, n)$ to the extent that they export to $(1, \ldots m)$; Temin's (1969) study of the

ante-bellum (pre-1861) American economy contains interesting illustrations. But importers in economy $(m+1)$, for example, are
worse off: terms of trade have turned against them. And, if the latter
effect is more important than the former, the $(m+1)$ st trade balance
may *deteriorate* – and the mth improve – *pace* conventional specie-
flow-mechanism wisdom; especially if forward-looking consumers
try to maintain their living standards. (See the Laursen–Metzler
effect, Problem **66**.) So, on reflection, specie-flow effects make up a
mixed bag, although prices in economy $(m+1)$ are unambiguously
subject to upward pressure. (Pressures are transmitted more rapidly
the more important are traded goods. If economy $(m+2)$ were
London, powerful pressure on prices would be exerted very rapidly
indeed.) And at any 'node' upward pressure on prices is apt to look
like cost push: imports cost more; and home-market prices of export-
ables increase; see Girton and Roper (1978).

Remarks

1. Labour-intensive goods and services may transitorily experience
   higher demand, surely if money wages lag.
2. In what passes for formal economic theory, the processes just
   described finally restore initial equilibrium: for example, vector $\bar{\Gamma}$
   is regained. In real economic life one must be more guarded: for
   one thing, the biological components of the economies are in
   ceaseless flux so that the implicit analogy to physics is not robust;
   and, along similar lines, initial conditions may exert 'permanent'
   force in economic models – families, for example, are not readily
   comparable to groups of physical particles – see Burstein, 1988b,
   Chapter 2).

6.3   FIXED EXCHANGE RATES: FURTHER CHARACTERISTICS OF ADJUSTMENT PROCESSES

The following remarks by Friedman (1953b), made in a context
supplied by Section 6.4, add transparency to the discussion:

> If internal prices were as flexible as exchange rates, it would make
> little economic difference whether adjustments were brought about
> by changes in exchange rates or by equivalent changes in internal
> prices . . . [But] at least in the modern world, internal prices are

highly inflexible . . . The inflexibility of prices, or different degrees of flexibility, means a distortion of adjustments in response to changes in external conditions. The adjustment takes the form primarily of price changes in some sector, primarily of output changes in others.

Wage rates tend to be among the less flexible prices. In consequence, an incipient deficit that is countered by a policy of permitting or forcing prices to decline is likely to produce unemployment . . . [so that] the consequent decline in real income reduces demand for foreign goods . . . But this is clearly a highly inefficient method of adjusting to external changes.

Friedman (1953b, p. 165)

Under fixed rates, the pieces are jerkily put together in an erratic, inefficient sequence; relative-price relationships are distorted. And the underlying dynamic process entails even more tenebrous implications. Say, realistically enough, that the open system is subject to continuous shocks. If the shocks are generated randomly, the *j*th economy's relative price structure must always be distorted: resources cannot be efficiently allocated. In principle, non-random shocks are forecastable; but Friedman has just shown us that inertial systems cannot adapt efficiently – not even if the efficient path is identified. And in the real world the 'efficient path' is likely to be unidentifiable; and even those who think they know what the efficient path is will disagree. After all, the *raison d'être* of the Invisible Hand is based on transmission of information by price signals that inform otherwise ignorant transactors, who thus become collectively seized of information they are individually unable to gather. Price signals are fed into micro programmes (utility maximization is an example) that are coordinated along lines developed in general-equilibrium theory – leading to the prime welfare-economics proposition that all competitive equilibria (a mathematical idea) are optimal and that every optimal state is dual to a competitive equilibrium. All of this is smashed up in ways just explained by Friedman (1953b).

Must fixed-rate régimes be utterly condemned to allocative failure? Not on the plane of theory. Consider *tabular standards*, going back as far as Wheatley (1807) and quite recently interestingly discussed by Friedman (1984a). Recapitulating Lecture Two, agents confronting a *tabula rasa*, so far as accounting modalities go, and controlling advanced computer technology, would construct a synthetic unit of

account defined on fragments of thousands of goods and services –
elaborating on the European Currency Unit (ECU) concept. Call the
'imaginary' unit the *Aureus*;[1] a debt of one thousand Aurei (Ⱥ1,000)
is discharged by a tender – selected from a large class of eligible
tenders – commanding a basket of goods and services equivalent in
value to 1,000 Aureus units, each 'containing' c_1 ounces of Arabian
Light crude oil, c_2 grams of a certain type of steel, delivered at
location L_i, etc.

Under a global Aureus standard, only real structural changes or
shocks can cause derangement. The worst case for fixed exchange is
precluded: our prices *in general* will not require substantial adjustment, as they would if we had to adapt to global deflation in a
contemporary fixed-rate régime. True, if we are a banana republic
and world demand for bananas falls, it will be necessary for banana
prices (measured in Aurei) to fall; but, under floating rates in the
same circumstances, it seems inefficient for *all* our prices to fall *pari
passu* in order to correct 'banana imbalance'.

Among the economic substances whose prices are to be quoted in
Aurei are national currencies – dollars, pounds, yen, lire, francs, etc.
And, almost surely in the early days of the Reform, tenders dis-
charging debt will be ethnocentric: debts contracted in Britain are
likely to be discharged by transfer of claims against British banks.
Still, monetary authorities would be little more than competitive
'currency' sellers (issuers) in a nexus established by Klein (1974) and
Hayek (1976). Ideally the currencies would be convertible; and
issuers would hold Aureus-denominated securities, or real assets,
purchased with proceeds of currency sales, as *de facto* reserves. If the
pound becomes disfavoured and the Deutsche Mark favoured by the
markets, the Bank of England would purchase DM from the Bundes-
bank in exchange for Aureus-denominated securities, so that the
quantity of British issue would fall, and German issue would increase: rate-fluctuation can be confined to narrow bands. The game
thus played verges on being a sideshow.

To repeat, *relative* prices may be out of kilter so that, say, the
United States trade account is disequilibrated; American transactors
may, on net, be going into the red on the global giro (deficits being
measured in Aurei), either because of relative-price misalignment
or simple overabsorption. For reasons that are to me obscure, the
American government may make massive Aureus-denominated borrowings, selling the proceeds to Americans in exchange for their
IOUs; foreigners may welcome such financial intermediation, backed

by the American government's taxable capacity. But abstention by the American government would be consistent with the reformed régime. Emulating *ante-bellum* 19th-century American governments (over an interval on which the United States made dramatic economic progress) *laissez faire* could be practised; the situation could be treated like one in which residents of New Jersey have gone on a spending binge so that New Jersey accounts with ex-Jersey agents flash red – leading to spontaneous corrective processes being enforced by nervous creditors. The 'trick' is this. An economy's trade deficit, in the reformed order, implies *nothing* about demand for its currency, or other currencies. (See Lecture Ten for a related argument in a somewhat different context.) The transactional advantages of fixed exchange (whatever they may be) are retained without sensitizing real economic action to official-reserve crises. The monetary and real domains of economic action are partitioned by a process in which *money* is absorbed by *finance*.

6.4 FIXED EXCHANGE RATES: INTEREST-RATE EFFECTS AND BANK-RATE POLICY

Friedman (1953b) again illuminates the discussion:

> Interest-rate changes have in the past played a particularly important rôle in adjustment to external changes, partly because they have been susceptible to direct influence by the monetary authorities, and partly because, under a gold standard, the initial impact of [balance of payments disequilibrium] was a loss or gain of gold and a subsequent tightening or ease in the money market.

> Friedman (1953b, p. 166)

To the extent that interest rates move fluidly – and a number of key rates do move fluidly – and to the extent that prices of goods and wages are sticky(!), interest-rate (Bank Rate) policy can be relatively effective as a stop-gap device. And narrow bands for feasible exchange-rate fluctuation, following from close spacing of gold points for example, further promote the elasticity of response of capital flows to interest-rate differentials: risk of exchange-rate fluctuation is thus minimized.

Remark

Lecture Two deals with more or less secular capital flows, as does Lecture Seven. Both the *rationales* and the mechanics of such flows differ markedly from those governing bridging finance.

A Case History: The Salad Days of Bank Rate at London

The following authoritative remarks by Sayers (1957) concern Britain *circa* 1874–1914. The Bank Rate mechanism worked so powerfully that, if shocks died away fairly promptly, internal price adjustments could be averted.

> Three circumstances were particularly favourable to this [Bank Rate] link in the chain of control. First, the internal effect of high rates in drawing cash from the country banks [a channel explored by Henry Thornton] was probably at its maximum in the third quarter of the century . . . Secondly London's foreign lending was large and extremely sensitive to market rate. Thirdly, the world's total stock of gold was increasing.
>   . . . During the eighties [London's net foreign lending] soared . . . The pace at which new loans were floated was highly sensitive to interest rates. Borrowers were usually able to wait a few weeks in the hope that a spell of dear money would pass . . . or, if the bonds had already been issued, high interest rates at London would make them slow to remit the proceeds abroad . . . So, in one way and another, a short spell of dear money would ease the strain on the exchanges before ever the balance of trade could be affected.
>
>   Sayers (1957, pp. 14–15)

Relying on its Bank Rate weapon, the Bank of England held paper-thin gold reserves over this period. Bagehot swept the intellectual board and his reputation soared, as his advice was spurned.

A Conjecture

Consider the possibility of a 'kink' in the supply curve determining the flow of funds towards London (as a function of Bank Rate). Then, if rates increased at London, other centres would not follow; but they would follow if rates fell at London. Such a kink would explain the remarkable power of the Bank Rate mechanism described by Sayers. And the conjecture is quite plausible: ex-British monetary authorities would typically find lower domestic interest rates attractive; and they typically held much more substantial reserves than those of the Bank, since a major source of indirect global liquidity consisted of London-securities holdings. Such *reserve pyramiding* – notably featuring the American national banking system, 1863–1914 – made the Bank's reserve-position all the dicier and the Bank Rate mechanism all the more important.

Hicks (1986, p. 21) goes so far as to write that London 'acted as a sort of central bank for the whole world economy'. (See the coverage of 'Bretton Woods', and what has been called its implicit dollar standard – a type of gold-exchange standard – in this chapter's problem set and its annotations.)

6.5   MONEY-SUPPLY THEORY IN FIXED-RATE RÉGIMES

(See Lectures Nine and Ten. There is obvious national autarchy over money-supply in floating-rate régimes. See Problem **61** and its annotation for the linkage between floating rates and Friedman's money-supply rule: floating rates are necessary for the rule to be feasible.)

The Standard Exposition

(See Rivera-Batiz and Rivera-Batiz, 1985, pp. 196–216. Their exposition is ISLM-based.)

The analysis keyed to equations (6.1)–(6.4) is a skeletal version of the work of this sub-section.

The jth economy's monetary base consists of claims against its central bank. These claims are the result of (dual to) the central bank's cumulative purchases of assets, including the following: foreign exchange and gold (international reserves, labelled x_1); domestic instruments, including loans, discounts, government bonds, etc.; (central-bank credit, labelled x_2). Labelling the monetary base x_3:

$$x_3 = x_1 + x_2 \tag{6.5}$$

And assigning a simplistic money-multiplier, μ:

$$dM^s = \mu dx_3 = \mu(dx_1 + dx_2) \tag{6.6}$$

Now consider demand for money (M^d) in equillibrium:

$$M^d = L(r^*, p^*, y^*) = M^* \tag{6.7}$$

Equation (6.7) pertains to a small open economy under fixed exchange – so that feedback from the economy to the rest of the world can be ignored; the equilibrium state of the economy conforms to global norms for interest rates and prices and embraces full employment. In equilibrium $M^d = M^s$. So, recalling equation (6.6),

$$0 = \mu(dx_1 + dx_2); \quad dx_1 = -dx_2 \tag{6.8}$$

The central bank cannot control money supply.

The dynamics of the 'standard drill' pivot on Inequality (6.9), establishing a *prudential criterion*:

$$M^* \leq \lambda x_1 \tag{6.9}$$

For simplicity, write (6.9) as an equality:

$$M^* = \lambda x_1 \tag{6.10}$$

Solving equation (6.10) for x_1 (cf. x_1^*) and plugging x_1^* into equation (6.5), the required value for x_2 is easily extracted:

$$M^* = x_1^* + x_2^* \tag{6.11}$$

Define $x_1 - x_1^*$ as χ; and $m = M - M^*$. The dynamic law for χ_1 is:

$$\dot{\chi} = f(m); \quad f'(m) < 0; \quad f(0) = 0 \tag{6.12}$$

The authorities contract their control variable, x_2, when the prudential rule is violated; and, in a fractional reserve system, the rule will finally become violated as reserves leak out–if not at once. We posit that for $m > 0$, $\dot{x}_2 < 0$. So:

$$\dot{m} = g(\dot{\chi}) = g[f(m)] = \phi(m); \quad \phi'() < 0; \phi(0) = 0 \tag{6.13}$$

In words, when money supply exceeds its norm, the proximate determinants of money-growth are decreasing: international reserves are draining away; the Bank contracts its loans and discounts (makes open-market sales) when the prudential ratio is violated.

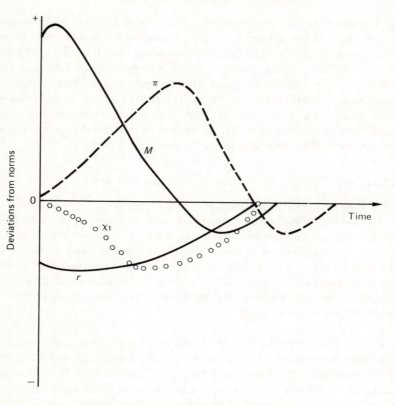

Figure 6.2   An expansionary episode

As for the underlying relationship, $\dot{\chi} \lesseqgtr$ as $m \gtreqless 0$, the standard drill relies on depressing effects of expanded money supply on interest rates and the trade balance (cf. stimulus to imports) as prices rise and absorption exceeds gross domestic product. The specie-flow mechanism modelled by equations (6.1)–(6.4) controls the analysis; see Lecture Nine. In sum, *monetary autarchy is surrendered*.

An Expansionary Episode

Consult Figure (6.2). The central bank, perhaps under intense political pressure, violates its prudential criterion and sharply increases x_2; it makes large open-market security purchases. Then the Bank regains its composure and restores its control system. Time-paths of key variables are traced in Figure (6.2). The reserve position

(x_1) appears to behave strangely; the reason is that, until money supply falls *below* its norm, reserves leak away. So M must overshoot: money supply must fall below its norm, and then rise up to the norm, for the reserve position to be restored. Price inflation (π) follows a serpentine path and also overshoots, reflecting inertial influences, including complex lags. Interest rates are plotted unimaginatively; but more arcane paths, including overshooting, can easily be conjured up. Finally, we have seen that the dynamic process works very differently in a Bank Rate régime.

Hypothetical Examples Counter to the Standard Drill

(See Burstein, 1986, Chapter. 3.)

Underlying stipulations differ from those controlling the standard drill – but inhere in modern monetary theory and evolving institutions. Money, however defined, is to yield interest. And public-debt issue and whatever is called money are not sharply distinguished: the analysis spans a wide spectrum of readily marketable (liquid) assets. Central banks pay interest on deposits and, of course, charge interest on credit taken from them.

Example One   Fiscal policy becomes more expansive: public-sector spending (say, on defence) increases; and tax-rates are cut. Lecture Two explains why domestic sources of finance will fall short of demand for finance, so that capital inflow, dual to an increase in the trade deficit, is required. Even if we stipulate that capital flows respond perfectly elastically to *risk-adjusted* global interest rates, interest rates in 'our' economy will increase: portfolio compositions must tilt towards holdings of our debt (or shares in our assets, etc.); investors must be compensated for concomitant risks. *Among the higher interest rates are those commanded by money.* The upshot might be called a fiscalized Bank Rate policy.

Higher interest rates, integral to the process, validate 'secondary' capital inflow, balanced by central-bank accumulation of *devisen* not taken into private portfolios: the change in the consolidated capital account is *nil*, but the reserve base increases. (The consolidated capital account encompasses changes in official reserves. Our central bank's reserves increase; foreign holdings of claims against our private sector increase 1:1 with the increase in official reserves.) And the multiplier on high powered money (the reserve base) will kick in so that, if interest rates on monetary balances are pitched up high enough (recall the underlying underdetermined model), there will be multiplied increases in money stocks in the new equilibrium.

Example Two   The central bank raises its lending rate (Bank Rate). It is now less attractive to borrow from the Bank; banks offer higher deposit rates, planning to reduce their debits at the central bank with the proceeds. In the upshot, the interest rate on money in our economy is higher . . . and the analysis offered in Example One takes over.

Abandonment of the stipulation that money does not yield interest flexibly suffices to pulverize the principal proposition of the standard exposition. And there are many other paths, in the scheme of analysis associated with the underdetermined models of Lecture Four, to this result.

6.6 PRINCIPAL PROPERTIES OF FLOATING (FLEXIBLE)-RATE RÉGIMES

Friedman's classic (1953b) study's results can be organized into six 'boxes' of material.

1. Floating rates promote monetary autarchy: deviant behaviour of our general price level, relative to global inflation-performance, is compensated by contra-variant behaviour of our exchange rate; if we maintain local price stability over an interval on which world inflation increases, our currency will appreciate, etc.

Remarks

The annotation of Problem **60** explains that freely-floating exchange rates do not purchase immunity from effects of *real* economic changes o'er the world: if foreign markets slump, demand for our exports will shrink; shifts in tastes and innovations in technique affect relative prices of our products and the ones we import; and to the extent that capital flows substitute for ultimately necessary price adjustments in any régime, real relationships among prices and quantities are disequilibrated over the prolonged adjustment process.

If *relative* prices are inertial, exchange-rate changes provoke allocative distortion: *all* our goods become cheaper compared to foreign goods if our exchange rate depreciates. Rate-flexibility triggers a blunderbuss adjustment process.

The fault in adjustment to *real* change in either fixed or floating rate régimes lies in an inept choice of numéraire: the Aureus prices of various paper monies vibrate violently – and these substances are numéraires. If the Aureus is numéraire, there can be no money illusion; and only *relative* price changes matter. The following example clarifies these points.

Our trade balance sharply deteriorates because of a fall in demand for an important export (see the Banana Republic of Chapter 7) whose local-currency price is sticky. An ensuing 15% (say) depreciation of our currency may correct the trade deficit by making *all* our goods cheaper in foreign measures, thereby distorting relative prices in our economy.

2. Exchange-rate volatility is a symptom, not a cause, of underlying 'instability' in a régime of clean floating.

Remarks

If expectations of others' expectations (interactive expectations) are ignored, this seems true with respect to effects of differing monetary régimes, e.g. disparate inflation rates. But for some years foreign-exchange markets have resembled stock-exchanges more than tâtonnements equilibrating 'real' forces. It is plausible that a major portion of post-Bretton Woods currency-rate variance has been due to autonomous speculative forces, often divorced from 'fundamentals'; it appears that the most critical expectations concern those of other traders. Exchange rates are propelled up and down the way growth stocks are; 'fundamentals' may amount to little more than they do at Sotheby's auctions of paintings . . . See Frydman and Phelps (eds., 1983) for an excellent set of papers on estimating others' expectations, *inter alia*.

By way of summary, see my earlier remarks:

> The open equivalent to the neurasthenic bourse of the *General Theory* is a quasi-exogenous process determining real rates of interest and foreign exchange rates. To the extent that foreign exchange-rate fluctuation is heavily influenced by the action, and expected action, on financial markets, an economy operating under floating rates may behave like one whose wages and prices are not fully adapted to levels required by the equilibrium

of a fixed-rate system – unless its wages and prices are perfectly flexible(!). Successful adaptation of open economies to asset-market-driven exchange-rate fluctuations requires wage-price flexibility! This upshot, so alien to orthodox paradigms for floating-rate régimes, and contradicting their *raison d'être*, is the most salient feature of the post-Bretton Woods world economy.

Burstein (1986, p. 155)

3. Exchange rates are far less inertial (i.e. more flexible) than prices of goods and services, especially wages; the adjustment process is more rapid under cleanly-floating rates. And prices of goods and services are inertial to varying degrees: general-price-level adjustment exacerbates relative-price distortions under fixed rates. (See Section 6.3.)

Remarks

The case for fixed rates is enhanced in the following way. Very substantial 'bridging' work is accomplished by *capital flows*. And elasticity of response to interest-rate differentials is also very substantial; *and* shorter-term interest rates' motions are not inertial.

Indeed capital flows may bridge *fundamental* trade deficits for quite lengthy intervals, with mixed results. Say that trade fundamentals change adversely for our trade balance. If capital flows were barred, and prices and wages were inflexible, a crisis well might ensue, perhaps causing a collapse of the financial framework so that numerous bankruptcies led to break down of coordination of real activity. Capital flows do useful work! On the other hand, the availability of foreign loans may exacerbate unsound political tendencies so that adjustment-efforts are the more feeble and protracted; think of an over-absorption episode in a country whose government faces an election, perhaps under the glower of a politicized army. More mundanely, Lecture Four explains how the social costs of disequilibrium episodes are reckoned: for one thing, accumulated borrowings may comprise a burden like that of reparations imposed on a losing power; for another, price/quantity distortions of disequilibrium episodes are socially costly. Finally, refer back to Lecture Four's 'deconstruction' of the idea of equilibrium (or disequilibrium). In a proper theory of economic policy, *equilibrium* describes a saddle-point of an *n*-person game; and is not equivalent to the equilibrium state of a gas relative to locked-in controls.

'Long-term' feasibility of capital-inflows is studied in Lecture Two and by Burstein (1986, Chapter 10).

I do not seek to make a case for fixed rates on net: the immensity of contemporary capital flows seems to assure that fixed-rate control-schemae would be drowned. There seems to be no turning back.

4. Capital flows are surprisingly important to transient adjustment processes even in cleanly-floating régimes. Friedman trenchantly explains why:

> If a rise in the exchange rate is expected to be temporary, there is an incentive for holders of the country's currency to sell some of their holdings for foreign currency in order to buy back the currency later on at a lower price . . . they absorb some of what would have been surplus receipts . . . Conversely, if a decline is expected to be temporary, there is an incentive to buy domestic currency for resale at a higher price.
>
> Friedman (1953b, p. 162)

> [Overshooting of the exchange rate] offers an opportunity to make a profit by buying the currency now . . . But this is precisely equivalent to lending by speculators to the country whose currency has depreciated. The return to the speculators is equal to the rate at which the currency they hold appreciates. In a free market with correct foresight, this will tend . . . to approach the interest rate . . . [s]peculation with a flexible exchange rate produces the same effect as explicit borrowing by a country whose currency has depreciated or explicit lending by one whose currency has appreciated . . . There is, however, this important difference: under flexible exchange rates the inducement to foreign lenders need involve no change in the interest rate on domestic loans; . . . a particular example of the independence of domestic monetary policy under flexible exchange rates.
>
> Friedman (1953b, p. 184).

Remarks

The *interest-parity* analysis of Lecture Three illuminates Friedman's point. Our interest rates cannot stay in place if our exchange rate is to overshoot (in one direction or the other) for an incremental capital flow to be activated. And the overshooting episode distorts terms of trade; Friedman may overstate his case.

Under fixed or floating rates, then, shock waves are substantially absorbed by capital flows. But the alternative régimes respond differently to changes in 'fundamentals': adaptation of the general price level under fixed rates is clumsy and slow – although relative prices, subject to different degrees of inertia, become distorted in both régimes.

An Illustration of the Argument

(See Burstein, 1986, pp. 158–9 and Burstein, 1988b, pp. 81–2.)

Following Allen (1967), the Canadian economy is to exhibit an *intrinsic oscillation*. The American economy has its own intrinsic oscillation, but effects of the Canadian on the American economy are ignored. However, the American economy transmits a *forced oscillation* to the Canadian economy *via* the trade account of the Canadian balance of payments. Canadian exports surge during upswings of the American economy and sag during American downswings, and Canadian imports oscillate sympathetically with the Canadian economy. As for effects of foreign-exchange-rate fluctuations, when the American economy surges, the Canadian dollar appreciates (to the extent that 'trade events' matter). Appreciation of the Canadian dollar damps stimulative effects of an American economic expansion; reversing the thrust of the American engine, depreciation of the Canadian dollar damps the resulting negative shock to the Canadian economy. But this scenario ignores unexploited opportunities for profit; it depicts a market that neglects opportunities to accumulate American (Canadian) dollars during booms (recessions) of the American economy. In a corrected scenario, the amplitude of the 'exchange-rate cycle' will be less.

So 'speculation' *à la* Friedman (1953b), makes the fixed- and floating-rate processes imitate each other; and indeed 'speculators' under the floating-rate régimes organize virtual capital flows. But that is not all. If buoyancy of the American economy boosts Wall Street, and if expectations are elastic so that the Market's appetite grows on what it feeds, foreign investors will seek 'dollars' to pour into Wall Street, so that the US dollar will *appreciate* because of the American boom. Then stimulus imparted to the Canadian economy by an American boom (or drag imparted by a slump) is *amplified* by floating rates. Floating rates then exercise perverse force, amplifying waves that are damped in Friedman's model.

5.   *Speculation Encore* The sense in which speculation (or, better, the speculative dimension of transactors' activities) may be destabilizing is often misunderstood.

   Destabilizing Speculation [?] The annotation of Problem **62** concerns Friedman's famous contention that, for currency speculation to be generically destabilizing, speculators have to lose money on average. And indeed the proto-type analysis of exchange stability obeys the $dX/dt = f(X)$ paradigm – where X measures excess demand for a currency. Stability hinges on whether $f'(X)$ is negative or positive; the exchange market is stable or unstable as $f'(X)$ is negative or positive.

   Today the 'speculation' issue has a quite different purport. The crux is *not* whether speculation makes for instability. Rather it concerns the extent to which speculation transforms markets into casinos like those of Chapter 12 of the *General Theory*. Does speculation distract currency markets from 'real' fundamentals? Today we are not concerned with stability in its proper (mathematical) sense; rather we are concerned with the controlling *motivation* of exchange-rate fluctuation – especially with ways in which some damping processes may be broken up so that adjustment processes become dysfunctionally erratic, albeit not unstable mathematically.

6.   Currency depreciation inevitably ratchets up the price level. The upshot is often confused with *inflation*; and writers often mistakenly infer from this that currency depreciation is self-defeating. This misperception will shortly be corrected – after we dispose of a related confusion. Passive or induced depreciations are often confused with active ones (of the sort deployed in the competitive depreciations of Beggar My Neighbour policies). The purpose of a passive depreciation is to *restore* terms of trade: think of a dirty-floating régime in which Economy E's rapid inflation has left the E-dollar overvalued, so that E finally depreciates its dollar. The

depreciation will give a fillip to the E price *level*; but this implies nothing about continuing inflation; and surely does not imply that terms-of-trade effects are nugatory. (Retaliatory action by other economies is another matter.)

Price Effects of Currency Depreciation

See my related analyses of a proposed tax reform in Cambodia *circa* 1974 (in Allingham and Burstein (eds), 1976, pp. 61–71) and of the oil shocks of the 1970s (in Burstein, 1986, Chapter 5).

Equation (6.24) determines an economy's general price level; prices are expressed in its own currency, in the sense that a unit of currency measures out at unity on the value scale:

$$p = w_1\lambda_1 + w_2\lambda_2 \tag{6.24}$$

where

p = the price of a unit of the final domestic product
w_1 = the price of a unit of domestic resources
w_2 = the price of a unit of imported resources
λ_1 = the quantity of domestic resources required to produce one unit of domestic output
λ_2 = the quantity of imported resources required to produce one unit of domestic output

Assign specific values so that:

$$1 \cong (0.8)(0.7) + (1.47)(0.3) \tag{6.25}$$

The exchange rate (against a composite currency assigned to the 'rest of the world') is initially 1:1. *Now* two units of our currency are to exchange for one unit of foreign currency. Equation (6.24) requires that equation (6.26) should hold: in the simplistic competitive economy, unit price equals unit cost of production.

$$1.44 \cong (0.8)(0.7) + (2.94)(0.3) \tag{6.26}$$

Our price level increases by 44% – and, indeed, our real wage rate falls correspondingly: domestic inputs are now relatively cheaper. In a less simplistic formulation, there would be substitution against imported components in both production and consumption; and it would be appropriate for money supply to be expanded, by 44% if velocity of monetary circulation is invariant against the process, in order to avert a liquidity crunch – see Burstein (1986). Of course, such a once-and-for-all increase in money-supply portends *nothing* for continuing inflation.

In the upshot the terms of trade deteriorate, although the once-over 44% price rise abates the fall. (For one of many illustrations of carelessness, even on the part of sophisticated economists, about distinction of passive from active depreciation, see Thirlwall, 1988.)

This process may be politically and socially awkward, if not disruptive. But such awkwardness is intrinsic to any process reducing mass living standards; and reductions in money wages are *more* disruptive. It follows that, under a system of (perhaps dirty) floating exchange rates, money illusion may mandate that money supply be expanded enough to validate an equilibrium in which money wages substantially increase; and the exchange rate falls all the more so that the targeted terms-of-trade change is accomplished. The analysis illustrates a principal long-standing characteristic of floating rates: monetary autarchy is greater under floating rates (although it is not *nil* under fixed rates, especially when monetary balances flexibly yield interest).

Note

Problems 67–73 and their annotations deal with 'Bretton Woods' and its aftermath – régimes of policy unable to reconcile obsession over 'adequate international liquidity' with installation of sufficiently robust constraints on profligate official borrowers and banks, lickerish over 'sovereign lending', Samsons threatening to pull down the global financial system if their otherwise worthless loans are not validated by official exchequers.

An Annotated Problem Set For Lecture Six

PROBLEMS

The following problems, attached to previous lectures, should be reviewed at this point:

Lecture Two: **4**, **11**
Lecture Three: **18–19**, **22–27**, **29–31**
Lecture Five: **50**

Small Open Economies

57. (See the annotation of Problem **4**, Lecture Two.) Which of the following are properties of small open economies (SOEs)?:

    (a) wage-price flexibility assures full employment;
    (b) real income is sensitive to global events;
    (c) open-market operations by its central bank do not affect its secular real growth rate;
    (d) two of the above choices are correct;
    (E) choices (a), (b) and (c) are correct.

Keynesian Adjustment Processes

58. (See Lecture Four.) In a Keynesian adjustment process:

    (a) relative prices of commodities bear most of the weight of international adjustment processes;
    (B) imbalances of trade transmit income disturbances from economy to economy;
    (c) debt issues cannot be in local currencies;
    (d) two of the above choices are correct;
    (e) none of the above choices is correct.

Currency Zones

59. (See Burstein, 1986, Chapter 11, and its references.) As for adjustment in an integrated monetary area:

  (a) integration is undesirable unless foreign-exchange risk can be obtained cheaply;
  (b) fluid factor migration is a necessary condition for protection of real incomes of other, immobile, factors;
  (c) such a scheme will almost surely collapse if economic fluctuations in sub-regions are negatively correlated or uncorrelated;
  (d) all of the above choices are correct;
  (E) none of the above choices is correct.

Floating Exchange Rates

60. Under floating (flexible) exchange rates:

  (a) national policies do not have real effects;
  (B) the 'J'-curve may deter prompt adjustment;
  (c) capital inflows are nil;
  (d) two of the above choices are correct;
  (e) choices **(a)**, **(b)** and **(c)** are correct.

61. Choose the correct statement:

  (a) obedience to Friedman's Rule requires that one's foreign-exchange rate be trendless;
  (B) in an open economy under fixed exchange rates, the central bank cannot control monetary growth;
  (c) in an open economy under fixed exchange rates, fiscal policy determines inflation;
  (d) all of the above choices are correct;
  (e) none of the above choices is correct.

62. Choose the correct statement:

  (a) Friedman (1953b) argues that currency speculation is destabilizing;
  (B) Friedman (1953b) also argues that flexible exchange rates promote national policy independence;

(c) if foreign-exchange rates are typically dominated by 'asset market events', adherence to purchasing power parity is much facilitated;

(d) two of the above choices are correct;

(e) none of the above choices is correct.

63. Choose the correct statement:

(A) the *Dutch disease* concerns effects on traditional export sectors of rapid development of natural gas or crude oil exporting activity;

(b) Appreciation of the exchange rate is a major link in deindustrialization effects of an oil boom;

(c) in general, currency appreciation is highly adverse to living standards;

(d) two of the above choices are correct;

(e) choices **(a)**, **(b)** and **(c)** are correct.

64. (See Burstein, 1986, Chapter 10.) Choose the correct statement:

(A) if terms of trade changes are dominated by financial-market events, floating rate régimes imitate neurasthenic fixed-rate ones;

(b) stagflation supplies convincing proof that, in the modern global economy, monetary forces do not influence price behaviour;

(c) in Mundell's model, American monetary expansion stimulates Europe;

(d) two of the above choices are correct;

(e) none of the above choices is correct.

Stagflation, etc.

65. (See Burstein, 1986, Chapter 10.) Choose the correct statement:

(a) stagflation is more likely if lags are short and business cycles are in phase;

(B) Mr Heath's fate illustrates that inflation is an essentially monetary phenomenon;

(c) the fate of M. Mitterrand's first economic policy illustrates how the post-Bretton Woods régime confers autarchy on medium-sized economies;

(d) all of the above choices are correct;
(e) none of the above choices is correct.

Selected Topics

66. Choose the correct statement:

(a) the Marshall–Lerner condition is met if the absolute sum of demand elasticities exceeds unity;
(b) imperfect capital mobility leads to massive floods of funds in response to interest-rate disparities – and indeed is *imperfect* for that reason;
(c) the Laursen–Metzler effect arises from efforts to maintain living standards in the face of changes in the purchasing power of incomes – and so concerns stimulus to absorption from currency depreciation;
(D) at least two of the above choices are correct;
(e) none of the above choices is correct.

Bretton Woods and After; International Liquidity Régimes (See also Lecture Four, Section 4.1.3)

67. Which of the following leads to decreased demand for international reserves?

(a) replacement of a gold standard by a floating-rate régime;
(b) massive swap agreements between central banks;
(c) less covariance between business cycles;
(D) two of the above choices are correct;
(e) choices (a), (b) and (c) are correct.

68. The Bretton Woods System:

(a) deployed adjustable pegs, if erratically;
(b) imposed the brunt of the adjustment burden on non-reserve currencies;
(c) yielded seigneurage profits to the United States – surely according to General de Gaulle;
(d) two of the above choices are correct;

(E) choices **(a)**, **(b)** and **(c)** are correct.

69. As for the Bretton Woods system:

    (A) the United States effectively acquired two essential rôles;
    (b) one rôle concerned provision of inconvertible US dollars;
    (c) the Triffin dilemma was solved when Mr Nixon inexplicably took the United States off gold in 1971;
    (d) all of the above choices are correct;
    (e) none of the above choices is correct.

70. Choose the correct statement:

    (A) in an open economy under fixed exchange rates, money-supply growth has no clear-cut causal effect on domestic inflation;
    (b) under Bretton Woods, the American dollar was inconvertible;
    (c) under Bretton Woods, adjustment burdens were borne almost entirely by reserve-currency economies;
    (d) two of the above choices are correct;
    (e) choices **(a)**, **(b)** and **(c)** are correct.

71. Post-Bretton Woods (post-1971) experience with floating rates has:

    (A) been substantially inconsistent with purchasing power parity theorems;
    (b) found the exchange value of the US dollar (USD) almost perfectly inversely correlated with the American business cycle;
    (c) found asset-market events irrelevant for foreign-exchange-rate movements;
    (d) all of the above choices are correct;
    (e) none of the above choices is correct.

72. As for post-Bretton Woods exchange-rate turbulence:

    (a) outcomes have been pretty much in line with 'academic' forecasts;

(B) speculation cannot be rejected as a driving force;

(c) non-sterilizing central-bank intervention occurs when the central bank does not allow changes in foreign-exchange reserves to affect domestic money supply;

(d) all of the above choices are correct;

(e) none of the above choices is correct.

73. Choose the correct statement:

(a) the domestic-credit-expansion (DCE) criterion is a necessary corollary to Friedman's money-growth Rule under a régime of floating exchange rates;

(B) domestic-credit-expansion criteria sensitize monetary policy to the balance of payments;

(c) J. S. Mill, perhaps the most fanatic of the currency schoolmen, is the father of the International Monetary Fund's *domestic credit expansion* criterion;

(d) all of the above choices are correct;

(e) none of the above choices is correct.

SELECTIVE ANNOTATIONS

Problem 57

57(a) This choice was quite fully analysed in the annotation of Problem **4** (Lecture Two).

57(b) An economy possessing a stable point of full-employment equilibrium may be immiserated; its labour force may be absorbed in producing primary products for export that are what was quaintly called 'drugs on the market' – and, for the rest, taking in each other's washing. In any event, a small open economy's 'trade cycle' is sensitized to terms-of-trade movements – as is obvious from American economic history from say 1730–1870. The 'classical' formula for economic growth of a small open economy emphasizes capital build-up, especially human-capital build-up, permitting the labour force to be absorbed in high-value-added action.

57(c) Indeed, a principal proposition of classical economic theory concerns the neutrality of real economic action, surely secular action, against money-growth. The proper problem, explored in Lecture Six, concerns the ability of a central bank to control money supply. Under floating rates, such control is easily obtained. Under fixed rates, rather simplistic, but widely diffused, analysis concludes that there would be no control of money supply. Less simplistic analysis, defining 'money' much more broadly, yields a rather clotted result permitting some control of 'money supply', subject to severe constraint. The more sophisticated analysis of Lecture Ten shatters the paradigms so far explored; 'money supply' becomes a quite vacuous notion.

Problem 58

58(c) No! Indeed the debt burdens of Mexico, Argentina, Brazil *et al.* are so critical for these economies, and their bankers, precisely because their foreign debts are largely denominated in US dollars – and, more important, payable in 'hard currencies'. In the upshot, then, capital flows do not necessarily influence the *j*-dollar exchange rate: US dollar borrowings are directly spent on imported goods; and subsequent exports are sold for hard currencies, which are diverted towards debt-repayment; *j*-dollar flows are simply not in play.

Problem 59

Context is supplied by Friedman (1953b):

> In a sense, any flexible exchange system is . . . a mixed system, since there are rigid rates between the different sections of one nation . . . A group of politically independent nations all of which firmly adhered to, say, the gold standard would thereby in effect submit themselves to a central monetary authority, albeit an impersonal one. If, in addition, they firmly adhered to the free movement of goods, people and capital without restrictions, and economic conditions rendered such movement easy, they would, in effect, be an economic unit for which a single currency – which is the equivalent of rigid exchange rates – would be appropriate.

> Friedman (1953b, p. 193, note 16)

So feasibility of flexible exchange is determined, to some extent at least, by *transactions cost*. The following stylized example from Burstein (1986, p. 188) illustrates central issues of determination of *optimal currency zones*.

After Irish independence the Irish pound remained tied to the British pound for some time. The economic rationale must have been compelling.

Assume, counterfactually, that Irish exports mostly went to Britain *and* that the Irish and British pounds floated against each other. Then Irish pound proceeds of Irish exports might fluctuate substantially. And, to the extent that wage bargains are stickily set in Irish pounds, exporters' net proceeds fluctuate still more erratically. Indeed, their variance might be dominated by currency rate fluctuations so that Irish exporters, if they could not purchase cheap insurance, willy nilly would be currency speculators. Nor would so thin a market work smoothly: only a few futures contracts can be written efficiently (see Telser, 1981).

After Ireland joined the Common Market (EEC), the links between Irish and British currency were severed. (A proximate cause was Britain's refusal to join the European currency 'snake'.) Since Irish trade drifted towards the continent after Ireland joined the EEC, the 'variance minimization' hypothesis is supported both by the Irish-British currency link, while it lasted, and its severance.

Choice of Metric

Lecture Ten illuminates the following conjecture. Say that, on average, producers in region z competitively sell their outputs on British, French, American and German markets in fairly stable value-weighted proportions. If these markets are dominated by their national currencies, socioeconomic stability is promoted by expressing wage bargains in an imaginary currency unit, 'comprising' British, French, etc. currency-unit fragments – the Pfolmar. And Pfolmar-denominated debt may be ordinarily discharged by z-dollar tenders. Life imitates Art: the fable substantially describes the *raison d'être* of the European Currency Unit (ECU).

59(a)　The introductory material just above fully explains why **59(a)** is rejected.

59(b)　The Stolper–Samuelson theorem postulates a contrary conclusion. (The theorem is limned at pp. 208–9.) Not that the theorem is all that robust: the rejection of **59(b)** should be treated diffidently. Thus, if factors are not mobile between two points and if, so to speak, the economic temperatures of the points change oppositely, a macropolicy intended to stabilize one point will destabilize the other. Perfect factor mobility would (here) assure even heat distribution; and make uniform macropolicy more attractive.

59(c) This response too is rather problematical. 'Unregulated' adjustment is abetted by negative or nil correlation of subregional fluctuations. Then the localities will not drag each other down; a slump at one point will be mitigated by buoyant demand for imports at another. The effects on economic regulation (say, fiscal policy) are quite different: if the trade cycles of two members of a currency zone are in counterphase, a policy directed towards cooling off one 'point economy' will exacerbate unemployment at the other – in the Keynesian paradigm.

The Variance Minimization Hypothesis

The idea that, in some sense, 'economic variance' is minimized if currency zones are defined optimally is heuristically appealing. In 1986 I sought a more systematic explanation:

> When will a common unit of account minimize variance of regional income, prices or some other variable X? Consider an economic domain. Points belonging to it that are coloured red share a particular unit of account – and belong to subset R. Violet point p does not belong to R. If the variance of X, a composite based on the value of X reckoned at each point belonging to R, would fall if p were to join R, p should join R – relative to the variance-minimization criterion. Next consider red point q. If q were removed from R, the variance of X, reckoned as before, would fall: the criterion requires removal of q from R. Boundaries constructed this way are unlikely to conform to political ones.
>
> Burstein (1986, p. 187)

Problem 60

60(a) This improper choice seems to have a sinister appeal. But the spell is readily broken. Thus we have seen that, in mathematical modelling, one solves for *terms of trade*. If the solution of a problem in comparative statics requires revised terms of trade, the upshot may be accomplished either by proportionate changes in prices (!) or by exchange rate adjustment. The mathematics are blind to the exchange-rate régime.

Now consider a counterexample. Real public-sector spending on goods and services increases in the jth economy. Under a 'full employment' stipulation, equilibrium terms of trade improve–at least in the standard format.

60(B) The 'J-Curve' is glossed in Lecture Two. Any newspaper reader knows that real-world balance-of-payments adjustment is subject to long, erratic lags, so that relative prices are significantly distorted over lengthy intervals.

60(c) Another improper choice that seems to exert sinister appeal. Perhaps one reason for confusion on this point lies in the intrinsic ambiguity of the idea of *equilibrium* in this setting: 'equilibrium' capital flows ensue from strategic choices – see Lecture Four.

Problem 61

61(a) This choice is, so to speak, precisely wrong. A prime rationale for floating rates is that they confer powers of monetary autarchy; if Economy E elects more rapid monetary expansion than the global norm, the E-dollar rate(s) will fall secularly; the E-dollar rate(s) will trend down.

Friedman knows that his Rule makes no sense under fixed-exchange. Floating rates are an acknowledgedly indispensable companion to his money-supply(or central-bank-credit) Rule.

61(B) There are few consensuses in economics as strong as this one. This is the standard drill (solidified by the commentary on Problem **73**). An increase in domestic credit expansion is offset by a loss of foreign assets, reflecting disposition abroad of unwanted monetary assets, reflected by a balance-of-payments

deficit; purchases of assets from aliens comprise capital outflow, offset by national reserve loss. The result described by
the lecture is more guarded. (It describes an equilibrium like
that of a bank–oligopoly model; and it evokes systems of
currency-competition.)

61(c) No! In such an economy, inflation is determined by global
forces. This is made especially clear in Lecture Eight (on the
classical theory of money.)

Problem 62

62(a) *Au contraire*! Indeed Friedman's (1953b) discussion remains of
particular interest – even in the light of the massive literature
that has flowed from his early study.

> People who argue that speculation is generally destabilizing
> seldom realize that this is largely equivalent to saying that
> speculators lose money, since speculation can be destabiliz-
> ing in general only if speculators on the average sell when
> the currency is low in price and buy when it is high.

Friedman (1953b, p. 175)

Friedman's analysis tacitly stipulates existence of a well-
defined equilibrium state based on such 'real' factors as purchasing power parity. Experience in the 1980s has been of
exchange rates that fluctuate like share prices; of markets
dominated by capital-account transactions. It is not preposterous to suggest that the upshot resembles a pseudo-fixed-
exchange system in which exchange-rate pars lurch about
drunkenly, leading to ceaseless distortion of real values.

62(B) The choice must be obviously correct to any of Friedman's
readers, but reflection erodes the importance of the point.
True, floating rates afford much more latitude to money-
supply policy, on the tacit assumption that inflation is closely
linked to money-growth. But many libertarians conclude that
liberty is better served by the impersonality of the gold standard's drive-mechanism than by a national autarchy that lib-
erates a nation's 'directorate' so that perhaps the 'directorate'

is better able to impose its will – or its caprices – on the people. A member of a nation state who does not wish to be subject to others' wills is hardly better off because he is dominated by an authoritative fellow citizen instead of the impersonal constraints of, say, a gold-standard ordering.

62(c) the absurdity of the choice perhaps drives home the importance of the point. See the commentary on **Problem 62(a)**. Many economists cling to purchasing power parity as a norm regardless of the lessons of experience.

Problem 63

63(A), (b) See Rivera-Batiz and Rivera-Batiz (1985, pp. 265–7) and their citations. The putative driving force is currency *appreciation*: choice **(63b)** is incorrect.

The *Dutch Disease* – a term reflecting a misreading of Dutch and Norwegian experience after discovery of oil and gas deposits under their territorial waters – is *not* a disease; it is a beneficent syndrome that appears hard to decipher. To the extent that enhanced wealth stimulates imports and new wealth is placed abroad, there is no upward pressure on our exchange rate. Such pressure works to fill in the gap between foreign-exchange inflows and the induced outflows just limned. And indeed, if countervailing policy measures are excluded, there will be *some* excess supply of foreign currency – at least, by conventional reckoning; see Lecture Ten – unless our currency appreciates. The currency appreciation (an improvement in terms of trade) diverts *excess demand* for our manufactured goods abroad, and diverts our exports to the home market – hardly an example of deindustrialization. Thus if home-produced services are more income elastic than home goods, some labour may be diverted from manufacturing to services, a benign enough process.

Pressure against domestic manufacturing results from the improvement in terms of trade; it is an ancillary effect of a follow-on benefit from say oil and natural gas discoveries. Labour is released from manufacturing only because the opportunity cost of retaining such labour has increased; the release further enhances our welfare.

63(c) Recall Lecture Four: all else the same, currency appreciation *enhances* living standards: our resource-expenditure commands more goods. The theory of policy concerns trade-offs that may exist between this beneficent effect and negatively valued consequences such as reduced manufacturing employment (perhaps). An instinctually mercantilist mind set, rife among City men and politicians, lauds the 'stimulus' of worse terms of trade, permitting (!) us to obtain less utility from a unit of resource expenditure. Keynes's 'Notes on Mercantilism' (Ch 23 of the *General Theory*) continue to supply a fillip to perverse reasoning about these matters.

Problem 64

64(A) See the annotation of Choice **62(c)**.

64(b) (and choice **65(a)**) The term *stagflation* implies a blunder; it implies persistent belief in the discredited 'Phillips Curve' trade-off between employment or real growth and inflation. It is now amply established that the Phillips trade-off is an illusion: at most an unexpected price acceleration (inflation-rate increase) may supply temporary stimulus; or an unexpected price deceleration may temporarily damp real growth. The correct analysis is based on the complex lead–lag processes governing real-world evolutions of economic data. Think of a pulsator randomly emanating energy waves. Interference predominates so that fluctuation in observed energy-intensity of received radiation may inspire elaborate, if baseless, conjectures.

Consider this example (based on Burstein, 1986, p. 157). *B* may be stimulated by orders placed during *A*'s boom, and filled during the *A* recession. *B* prices may not accelerate until its boom is well along; or only towards the end of *B*'s boom, continuing to accelerate well into the ensuing recession. Costs of production thus tend to fall during early stages of recoveries as physical capital and 'tenured' labour fall. Economies *A* and *B* may have identical growth and inflation norms; and cycles that are in counterphase.

64(c) Swoboda's (1983, pp. 94–5) succinct summary of Mundell's

(1968) model emphatically refutes choice **64(c)** The model is intensely Keynesian: real rates of interest are determined by monetary phenomena:

> A fiscal boom is transmitted abroad, whereas a monetary expansion at home increases income there but reduces it abroad. The reason is that a fiscal expansion that raises the domestic interest rate creates a capital inflow, a depreciation of the foreign currency, and an increase in net foreign exports. In contrast, a domestic monetary expansion induces a depreciation of the domestic currency, a capital outflow, and an increase in domestic net exports, the counterpart to which is a fall in foreign exports and capital.

> Swoboda (1983, pp. 94–5)

Problem 65

65(a)   See the annotation of choice **64(b)**.

65(B)   In 1986 (pp. 160–2) I outlined two episodes that go far to explain the political economy of stagflation: 'Mr Heath's Fate and the aftermath of M. Mitterrand's 1981 triumph'. (This is written soon after M. Mitterrand's 1988 triumph, based on the perceived sincerity of his recantation of the principles he espoused in 1981.)

Mr Edward Heath, British Prime Minister, 1970–4, denied responsibility for British inflation, insisting that it was imported: rising prices of imports, measured in sterling, were his government's fate, not its fault. And inflation often looks cost-based – however speciously.

Early in Mr Heath's term fiscal policy became expansive; and rising expenditures were readily accommodated by correspondingly expansive monetary policy. Massive increases in consumption expenditure led to current-account deficits easily financed by external borrowing. Imported supply floated up to meet intensified demand; in early stages of the expansion, goods markets were not disequilibrated.

Recently-discovered North Sea oil deposits shot up in value in the wake of the 1973 oil shocks. It was easy to finance the current-account deficits; capital inflow supported sterling. But, quite soon, rapidly growing external British debt alarmed creditors – *in esse* and *in posse*. The British government became concerned about its mounting external debt. It became prudent, if not mandatory, to abandon efforts to support sterling through foreign borrowing. Prescient speculators who sold sterling short, and held on, scored heavily.

The imported inflation chimera came into play. Depreciation of sterling led to higher prices of imports; the upshot looked like cost-push. As the annotation of choice **64(b)** shows controlling lags are characteristically complex. So the dénouement is reached: stagflation! Real wages eroded as prices increased, i.e. as effects of sterling depreciation worked their way through pipelines. Labour unrest followed. Mr Heath's confrontation with the miners led to his fall.

65(c) Events in France, following M. Mitterrand's election in 1981, mirrored the British story – and, indeed, moved faster to a more dramatic economic conclusion (but, as we have seen, to a very different political conclusion – one reason for the political difference perhaps lying in Mr Heath's election slogan: The Man of Principle). The first Mitterrand government operated a *closed* Keynesian model. Expansive fiscal policy provoked a huge trade deficit and a flight from the franc – as would be forecast by even a simplistic *open* Keynesian model.

Huge support operations, contributing to an unprecedented level of foreign-held debt, failed to prop up the franc. In a few months the French economy went through the British cycle of the annotation of choice **65(b)**. And stagflation, as it seemed, persisted past Autumn 1984 . . . Finally M. Mitterrand abandoned his theories, changed his government, luckily lost the parliamentary election of 1985 and was returned triumphantly in 1988. There may be a moral in the tale.

Problem 66

66(a) We largely elide careful analysis of the famous *Marshall–Lerner condition*; fortunately resulting complexities lie outside our domain of discourse. A rather grotesque formula is supplied by Metzler (1948).

If the discrepancy between exports and imports is small,

relative to the total value of foreign trade, it can easily be shown that a depreciation of the currency of either country in the proportion K will bring about a change, positive or negative, in that country's balance of payments on current account, which has the following value, relative to the value of exports

$$K[\eta_1\eta_2(1+\sigma_1+\sigma_2)+\sigma_1\sigma_2(\eta_1+\eta_2-1)/$$
$$(\eta_1+\sigma_2)(\eta_2+\sigma_1)] \tag{6.27}$$

[The ηs are demand elasticities and the σs supply elasticities.] The foreign exchange market is obviously[!] unstable unless the expression in the brackets is positive: exchange stability requires that depreciation must increase a country's net supply of foreign exchange.

Metzler (1948, footnote 4)

The algebra for the case $\sigma_1 = \sigma_2 = \infty$, is more transparent. Assume that prices are parametric for both countries – that supply elasticities are indefinitely large. Then the condition for exchange stability in Metzler's special case is the Marshall–Lerner condition: the sum of absolute values of the demand elasticities, $\eta_1 + \eta_2$, should exceed unity. This result is established more firmly below. Meanwhile consider these remarks:

1. One tacitly assumes that the various industries are competitively organized so that potential monopolistic or monopsonistic power is not exploited. The realm of scientific tariffs, Beggar My Neighbour, reciprocal and demand curves, etc. is avoided.
2. The heuristics of the Marshall–Lerner condition, now understood to be a very special case, follow. If foreign demand for our imports were zero-elastic, a 1% depreciation reduces intake of foreign currency by 1%; the trade balance can stay intact if our elasticity of demand for imports is at least unity.

The reader should show how the Marshall–Lerner cross-over point is achieved when foreign and domestic demand-elasticities are each –0.5.

A More Rigorous Derivation of the Marshall–Lerner Condition

(See Sohmen, 1958, an appendix to Kindleberger, 1958, pp. 610–12).

Define the trade balance in terms of foreign currency:

$$B = f(p/\xi)(p/\xi) - g(\xi\,\pi)\pi \qquad (6.28)$$

Glossing equation (6.28), and taking the United States as the home country, p is the US price for exported goods, ξ the exchange rate, expressed as the number of units of domestic currency commanded by a composite unit of foreign currency; π is the price of American imports, expressed in the foreign measure. Of course the price of American goods in the composite foreign measure is p/ξ so that American receipts of foreign currency on trade account are given by the product $(X)(p/\xi)$, where $X = f(p/\xi)$. Similarly, American foreign-currency payments on trade account are given by $g(\xi\pi)$.

Differentiate the trade balance, B, with respect to ξ:

$$dB/d\xi = f'\,()\,[p/\xi^2(p/\xi)] + X(-p/\xi^2) - g'\,()\,[\pi^2] \qquad (6.29)$$

If Giffen goods can be excluded,

$$dB/d\xi = X(p/\xi^2(\eta_x - 1) + (J)\pi\eta_m/\xi \qquad (6.30)$$

where η_x and η_m are absolute values of elasticities of demand for American exports and imports.

Further algebraic manipulation leads to the condition for exchange depreciation to improve the trade balance, i.e. for $dB/d\xi > 0$ – where V_x and V_m are initial values of American exports and imports expressed in the foreign measure:

$$(V_j/V_x)\eta_x + \eta_m > 1 \qquad (6.31)$$

If trade were balanced *ab initio*, the Marshall–Lerner condition emerges. But if there is an initial trade deficit, 'a small depreciation still results in an improvement even if the sum of the demand elasticities falls below unity. The permissible deficiency depends on the size of the trade deficit') (Kindleberger, 1958, p. 612).

Multiple Equilibria

Friedman poses the following interesting conjecture:

> As a practical matter, the conditions necessary for any relevant range of rates to have the property that a rise increases excess demand seems to me highly unlikely to occur. But, if they should occur, it would merely mean that there might be two possible positions of equilibrium, one above, the other below, the existing . . . rate. If the higher is regarded as preferable, the implication for policy would be first to appreciate the . . . rate and then to set it free.
>
> Friedman (1953b, p. 160)

(The analysis is not concerned with 'autonomous' speculative episodes – see Burstein, 1986, Chapter 6. Rather it concerns parameter values *à la* the Marshall–Lerner condition analysis.)

First consider a physical analogy. Say that there are numerous sources of gravitational-like fields. Each field is weak: particles will often escape the attractive force of field F_i. But a free particle will, with a probability approaching unity, be sucked into Field F_j ($j \neq i$) within time-interval T. The system is weakly stable; the particles will not escape the finite space in which the analysis is conducted. The physical analogy translates into economics in an obvious way.

Figure (6.3) depicts Friedman's case. The exchange rate has been at the unstable equilibrium value *0b*; in Friedman's scenario, it has been held at *0b* via controls. Exchange rates *0a* and *0c* are stable equilibrium values. So the authorities can exploit the system's local instability by releasing the exchange rate in the appropriate direction. The upshot is similar to Nelson's (1956) analysis of low-equilibrium growth traps – see Branson (1979, pp. 487–90) and Burstein (1986, p. 124).

66(C) Rivera-Batiz and Rivera-Batiz (1985) – citing Laursen and Metzler (1950) and Dornbusch (1980) – ably describe the *Laursen–Metzler* effect:

> . . . Domestic residents may keep their real expenditure constant whenever they face a reduction in purchasing power. Then a devaluation [we prefer to say depreciation]

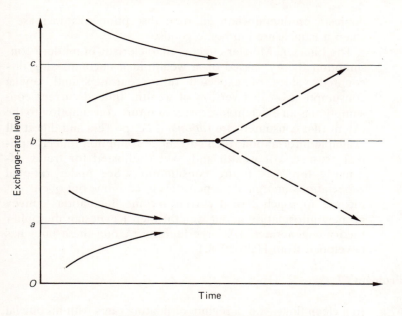

Figure 6.3   Friedman's scenario

The solid arrows simply indicate that the respective equilibria are stable. The dashed lines describe an 'evolution' such that, when control is abandoned, the controller need open only the upper or lower valve in order to send the system to the upper or lower equilibrium level.

> leads to an increase in absorption (i.e. an increase in expenditure measured in terms of domestic goods) in order to offset the decrease in purchasing power of domestic output . . . The [Laursen–Metzler] effect arises whenever domestic residents try to maintain their standard of living in the face of changes in the purchasing power of their income.
>
> Rivera-Batiz and Rivera-Batiz (1985, p. 176)

This is the 'trick' behind the analysis. Upon depreciating its currency, Economy E, surely if it is at full employment, faces a more confining budget constraint: it must surrender more home goods to obtain given quantums of foreign goods. If Economy E agents defy this decay in their real income, gross domestic product unchanged, their absorption must increase – when it is measured in home goods.

The Laursen–Metzler effect is characteristic of modern consumption theory, based on a wealth-idea encompassing discounted values of expected future earnings and keying consumption on this version of wealth. Indeed current consumption is an efficient forecaster of future consumption to the extent that consumers are *rational* – i.e. possess and digest all available information; then current consumption reflects optimal estimates of wealth and, when adjusted for trend, efficiently forecasts future consumption. So, under rational expectations, marginal propensities to consume out of current income approach *zero* if current-income fluctuations convey no new information about wealth; then Keynesian multiplier theory degenerates. (A large literature along these lines has developed from Hall, 1978.)

Problem 67

67(a) In a clean float – i.e. a régime of floating rates with nil official intervention – there would be no need for official reserves! And private 'speculators' would be strongly motivated to iron out transient fluctuations in exchange rates; so that indeed private agents manage reserve-stocks under a clean float in the way specialists hold 'stocks of shares' in Wall Street.

67(b) The choice is obviously correct. In the same way unused overdraft facility is a very close substitute for cash balances in the micro-analysis of a closed monetary system. The central banks in an open-economy model may be perceived as members of a clearing house in a giro schema.

67(c) If covariance between business (trade) cycles decreases, a reserve drain from Economy *A* is, of course, matched by reserve-accretions elsewhere. But recall the ancient banking adage, do not lend money to people who need it(!): terms may be onerous; and a slow leak may become a haemorrhage, especially if speculative possibilities are fully explored. High covariance reduces the likelihood of drains occurring; and so, on net, reduces demand for reserves.

Problem 68

68(a) Friedman's (1953b) appraisal of the Bretton Woods system proved prescient:

> In short, the system of occasional changes in temporarily rigid exchange rates seems to me the worst of two worlds: it provides neither the stability of expectations that a genuinely rigid and stable exchange rate could provide in a world of unrestricted trade and willingness and ability to adjust the internal price structure to external conditions nor the continuous sensitivity of a flexible exchange rate.

> Friedman (1953b, p. 164

Does Friedman consider the 'continuous sensitivity' that saw the US dollar soar to a $1.10/1 £ level in 1984 and plunge to $1.88/1 £ during 1988 to be entirely benign?

68(b) Both the Bretton Woods régime and its successor (with its stringent IMF drill, imposed on lagging debtors) rely on deficit-economy adjustment; in neither régime is there meaningful external pressure on economies running trade-surpluses to adjust – other than to react to the pointlessness of building up credits against bankrupts. Keynes's proposal *circa* 1943 to tax credit balances – in the context of his 'Bancor' plan – would indeed have shifted the adjustment-burden towards economies running trade surpluses – while perhaps neglecting necessary restraint on profligates.

68(c) (This annotation also pertains to choice **68(b)**.) So long as demand for US dollar balances for international reserve purposes grew, the United States was free to run trade deficits without coming under pressure; and, as a reserve-supplier under Bretton Woods, and as a debtor (*circa* 1988) whose debt is denominated in its own currency, the United States has never faced a convertibility crisis – with an important exception. The exception was in 1971, when Mr Nixon essentially demolished Bretton Woods. Obsessed by the 1972 election – the Watergate crisis was in the near future – Mr Nixon, advised by Mr Connolly, was highly averse towards Restraint.

In the post-war era, the United States has earned immense seigneurage profits, selling paper for real assets or, in the Reagan years, for consumption flows.

Two Remarks

1. In the heyday of American economic suzerainty the United States did *not* run trade deficits. Rather it effectively traded liquid assets, especially treasury securities, for real assets, especially in Europe.
2. Notably since 1986, capital inflows into the United States have taken the form of foreign purchase of *real* American assets. The upshot has not been entirely prodigal: American overabsorption should not be entirely ascribed to its undoubted consumption binge; much of the American trade deficit can be ascribed to indirect importation of capital goods (encompassing labour costs of construction) offset by tapping foreign savings. Agreed, it would not be necessary to tap foreign savings if American savings were larger!

Problem 69

69(A) It is indeed often said that, under Bretton Woods, the United States exercised two rôles: (1) maintaining convertibility of the dollar into gold; (2) supplying international liquidity. It was, of course, a pleasure for the US to discharge the second 'duty'. The first 'rôle' is more problematical; nor indeed is the second embedded in the Bretton Woods Agreement; both 'rôles' developed haphazardly. *All* members could discharge their obligations either by maintaining gold-convertibility (as the United States did at a 13.71 grains of gold per dollar rate) or by maintaining exchange rates *vis-à-vis* the other n-1 currencies at rates conforming to published gold parities (for all n currencies). In fact, as McKinnon (1979) explains, only the United States exercised the gold-convertibility option while eschewing intervention as a general rule. And the United States dollar was the intervention, and vehicle, currency. (See the commentary on problems **68(b)** and **68(c)**.)

69(c) The 'Triffin Dilemma' concerns steady decay over the 1953–1971 interval in the ratio borne by American gold reserves to American liabilities to official foreign agents. The second rôle became inconsistent with gold convertibility of the dollar, at least on the assumption that the *de facto* régime comprised a gold-exchange standard so that the dollar was, for official holders, an indirect, and interest yielding, way of holding gold. An alternative explanation to the Triffin dilemma is this: Messrs Nixon and Connolly wanted more freedom to undertake expansive monetary/fiscal-policy during the run-up to the 1972 election; the convertibility rôle was a clog on a gathering policy, but was not the root of an imminent crisis.

I studied the Triffin dilemma years ago; see Burstein (1963, pp. 852–61). Triffin's (1961) statement of the dilemma is lapidary:

> The most fundamental deficiency of the present system, and the main danger to its future stability lies in the fact that it leaves the satisfactory development of world monetary liquidity primarily dependent upon an admittedly insufficient supply of new gold and an admittedly dangerous and haphazard expansion in the short-term indebtedness of key-currency countries.
>
> Triffin (1961, pp. 100–1)

Three 'cures' were prominently in play. One, Harrod's, was to increase the gold-price: at a high-enough gold price, any liquidity 'shortage' is eliminated; indeed, at a high enough gold price a very small physical stock of gold is consistent with excess liquidity. Harrod's proposal was brushed aside, partly because it was so simple, partly because it would have reduced the importance of the IMF *fonctionnaires*.

Triffin's plan, and that of Dr E. M. Bernstein, would have enhanced IMF Powers. (See Triffin, 1961.) Triffin's plan would substitute 'IMF balances for balances in national currencies (mostly dollars and sterling) in all member countries' monetary reserves' (Triffin, 1961, p. 103). The IMF would exercise both the monetary and regulatory powers of a central bank.

Under the Bernstein plan, the IMF would have issued its own liabilities – long-term debt – in exchange for gold or scarce currency, lending the proceeds to member countries experiencing balance-of-payments trouble; an essentially unchanged global reserve-stock was to be deployed more efficiently.

The following remarks (mine) contain the thrust of this annotation:

> Triffin's institution could acquire claims payable in gold against surplus economies through open-market sales of securities, forcing them to tender dollar and sterling accretions to Triffin's Fund. Such intervention confirms Bernstein's concern that the Triffin institution would intervene forcefully in national affairs. I suspect this is the real rub: Triffin's proposals lead to IMF acquisition of many central-bank powers; the international institution would acquire no little suzerainity.
>
> Burstein (1963, p. 861)

Problem 70

70(A) An extreme, and chimerical, version of this proposition is the so-called *law of one price*, requiring that prices of traded goods be identical at all locations always, allowing only for transport and other such costs. The schemae of Lecture Eight are much more moderate; but they suffice to establish that, under fixed exchange rates, causality runs from behaviour of prices *part-out*, perhaps reflecting global trends in money-supply and money demand, to prices and money supply in 'our' economy. (See Burstein, 1986, Chapter 11 – much influenced by Girton and Roper, 1978.)

Problem 71

Problem 71 is inserted for review purposes; it breaks no new ground. But it is worth continuing to pound away at the point underlying choices **71(b)** and **71(c)**. The reasoning controlling the interest-parity controls stock-market investment generally. If share prices at New York are of a sudden expected to rise more rapidly than elsewhere, the dollar must shoot up (overshoot), so that total returns over holding periods are globally equalized; losses on dollar-exchange compensate for differential dividend-yield-plus-capital-gain at New York. More naively, enthusiasm about American investment prospects induces demand for dollar-assets eligible for tender for shares (but see Lecture Ten) and so pushes up the dollar; or gloom about American prospects pushes the dollar down.

It is well known that foreign-trade finance accounts only for a smallish part of the immense flows sloshing across the global financial grid.

Caveat

A 'high' dollar rate does not discourage portfolio investment; but the prospect of a *falling* dollar does. Direct investment is another story: if sterling is 'high' – as in May 1988 – it is unattractive to site plants, producing products shipped o'er the world, in Britain: costs, expressed in say complex (imaginary) trade-weighted currency units, are then too high in Britain.

Problem 72

72(a) 'Academic' forecasters have been disappointed in at least two ways. Exchange-rate movements, post-1971, have not been as closely keyed to 'trade events' (purchasing power parity for example) as theory had suggested. And forward rates have not been good predictors of spot rates in future.

72(B) We have spent much energy making this point. But 'speculation' is a vague concept. *All* transactors are influenced by expectations of price-behaviour of potential purchases or sales, unless relevant half lives of the goods are extremely short.

72(c) The choice is, so to speak, precisely wrong. Recall Keynes's forceful criticism of the sterilization policies of the United States and France in the 1920s, especially his *Treatise* (1930, II, Chapter 35).

Problem 73

73(a), (B) Since *domestic credit expansion* criteria sensitize money-growth to the trade balance, it is obviously inconsistent with Friedman's Rule. (See the annotation of Choice **61(a)**.) As for choice **73(B)**, see Burstein (1986, pp. 182–5). Newlyn and Bootle (1978) prepare the ground:

> It is convenient to distinguish an increase in the money supply from domestic-credit expansion . . . In a closed economy, $\Delta M = DCE$ and this is also the case if the over-all balance of payments is exactly in balance, leaving the *foreign assets* of the central bank unchanged. However, if [foreign assets increase] money supply will increase by more than domestic credit expansion; and [if foreign assets decrease] ΔM will be less than DCE.
>
> Newlyn and Bootle (1978, p. 26)

Thus, if money and DCE have been growing at a target rate of $x^*\%$ per annum, and if the current account, which had been in balance, goes into surplus, *and* if the x^* target for DCE is to be sustained, money growth must exceed x^*. If the current account deteriorates, so that the central bank is drained of foreign assets, money growth must fall below x^* if the DCE target is to be hit: DCE approximately equals the change in money supply plus the balance of payments deficit.

Newlyn and Bootle (1978, p. 176) interestingly discuss Britain's traumatic 1977 experience. The Chancellor had to issue a Letter of Intent committing Britain to meet the IMF's DCE conditions in order to obtain further IMF credits.

73(c) See Burstein (1986, p. 185), citing J. S. Mill. Mill was, if anything, sympathetic to the Banking School, opposing the currency principle. The Currency School, and later writers in its spirit, argue that narrowly-defined monetary-aggregate targeting can be effective, despite exclusion from the target of important liquid-asset categories (e.g., bank deposits). The Bank Charter Act debate (1844) concerns a *de facto* definition of money that excludes bank deposits. See Fetter (1965), Mints (1945) and Viner (1937).

Note

1. The aureus was a *full-bodied silver* coin of the Roman republic retained by Augustus at 42 to the Roman pound, debased by Nero and again by Caracalla, etc. My incongruous usage may be justified by its charm . . . There is an immense literature on classical economies; for an admirable quick reference, see the article on *Coinage, Roman* in the *Oxford Classical Dictionary*. The Aureus will be joined by another Roman coin, the Caesara, later on in the book.

7 Lecture Seven Neoclassical Foundations of Open-economy Macroeconomics

7.1 PRELIMINARY REMARKS

Lecture Seven contrasts strongly with Lecture Five: in neoclassical economics, relative-price changes motivate adjustment to parameter shifts or stochastic shocks – a burden borne by aggregate-income changes in the Keynesian paradigm. And Lecture Seven strongly complements Lecture Ten: Lecture Seven explains how the evolution of a global *enterprise* may be determined by spontaneous competitive processes; in Lecture Ten, *finance* is explained in the same way. Both processes are transnational; on the plane of theory, the influence of the state is obliterated; and so both supply components of the framework of a liberal world-order.

An Interpolation

Following Hayek (1960), 'spontaneous competitive processes' may be evolutionary in some sense. But, as Hayek also shows, political – economic processes evolve relative to ethical, legal and sociological structures that are *not* invariant against acts of human will: *survival* in political economy has an autonomous dimension excluded from purely biological, or natural, processes. Thus the interactive processes controlling the 'relative wealth(s) of nations' *infra* concern *emulation* more than *rivalry*. (For a perceptive discussion of this problem, from an angle more Darwinian than mine, see Hirshleifer, 1978, 'Natural Economy versus Political Economy'; and indeed all the essays collected in Hirshleifer, 1987. Also D. Friedman, 1977, whose 'The Size and Shape of Nations' is strikingly based on rivalrous instincts.)

For me, the neoclassical economic *Weltanschauung* belongs to a 'wilfully' generated set of values capable of transforming 'natural' impulses towards conflict into urges to cooperate – altruism and benevolence aside. Marx thought otherwise: 'Marx himself was an enthusiastic Darwinist. He saw in Darwin's exposition of the competitive struggle for existence a biological basis in natural science for the class struggle in history' (Hirshleifer, 1978/1987, p. 191, referring to Himmelfarb, 1959, Chapter 19).

7.2.   THE RELATIVE INVARIANCE OF THE WEALTH(S) OF NATIONS(?)

7.2.1   Analytics

Perhaps stationary states culminate classical economics; and steady-growth paths characterize the moving equilibria of neoclassical schemae – on the surface, a happier mode. But neoclassical theory risks awkwardness, if not disaster, for the analysis of open systems in one respect: in the limit, ratios of wealth(s) of economies growing at different rates do not converge – an implication that is both ugly and empirically problematical. (Still, asymptotic properties of models of human behaviour may be uninteresting, if not improper.) So a moving-equilibrium paradigm tenable for open economics must entail interactions between economic groups leading to convergence of growth rates in the limit. Nor is this an egregious demand upon the theory: in a comparable model for Britain, it would surely be impermissable for the ratio

$$\overline{Y}(t)_{\text{Hull}}/\overline{Y}(t)_{\text{Haslemere}} \rightarrow 0 \text{ as } t \rightarrow \infty,$$

where $Y_i(t)$ represents the equilibrium value of the ith locality's per capita income at date t.

Putting these ideas to work in a simple way, study the model comprising Equations (7.1)–(7.3):

$$\dot{W}_i = f^i(W,\varrho,\gamma) \qquad i=1, \ldots, n \tag{7.1}$$

$$\dot{\varrho} = g^i(W,\varrho,\gamma) \qquad i=1, \ldots, n \tag{7.2}$$

$$\dot{\gamma} = h^i(W,\varrho,\gamma) \qquad i=1, \ldots, n \tag{7.3}$$

Glossary

ϱ_i = growth rate of real GNP per capita in the ith economy
γ_i = index of public sector absorption in the ith economy
W_i = per capita all-inclusive (human and non-human) wealth in the ith economy

$\lambda_i = (\varrho_i - \bar{\varrho}_i)$
$\Omega_i = (W_i - \bar{W}_i)$
ω_i = the proportion borne by W_i to $\overset{n}{\Sigma} W_i$

We concentrate on the evolution of (ϱ_i). Convergence of (ϱ_i) onto a common value, ϱ^*, is necessary – but not sufficient – for convergence of ω_i onto $(\bar{\omega}_i)$: thus immediate convergence of growth rates onto ϱ^* here preserves an *arbitrary* initial vector (ω^0). The system's integral is likely to be complicated, if not downright messy.

Turn now to a special case explored in the problem set:

$$\dot{W} = \phi^i(W,\varrho;\gamma^*) \quad i=1, \ldots, n \tag{7.4}$$

$$\dot{\varrho} = \Psi^i(W,\varrho;\gamma^*) \quad i=1, \ldots, n \tag{7.5}$$

Public-sector expenditures, tax-rates and other aspects of 'fiscality', are parametric. The upshot is explained in the annotations and in the stability-discussion *infra*; so the following remarks suffice now. From the angle of the ith fairly small economy, its fiscal policy affects its relative and absolute wealth positions in equilibrium, but not its secular growth rate – determined the way equilibrium price is determined in an isolated competitive market; the secular growth rate is parametric for the ith economy.

The simplistic equation (7.6) reveals an interesting point.

$$f(W_1;\gamma_1) = g(W_2;\gamma_2) \tag{7.6}$$

In a two-economy world $f()$ and $g()$ determine growth rates of real GNP per head. It is stipulated that $\partial f/\partial \gamma_1 < 0$ and $\partial g/\partial \gamma_2 < 0$; it remains to consider partial derivatives (gradients) with respect to wealth. The thrust of neoclassical theory of closed systems is towards $\partial f/\partial W_1 = \partial g/\partial W_2 = 0$; homogeneity rules; the proportion of income saved should be a function of technological terms of trade between consumption now and consumption later in conjunction with time preference, determined by *ratios* of consumptions now to consumptions later. (If technology were modelled by Professor Knight's Crusonia plant, the plant's continuous growth-rate dominates the solution: if the plant grows at 2% per annum, the savings rate adjusts so that time preference is two per cent at the margin; the real rate of interest is 2%.)

We have seen that this result, however plausible in isolation, blows up in open-economy analysis unless the groups are identical. A way out of the conundrum is to specify that motivation to accumulate wealth weakens as wealth increases. Then, if $\gamma_2 > \gamma_1$, all else the same, $\bar{W}_1 > \bar{W}_2$; the negative impact on growth of Economy 2's higher public-sector absorption is offset by the negative impact of Economy 1's greater equilibrium wealth. (We show *infra* that the negative impact on accumulation-drive of higher wealth may be explained by *emulation*, rather than intrinsic attitudes; of course, little human action is explained by *isolated* behavioural traits.)

Remark

Our improvisation on the theory of saving broadly conforms to the classical outlook, but contrasts sharply with *simpliste* Keynesian – or for that matter, Marxian – paradigms. (Marx's capitalists are puritanical: 'Accumulate, accumulate; that is Moses and the prophets'.) In *simpliste* Keynesian analysis, the proportion of income saved increases with income (which may be taken as a proxy for wealth). But so crude an hypothesis belies Keynesian thought. Modigliani's life-cycle hypothesis suffices to quash the notion that consumption theory must be simplistic along a Keynesian azimuth; and there are important passages in the *General Theory* presaging modern consumption theory in both its life-cycle of permanent income and its forward looking (rational expectations) aspects.

Stability Analysis

Taking up stability, consider λ and ω relative to $\gamma = \gamma^*$. Arrowsmith and Place (1982) show that, if the eigenvalues are imaginary with negative real parts, Figure (7.1) describes the upshot of displacement from $(\bar{\varrho}_i, \bar{W}_i)$, the origin of Figure (7.1)

By way of ancillary comment, recall Friedman's (1953b) interesting construction for multiple exchange-rate equilibrium in which an isolated economy's exchange rate(s) might move quite freely until

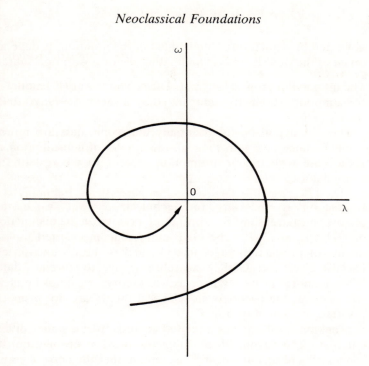

Figure 7.1　A stability analysis in (λ, ω) space

finally sucked into the field of force of a stable equilibrium point; it is implausible that there should be *no* stable rest point. (See Lecture Six.) Finally, local instability can be exploited in ways explained by Nelson (1956) – glossed by Branson (1979, pp. 487–90) and in a repressed (Soviet) inflation context, by Burstein (1986, pp. 123–4). The authorities may exert enough force to propel the system beyond the attractive field of force of an unsatisfactory rest point, relying on subsequent autonomous systemic action to achieve a more satisfactory rest point.

Further Annotation of the Schemae (see equations (7.1)–(7.3))

1. The 'mathematics' of the discussion are admittedly *verbal* – see Friedman (1946/1953a, p. 278, 'Lange on Price Flexibility and Employment'). But the format compactly organizes the material.
2. Interaction (of savings propensities across economies, thus

governed by emulation) is embedded in the notation: ϱ_i depends on *all* of the wealth, growth and public-sector-absorption values.

2.1 The interaction properly suggests Duesenberry's (1949) model of consumption, succinctly summarized by Branson (1979, p. 200):

> The . . . hypothesis is essentially that consumers are not so much concerned with their absolute level of consumption as they are with their consumption relative to the rest of the population.

2.2 Interaction is necessary for technical, as well as moral-philosophical, reasons. Section 7.3. elaborates on the disjunction of GDP_i from GNP_i. The GNP entry, 'income earned by our factors of production sited abroad', makes the disjunction especially clear: our GNP is acutely sensitive to 'foreign' data. What is more, in purely neoclassical theory, it cannot be clear who *we* are; the agents of neoclassical theory are not properly assorted by 'nation of origin'.

Svensson (1988) makes a related analysis from a rather different slant. The flavour of his interesting work is brought out by some of his results 'under the assumption that the home country has a higher . . . risk aversion than the foreign country' (p. 389). There is 'a tendency for the home country to import all assets and be a net lender; to export stocks [shares] since they are . . . more risky than the sure bond' (p. 389).

3. We focus on the *public sector*'s propensity to consume. In mixed, let alone socialist, economies, the public sector's capital accumulation is highly significant; so the productive operations of the Crown corporations are excluded from 'our' public sector.

3.1 Friedman (1984b) writes of 'The Taxes Called Deficits'; the consumption of the public sector comprises a drain – subject to an important qualification: if public consumption substitutes for private consumption (nationalized medicine is an example) the drain is abated (see Barro, 1984, Chapter 13). The public-sector-absorption parameter, γ_i, is difficult to compute. But, for $\gamma_i > 0$, the ith after-tax rate of return is reduced; and required after-tax rates of return (supply prices of capital so to speak) at Location L are, to say the least, strongly influenced by global alternatives. The higher is γ_i, the lower is the effective propensity to save in the *i*th economy, *ceteris paribus*; disposable net national income (including earnings from assets sited abroad) is less. (We follow the convention that global income of L residents is taxable by L.) And GDP growth at L is curtailed by lower after-tax rates of return at L, all else the same. So in neoclassical modelling the effect of '$\Delta \gamma > 0$' is to impede GNP growth or to stimulate GNP decay; in a global equilibrium in which growth is the same at all points, this effect must be offset by other partial effects, perhaps that of wealth, as has been explained.

4. As for *wealth*, refer to the Leontief model of Section 7.2.2. Direct and indirect effects of increased public-sector absorption conduce towards a lower level of wealth in a stationary equilibrium; and towards a lower relative wealth position in equilibrium-growth modelling.

Games

Policy-makers in the n economies, solving operational versions of our model, inevitably play a non-zero-sum n-person 'tax-policy' game. And it is quite plausible that political authorities should 'go into business for themselves', operating relative to criteria conflicting with those of private agents – as in the economic theory of government, alluded to in the problem set.

5. Keynes (1923) incisively criticized reliance on *asymptotic properties* in economics in a much-misunderstood passage including the phrase, 'in the long run we are all dead' (1923, p. 80). He is not attacking Virtue; Keynes merely urges economists to study transitional processes in connection with a putatively valid quantity theory of money, taken as a secular hypothesis. All this said, a model must achieve some sort of convergence or pass into chaos – although some conclude simply that formal modelling in economics is quixotic.

6. *Catastrophes and windfalls* have intrigued economists. See Samuelson (1947/1983), Archibald and Lipsey (1958), Clower and Burstein (1960), Hirshleifer (1987, Chapters 1–4) and Burstein (1988, Chapter 2). Economies display remarkable resilience; as Bagehot said, there is much ruin in a nation. And windfalls tend to be dissipated, so that bias towards models displaying convergence does have empirical support.

As for windfalls, it may seem bizarre that windfalls may have no long-run effects on collective balance sheets. But think of a born loser who receives a windfall and thriftily uses it to augment his sports-betting-business's working capital – and loses it. (Do not confuse systemic dissipation of windfalls with stochastic processes determining inequality in various spaces – see Gibrat's Law for example.)

The dissipation of a windfall does not tarnish its lustre; the path back to an economy's comparative-wealth position may be very pleasant. Nor is *dissipation* used pejoratively here; the value system of the West is consumption-rooted after all. (Such dissipation would be intensely regretted by mercantilists.)

Holism

Avoid holistic fallacies. Societies should not be endowed with individual traits so that a kind of pathetic fallacy is committed. The persistence exhibited by our models, and in life, must needs emerge from interaction of biological agents, themselves ceaselessly transisting, so that a society's cast of characters is forever changing. . . . Resolution of these deep ontological perplexes must be pursued elsewhere.

7.2.2 Heuristics

An Adaptation of Leontief's (1958) Model

(See Burstein, 1963, pp. 647–57.)

Relying on Irving Fisher, Leontief regards the savings decision as a choice to give up a quantum of present consumption in favour of a capital asset that generates 'a perpetual series of equal annual interest payments'. Figure (7.2) explains how the resulting intertemporal tussle is resolved. The horizontal axis measures current income and consumption; the vertical axis, annuity streams. At a point belonging to the 45° line, current consumption equals the perpetual annuity that can be purchased with initial capital; capital is neither increasing nor decreasing; persistence of a point like R represents a stationary state. And movement from initial-state R to P entails accumulation of capital. It leads to a new level of income, defined as the rate of consumption that leaves capital intact: $Y'_3 = Y'_3$; the next decision is made 'starting from T'. Starting at V, a movement to Q entails decumulation of capital, so that the 'next decision' is made 'lower down on the 45° line', at a point below V.

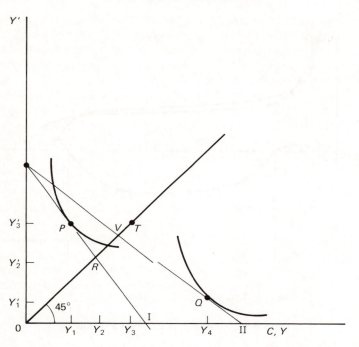

Figure 7.2 Marginal efficiency of capital and time preference

The terms of trade between current consumption and accretion to capital are given by the slopes of lines such as *I* and *II*. The flatter are these lines, the more current consumption must be sacrificed to increase the annuity stream by a given amount. In the scenario of Section 7.2.1, the effect of intensification of public-sector absorption is to flatten the transformation locus, so that, as we shall see, transient growth is slowed. Perhaps less obviously, higher public-sector absorption also leads to a rest point (stationary state) at which wealth is lower; but convergence onto *some* rest point is invariant against the level of public-sector absorption.

The indifference map concerns a representative agent; its rigorous underpinnings are fragile at best. Temporary equilibrium occurs at a point at which the transformation function, as perceived by private agents, is tangent to an indifference curve; the common rate of transformation maps into the equilibrium rate of interest. In temporary equilibrium, the marginal efficiency of capital (conceived as a rate of return over cost) equals the rate of time preference.

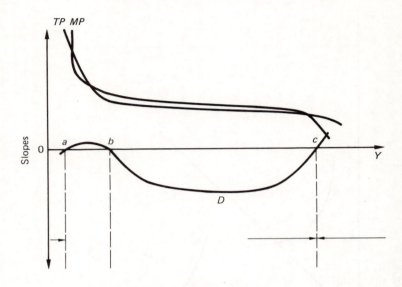

Source: Leontief (1958, p. 109)

Figure 7.3   Summary of Leontief's dynamics

Following Lerner (1952/1953), we distinguish the *marginal efficiency of capital* from the *marginal productivity of capital*. (Also see Friedman, 1962.) The latter is defined as the marginal efficiency of capital when the rate of investment is arbitrarily close to zero; as more of the economy's resources are shifted from consumption to investment activity, the rate of return over cost declines.

There are in Leontief's model two sets of basic structural relationships; one deals with time preference and the other with the marginal efficiency of capital. Figure (7.3) provides a simple way of understanding the dynamic upshot of interaction between the basic relationships. The *TP* curve reveals the slopes of indifference curves cutting the 45° line at points whose abscissa values are recorded on the horizontal axis of Figure (7.3). The *MP* curve, similarly derived, relates marginal efficiency of capital to levels of income (capital stocks) when the rate of investment is zero. The *D* curve registers differences between absolute values of the slopes of *TP* and *MP* curves (*TP-MP*). So long as *MP* exceeds *TP*, the capital stock increases; so long as *TP* exceeds *MP*, the capital stock decays; for *MP = TP*, the system is stationary. Points *a*, *b* and *c* on the *D* curve

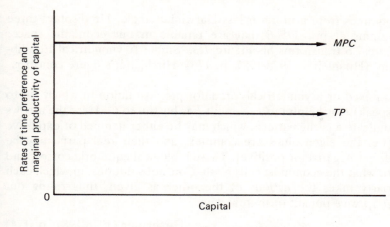

Figure 7.4   The Knightian version of Leontief's system

are rest points (equilibria). Point *a* represents a locally-stable equilibrium: *MP* exceeds *TP* to the left of *a*; and *TP* exceeds *MP* to the immediate right of *a*; income is growing if it is less than 0*a* and decaying if between 0*a* and 0*b*. Point *b* describes an unstable equilibrium: if income is displaced below 0*b*, in the neighbourhood of *b*, its time derivative is negative, and it converges on 0*a*; if it is displaced above 0*b*, it converges on 0*c*, another locally-stable rest point.

Finally, Figure (7.4) results from the strict homogeneity properties of the Knight–Friedman model; and implies indefinite steady growth of wealth and income – a result that is as uncomfortable for open-economy analysis as it is appealing in a closed analysis.

The analysis of Section 7.2. is crudely encapsulated by envisaging shifts in the *MP* curve of Figure 7.3 in response to changes in the intensity of public-sector absorption. An increase in γ_i shifts the *MP* curve leftward – the *MP* curve is now to be interpreted in terms of privately-perceived after-tax returns to investment when the after-tax cost of capital is very strongly influenced by a global market. Capital accumulation will ultimately converge on a smaller total mass as a result.

An Adaptation of a Hirshleifer (1978/1987) Model of Cooperation and Conflict

Hirshleifer (1978/1987, pp. 164–91) models natural (vs political) economies from a more-or-less-Darwinian angle. He displays three diagrams at pp. 175–6 that are tenable in our economic space; Figure 7.5 transforms his Figure 7.3, 'Stable Asymmetrical Equilibrium' (Hirshleifer, 1978/1987, p. 176). Hirshleifer's figure concerns

> a mixed or asymmetrical 'predator-prey' situation in which (so to speak) *G* is helpful to *F* . . . but *F* is hurtful to *G*. Here the arrows indicate a cyclic pattern, which may be either damped or explosive [i.e. the eigenvalues are complex; and their real parts may be either negative or positive]. These biological equilibria correspond to what the economist calls Nash–Cournot solutions, in which each party takes the actions of the other as given, thus ruling out *purposive* pursuit of mutual gain.

Hirshleifer (1978/1987, p. 174)

(Recall the lecture's preliminary remarks: political economy is concerned *au fond* with purposive action, with the exercise of Will.)

Points belonging to α are wealth-pairs for which W_F is stationary; and points belonging to β are wealth-pairs for which W_G is stationary. And equations (7.7) and (7.8) display the gradient (partial derivative) background:

$$\dot{W}_F = f(\overset{(-)}{W}_F, \overset{(+)}{W}_G, \overset{(-)}{\gamma}_F) \tag{7.7}$$

$$\dot{W}_G = g(\overset{(-)}{W}_F, \overset{(-)}{W}_G, \overset{(-)}{\gamma}_G) \tag{7.8}$$

By way of annotation, '$\overset{(-)}{\gamma}_F$' indicates that, all else the same, the rate of growth of *F per capita* wealth is a decreasing function of F's public-sector absorption. And '$\overset{(+)}{W}_G$' in equation (7.7) may imply *emulation*; while '$\overset{(-)}{W}_F$' in equation (7.8) implies more-or-less natural *competition*.

The emulative aspect of the α curve is more or less as in Duesenberry (see Section 7.2). The β curve may reveal that *F* has a love-hate relationship with *G*: *F* both emulates and preys on *G*: higher W_F values reflect more-successful *F* exploitation of competitive advantages over *G*.

The β' curve reflects an increase in γ_G; and interestingly implies that *both* are worse off at the new rest point. (The leftward shift of the β curve, β', reflects the fact that W_G in equation (7.8) is now more negative for any (W_F, W_G) pair.)

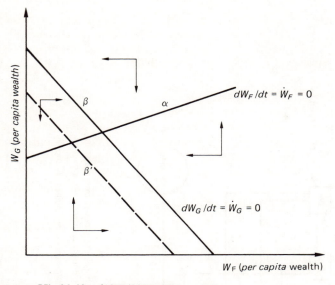

Source: Hirshleifer (1978/1987, Figure 7.3)

Figure 7.5   Emulation and competition in an open political economy

7.3 PRINCIPAL PROPERTIES OF AN ELEMENTARY OPEN ECONOMY ANALYSED IN A NEOCLASSICAL MODE

The admittedly *simpliste* Figure (7.6) suggests the myriad substitutions, motivated by relative-price changes, making for adjustment to shocks or parameter shifts *via* equilibration of markets. Figure 7.6 keys on the economy's openness and was indeed evoked by memory of a Wisconsin factory town. Exports are the mainspring of the town's prosperity *cum* population growth. (See the novels of Sinclair Lewis, a Minnesotan, for definitive depictions of boosterism.) How much Kleenex © and Delsey © can even fanatically loyal townsmen consume? Moving onto a more general plane, a surge in demand for Economy *E*'s exports induces increased demand for wage-goods and personal services even if the owners of its non-human resources are non-residents. Similarly, contraction of demand for *E* exports induces contraction of demand for *E* generated services, especially income-elastic ones; incomes of restaurateurs, barbers *et al.* and rents

186

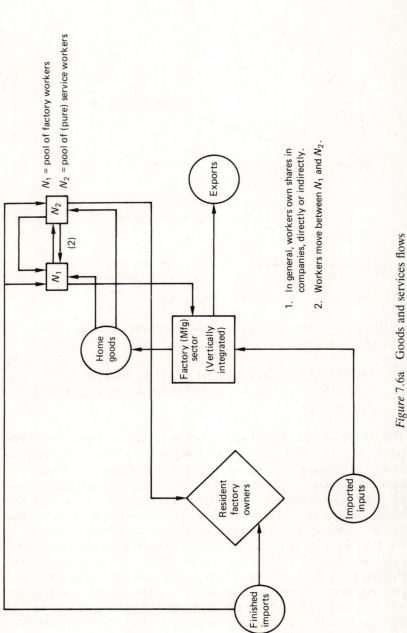

N_1 = pool of factory workers
N_2 = pool of (pure) service workers

Exports

N_2

(2)

N_1

Factory (Mfg) sector (Vertically integrated)

Home goods

1. In general, workers own shares in companies, directly or indirectly.

2. Workers move between N_1 and N_2.

Resident factory owners

Imported inputs

Finished imports

Figure 7.6a   Goods and services flows

187

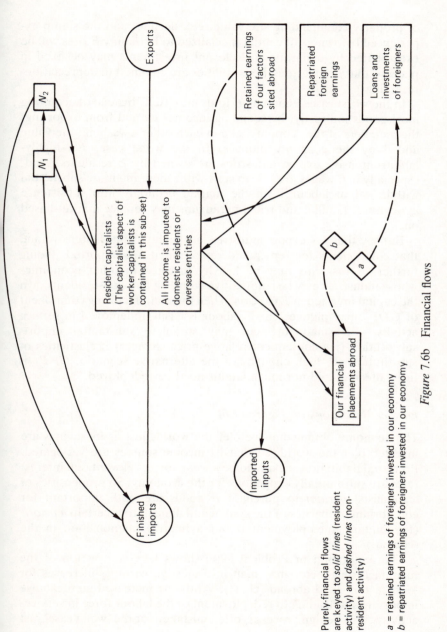

Figure 7.6b Financial flows

Purely-financial flows
are keyed to *solid lines* (resident
activity) and *dashed lines* (non-
resident activity)

a = retained earnings of foreigners invested in our economy
b = repatriated earnings of foreigners invested in our economy

of property commanding site-value, etc. decline, and the slump experienced by owners of capital specialized to Economy E sites will be exacerbated by emigration. (Relevant investments may be fixed in place so that disinvestment possibilities are confined to depreciation-reserving.)

In the worst case, Economy E folds into itself. Instead of acquiring most goods indirectly, by spending incomes earned from exporting, the members of the economy take in each other's washing; the value added by the economy plunges. In the worst case, E's highly-labour-intensive export industries are owned by E residents. And, especially if E wages are low to start with, there might be substantial withdrawal of labour from the market economy into subsistence agriculture; familial and tribal paradigms may replace market-based ones.

But say that E's export industries are highly capital-intensive and that components for repair and replacement are imported. Going further, E residents may be heavily invested in other economies whose industries may be competitive with E's; and non-residents own the capital invested in E exports. Then the manufacturing component of GDP_E may plunge; but E labour is easily redeployed in service activity – a small wage-cut may stimulate substantial import-substitution (*via* consequent relative-price changes) if elasticities of substitution are high enough. In the alternative scenario, GNP_E is little affected; and not much labour need be redeployed.

Further Reflections on Figure (7.6)

The economy obtains finance o'er the world, just as its savings are invested o'er the world, so that its income sources are variegated. Preferred habitation is likely to be a weak force; relevant real interest rates are substantially exogenous for the economy. So propensities of 'capitalists' *partout* to purchase E goods are both important for equilibrium properties of the system and difficult to ascertain *a priori*. (Involuntary unemployment is but a fugitive phenomenon in the schema.)

The annotation of Problem **80(c)** shows how contraction of the manufacturing sector may map into massive earnings-increases for 'our' factors sited abroad (cf. y'), validating increased merchandise importing and leading to redeployment of the labour force in service-activity. This benign process is often mistaken for the 'worst case' just explained.

Finally Becker (1971) illuminates the model depicted by Figure (7.6); also see Burstein (1978, 1986, Chapter 6). There are to be two nations coexisting in one economy. One, W, is few in number but owns almost all the economy's non-human capital. The other nation, N, is numerous. The equilibrium real wage rate, at any time, is determined by W and N tastes for capital- and labour-intensive goods and elasticities of substitution in consumption between home-manufactured goods, imports and services. Again, disjunction of the GNP and GDP measures makes impossible an *a priori* assessment of effects of shifts in demand for exports or of oil shocks on the W and N nations.

(The problem set and its annotations further explore interactions between the nodes of Figure 7.6.)

The Rôle of Keynesian Economics

Keynesian paradigms are not fruitful for analysis of the model of Figure 7.6. In the worst-case scenario entailing contraction of demand for E exports, the economy regresses; and may, at the culmination of the regression, implode so that aggregate value-added by domestic processes amounts to little more than mutual services (A teaches B chess; B gardens for C; etc.). But the worst-case scenario is comfortably accommodated by 'classical' economics – once known as the dismal science, after all.

7.4 CLASSICAL AND NEOCLASSICAL MONETARY THEORY AND SUFFICIENCY OF AGGREGATE DEMAND (cf. SAY's LAW)

A Classical Parable

In order to fix ideas, explore the elementary flow-of-funds matrix of Table 7.1.

The *dramatis personae* are a baker (B_1), a pair of barbers (B_2) and a banker (B_3). B_1 and B_2 spend 90 pence in the pound on each other's products and bank the rest. The banker (who may be the Crown) is a monopolist issuer of inconvertible paper; she rolls her own liquidity, just as the baker bakes his own bread and the barbers cut each other's hair. The goods and services obtained by the banker in exchange for paper-issue comprise her seigneurage profit.

Table 7.1   An elementary flow-of-funds matrix

Revenues Expenditures	B_1	B_2	B_3	Expenditure sums
B_1	–	0.90	0.10:	1.00
B_2	0.90	–	0.10:	1.00
B_3	0.10	0.10	– :	0.20
Revenue sums	1.00	1.00	0.20:	2.20

Interpolation

A properly-classical economy is on a commodity (or commodity-exchange) standard. Then, as Keynes (1936, Chapter 17) points out, excess demand for money is on a par with excess demand for steel girders – subject to effects of inelasticity of say, gold production with respect to gold's purchasing power; along with effects of sticky prices.

In principle, inelasticity of 'gold' production may provoke a crisis: transactors, unable to attain desired specie-holdings, may retain specie as it flows in or postpone or cancel outlays; indeed classical theorists were sensitive to this perplex. *But* in fact crises were never provoked by plans, on aggregate, to convert goods into money. Rather crises were provoked by efforts to convert non-monetary paper assets into money – or to convert junk securities into gilts. *Such* crises were fairly common. (See Lectures Two and Six.)

Resumption of the Main Line of Argument

Standard Keynesian descriptions of admittedly more sophisticated models of this sort forget that the bankers obtain income from the savings process. If bankers have bankers, the regress may end at the Crown – always an overabsorber, greedy for seigneurage profit, to finance its Danain jar of projects.

Transisting to the argument's next stage: (1) if savings plans concern produced goods, there can be no Keynesian effective-demand deficiency, as Keynes (1936, Chapter 17) pointed out; (2) the parable concerns issue of *additional* money – once the money stock equals stock-demand, the banker must shut down her printing press and live off capital accumulated from durable-goods purchases on the money-growth interval. (Classical arguments tend to culminate in stationary states.)

Say's Law Redux

Schumpeter (1954) suggests that Say's *law* is properly a *theorem*:

> The law asserts that the aggregate demand price of output as a whole is *capable of being equal* to its aggregate supply price for all volumes of total output.
>
> Schumpeter (1954, p. 624)

The analysis hinges on the decision to save. Agents choose between spending on sources or on services of sources. The properly-specified decision concerns profiles of service-flows yielded by uses of current income. It is easy to misspecify *thrift*.

Sources sought by savers might, like Marshall's meteoric stones, be non-reproducible; or they might not require labour and other productive services to be created – cf. currency, other government securities, private-sector bonds, etc. Keynes (1936) went some distance along this azimuth:

> That the world after several millennia of steady individual saving is so poor as it is in accumulated capital assets is to be explained . . . by the high liquidity premiums formerly attaching to the ownership of land and now attaching to money.
>
> Keynes (1936, p. 242)

But Lerner's (1952/1953) rebuke to this 'intriguing speculation' is quite decisive:

> There is nothing to stop the value of land from rising rapidly in the way in which money-wage stickiness stops the value of money from rising rapidly . . . Any conceivable desire for holding wealth in the form of land can therefore be filled until it overflows into the demand for other forms of wealth that *can* be produced.
>
> Lerner (1952/1953, p. 377)

(Also see Kaldor, 1960, pp. 59–74.)

One form of wealth that can be produced is non-industrial durables. As asset holders become satiated with real cash balances, as prices fall in a laissez-faire economy – or frustrated by their inability to obtain more real cash because of general-price-level stickiness – they will plan to increase holdings of such sources of services as houses-and-gardens, athletic skills, literary knowledge (cf. human capital) or, more subtly, to endow colleges, contribute to new church buildings or to environmental renewal (all source-building actions) yielding service streams.

Remark

In a more interesting, and realistic, case, increased demand for liquidity forces down yields of highly-liquid assets and provokes more financial intermediation and restructuring of debt towards the short end, in response to wider spreads between the 'mercantile rate of profit' and depressed yields of highly-liquid claims. Cf. *infra*.

The skeletal framework of the analysis is found in the *Wealth of Nations*, albeit in a context including the egregious unproductive-consumption idea:

> The revenue of an individual . . . may be spent on things more durable . . . A man of fortune [may content] himself with a frugal table and few attendants; he may lay out the greater part of it adorning his house or country villa . . . in collecting books, statues, pictures; or in things more frivolous . . .; or, in what is most trifling of all, in massing a great wardrobe of fine clothes, like the favourite and minister of a great prince who died a few years ago.

Adam Smith (1776/1910/1970, 1, p. 310)

Remark

Services of stocks can be marketed. You may tour my stately home, for a fee. I shall buy handblown *objets* from your glazier. Others offer instruction in Greek, chess, etc.

Financial-Asset Accumulation as a Clog on Accumulation of Real Capital (?)

The issue looks more prosaic under its more proper rubric: 'is demand for intermediation a potential clog on accumulation of real capital?'. The neoclassical reply is 'No'. First consider demand for public debt – referring to Sargent and Wallace, 1981. Issue convertible into particular fiat paper is tenable for monetary analysis. And, if public debt is not to be monetized, its total is bounded from above by taxable capacity – a stringent condition indeed in earlier times; and significant now. (Of course, as total real return on public debt falls at the margin, investors have incentive to adorn country villas and amass great wardrobes rather than buy public paper.)

As for demand for private debt – excluding 'currency writing', analysed by annotation of the parable – investors must see that their paper-holdings comprise direct and indirect claims on real assets and that real assets are the basis for companies' ability to service such paper. Closure is imposed from two directions: (1) a company properly capitalizes only the assets it operates – but cf. stock watering; (2) leverage(gearing) is constrained by increasing danger of ruin as a company's debt/equity ratio increases. So, to repeat, increased liquidity preference merely implies that the volume of intermediation will increase and that spreads obtainable by financial houses will widen.

(It has long been recognized, along lines initiated by Keynes and Hicks, that systematic liquidity preference may impose a *backwardation* on the yield curve so that long-term interest rates quoted today are biased implicit estimators of short rate in future. See Lecture Three.)

An Annotated Problem Set For Lecture Seven

PROBLEMS

74. In neoclassical modelling of open-economy problems:

   (a) multinational enterprise is a norm;

   (b) an increase in global preference for our goods causes our terms of trade to improve;

   (c) an increase in our tax rate leads to a decrease in the rate of growth of our total wealth only if incremental tax proceeds are invested in the open market;

   (D) two of the above choices are correct;

   (e) none of the above choices is correct.

75. If preferred habitation is a weak force:

   (A) marginal efficiencies of capital will tend to be strongly aligned;

   (b) the jth government's tax policies will be weakly constrained by global norms;

   (c) the relationship between GNP_i and GDP_i becomes almost 1:1;

   (d) all of the above choices are correct;

   (e) none of the above choices is correct.

76. A massive increase in foreign investment in Economy E will:

   (A) tend to increase prices of pure services in E;

   (b) lead to an increase in GNP_E that is large relative to that in GDP_E;

   (c) if the new industries are highly automated, lead to strongly positive effects on demand for E home goods, especially if new plant and equipment has a high import content;

   (d) two of the above choices are correct;

195

(e) none of the above choices is correct.

77. If our economy's propensity to save decreases:

   (a) short-run effects on our home-goods and services industries are negative;
   (b) in the short run, our exporting industries will be stimulated by lower wages;
   (C) in the long run, our living standards may fail to keep up
   with those of comparable economies;
   (d) two of the above choices are correct;
   (e) choices **(a)**, **(b)** and **(c)** are correct.

78. Choose the correct statement about the Banana Republic
   (*BR*):

   (a) if *BR* capitalists' propensities to save permanently increase, *BR* wage rates will increase in the long run,
   especially if the capitalists' propensity to consume home
   goods and services is weak;
   (B) a permanent increase in demand for *BR* exports maps
   into a corresponding permanent increase in *BR* capital
   outflow;
   (c) the capital outflow of choice (*B*) will be smaller if *BR*
   workers have a very low propensity to consume goods
   with high import content;
   (d) all of the above choices are correct;
   (e) none of the above choices is correct.

79. The neoclassical theory implies that:

   (A) in equilibrium, wealthier economies have higher GNP
   per capita than less wealthy ones – but GDP *per capita*
   may not reflect this;
   (b) repatriation rates of external company earnings must be
   rigidly fixed for the global economy to be efficient;
   (c) if Economy *E*'s savers come to prefer financial over real
   wealth, Economy *E*'s *per capita* GNP will fall even if it
   becomes more thrifty;
   (d) all of the above choices are correct;

(e) none of the above choices is correct.

80. The neoclassical theory also implies that:

   (a) the rate of growth of our total wealth will fall if our domestic 'marginal productivity of capital' falls, unless our propensity to save simultaneously decreases;
   (b) liquidity preference determines real rates of interest;
   (c) if 'our' capitalists relocate manufacturing activity in low-wage third-world economies, our gross national product per head will fall, although our gross domestic product per head is apt to increase;
   (d) all of the above choices are correct;
   (E) none of the above choices is correct.

81. The neoclassical theory implies that a global increase in preference for our goods:

   (A) has an impact on GNP that depends on who owns the capital operating in our economy;
   (b) leads to our catching the 'Dutch disease';
   (c) is less likely to lead to an increase in prices of services in our economy if owners of specialized resources producing such goods are local rather than alien;
   (d) all of the above choices are correct;
   (e) none of the above choices is correct.

82. According to neoclassical theory:

   (a) an economy whose capitalists strongly prefer 'home' as an investment habitat will be wealthier in equilibrium than one whose capitalists do not have preferred habitats;
   (B) in an idealized neoclassical world, *sans* preferred habitation, GDP and GNP may be weakly, if not negatively correlated;
   (c) the results of the Stalin régime in Russia prove that higher public-sector absorption deters wealth creation;
   (d) two of the above choices are correct;
   (e) choices **(a)**, **(b)** and **(c)** are correct.

83. If global demand for exports specialized to Economy *E* falls:

- **(a)** GNP_E effects must be more negative than GDP_E ones;
- **(B)** 'pure services' prices tend to fall relative to prices of goods with high import content;
- **(c)** the *E* government should run a higher real deficit, unless the fall-off in demand is temporary;
- **(d)** two of the above choices are correct;
- **(e)** none of the above choices is correct.

ANNOTATIONS

Problem 74

74(a) In neoclassical theory, one asks why a firm does *not* pursue business everywhere. Each company scans the world; it does not do business at Point *P* because of transactional factors – linguistics, costs of adapting to alien specifications – or perhaps for political reasons. Preferred habitation enters into constraint sets, but not into objective functions (crudely, utility functions); it is not that I prefer France intrinsically, but rather that they order this matter better in France (Sterne). Preferred habitation permits differential marginal rates of return – granting that, in principle, *some* location-neutral investors can impose location-neutrality on the market in the way that *some* adequately-funded investors may impose 'rationality' on a stock market.

74(b) No: what if the proceeds are poured into military adventures in Africa? But the context is full of substance. Begin with the sort of *tax-game* played by American states or Canadian provinces or, indeed, European nations and sub-groups. A New Hampshire tax-cut will be more successful if Massachusetts does not follow; Canada's marginal income tax rates are likely to follow American ones down. Tax-games are readily modelled on Cournot–Nash lines. (The games can be artificially, and dangerously, simplified by assuming that taxation is confined to points of origin of income; although, in life, residents of *X* must typically report global income to *X* tax authorities.)

An increase in X government expenditure may be easily financed by higher taxes if there is strong preferred habitation in X. (Or consider a tax increase as part of a plan to retire external debt, as in Ceausescu's Romania – see Lecture Two.) Now consider a case in which habitation-preference is weak. New taxes are apt to be laid on labour (highly immobile in Romania) and land, together with resources specialized to land – according to an ancient paradigm; the key to the exercise in an open economy is that activity not be readily transferable to the same quality of land elsewhere. Say that this is successfully done. There may be intriguing effects on resource-use. Prices of resources complementary with non-traded-goods production may rise: higher taxation leads foreign capitalists to eschew X so that more labour is available to build palaces like Versailles – leading to increased demand for resources complementary with labour in luxury construction.

Remarks

Governments might cooperate, avoiding tax-abatement competition in order to promote global tax revenues. Intergovernmental cooperation here is analogous to that in classic cartels; and starkly exemplifies the new economic theory of government: an international consortium of officials conspires against their citizens in plausible variations of the principal subject . . . Finally, there is room for the A government to depress the after-tax rate of return in A if habitat preference is strong; in the contrary case there would be massive capital-flight.

Problem 75

75(c) Since the annotations of Problem **74** obviously pertain to Problem **75**, annotation is continued to choice **75(c)**. The analysis hinges on distinction of gross domestic product (y) from gross national product ($y + y'$) – see Lecture Two. Thus, if preferred habitation can be ignored, capital flows equate marginal rates of return so that X residents may be heavily invested in Z, and may reinvest massive Z revenues in Z, and divert others to Y, so that GNP_x rises rapidly relative to

GDP_X. An important complementary concept is the *repatria-tion rate*; see Lecture Two. Even quite-sophisticated open-economy exercises often assume that earnings from resources sited abroad automatically flow into channels of demand for 'our' currency – an improper stipulation. Furthermore, proper definitions of saving bar equation of X economy savings streams (flows) with withdrawals from the X expenditure circuit (as in a simple closed Keynesian system): much X income is generated abroad and much investment-placement comes from abroad – all this being a reprise of a principal argument of Lecture Two.

Problem 76

76(A) By hypothesis, pure services are produced by labour; and the investment-surge reckons to increase our wage rates. Effects on home-goods industries are more complex. If the investments absorb inputs specialized to our economy – as do home goods – the relative price(s) of home goods will increase, leading to substitution by imports, so that capital inflow receives an indirect, as well as a direct, fillip. Alternatively, the investment-surge may be heavily import-based. Then effects on local markets may be quite slight; and if the outputs of the new plants, once they come on stream, are substantially exported *and* the investors are aliens, the process becomes a mere fugitive.

76(b) No! There is no reason for the new capital to belong to residents of E. Furthermore effects on GDP_E are sensitive to complicated measurements incident to shifts of labour from one sector to another. In order to fix ideas, think of an economy in which capital operated within its confines is mostly owned by foreigners, just as capital owned by E residents is deployed abroad. GNP_E effects may be quite slight. Of course, in neoclassical modelling, parameter shifts lead to labour-use switches rather than to changes in (un)employment.

76(c) Recall the fugitive process of choice **76(a)**. Income from the new processes is imputed to aliens who have very low propensities to consume E goods and services.

Problem 77

77(a) *Saving*, and the *propensity to save*, must be distinguished from their closed-economy counterparts. The source of saving is GNP, not GDP; in a highly open economy (say London's) switches in local savings propensities are far less important than switches of external ones, even in a strictly-Keynesian paradigm. In the neoclassical analysis, if the local propensity to consume increases (decreases), resources flow away from (towards) exports, reducing (increasing) the marginal efficiency of capital deployed in exporting. True, if the local propensity to consume were to fall in an economy that is not 'too open', workers' incomes may fall as they go into gardening, tennis coaching, etc.

Now consider the following classical, or neoclassical, scenario, consulting the *flow charts* of Lecture Seven (Figure 7.6a and 7.6b). Assume that capitalists (multinational companies) reduce repatriation of earnings from overseas projects and that demand for our exports falls (in the schedule sense). In the short run, more of our labour must be absorbed by home-goods production and pure-services activity. Wage cuts are required – and can be accomplished by exchange-rate depreciation under floating rates. Wage cuts restore investment in our export industries (partially); there may be some redirection of retained company earnings towards capital accumulation at our export points.

In any event, if the elasticity of demand for pure services is as great as unity, consumption of services out of profits can absorb released workers: resident capitalists add to their household staffs, dine out more in first-class (highly labour-intensive) restaurants, mass great wardrobes of fine clothes, etc.

77(b) No! Since the savings propensity has decreased, wages may well increase in the short run. If so, increased domestic absorption will impinge upon exporting (cf. dragging effects of higher wages).

77(c) The situation is obverse to the 'Japan' scenario of Lecture Four. In that scenario, higher Japanese savings rates map into more rapid accumulation of wealth; and, finally, to higher levels of consumption. Here a decline in the rate at which we accumulate wealth o'er the world leads in due course to lower levels of consumption relative to the consumption-path generated by greater thriftiness.

Problem 78

Banana Republic (*BR*) capitalists invest nothing at home not required for expansion of banana planting; and indeed we assume that the banana industry is stationary. Assume further that planters' domestic purchases are confined to pure services. And wage goods are to have a high import content; workers do not live on bananas, as they would if the model imitated Ricardo's.

At least in the short run, an increase in the propensity to save appears to make *BR* workers worse off: demand for personal services falls, *ceteris paribus*. As the planters' wealth grows, their expenditures in *BR* grow feebly. And their net BR investment is *nil*; proceeds of banana exports flow into foreign assets; GNP_{BR} and GDP_{BR} diverge sharply. (Still, in the limit, in the very long run, planter-wealth may stabilize at a high enough level to induce very substantial purchases of *BR* services.)

78(c)   It suffices here to explain why choice **78(c)** is ambiguous. The higher is the propensity of *BR* workers to consume bananas, instead of imports, the smaller is the portion of the banana crop that is available for exportation, and the larger is the portion of export proceeds available for capital outflow.

Say the *BR* workers' propensity to consume bananas is 0.5. Then the activity of producing one banana entails *net* exportation of 1/2 banana; and proceeds are further drained by the expense of importing some wage goods. (Foreign goods may be prohibitively expensive for workers; *cf.* some socialist-bloc situations.)

Problem 79

79(A)   In neoclassical theory, gross domestic product and gross national product need not be highly correlated. Indeed, as the annotation of choice **80(c)** shows, very wealthy economies may generate little output, relying instead on their vast overseas wealth.

79(b) Global efficiency requires that each dollar earned at Point *P* be eligible for transformation into investment anywhere in the world.

79(c) No! The problem highlights the sharpest of the contrasts between 'classical' and Keynesian paradigms. (Again, Keynes said that his theory was not meant to apply to an open economy, but rather to a closed set of economies.) Lecture Seven refutes the conclusion of choice **79(c)** even in a strictly-closed economy; and the argument is especially transparent in an open economy.

All that may be entailed is switches of direct overseas-assets positions into portfolio-investments; and direct domestic investments may be swapped with foreigners so that our portfolio holders end up with marketable claims (including listed shares, if any equity is retained) on restructured enterprises. And recall that, in the lecture's closed-economy analysis, an upshot of the asset-preferences switch is recapitalization of enterprises, increasing debt/equity ratios. Finally, liquidity may be imported like any other good (see Svensson, 1988): our gold holdings can be augmented by selling non-monetary assets for gold o'er the world; higher liquidity premia induce foreigners to reduce their liquidity in order to supply more to us.

The following remarks (based on Burstein 1986, Chapters 3 and 11) establish a more-general monetary-theoretic basis for the annotation of choice **79(c)**. Changes in demand for money evoke sympathetic supply-changes. Thus, in a pure paper-money system, increased demand for money leads to wider spreads for bankers (deposit rate falls relative to open-market rates); bankers respond by increasing their liabilities . . . Some of the increased proceeds from export sales (induced by weaker home markets) will be spent on gold-imports.

Problem 80

80(a) The reader may fall into a trap. She intuits that deterioration of the terms of transformation of consumption goods into capital (i.e. lower rewards for 'waiting') is adverse for wealth-accumulation. And she may have been taught, or think that she has been taught, that clogs on growth are dissolved by stimulus to aggregate demand, here supplied by a fall in the propensity to save.

At least two lines of attack can be successfully deployed against this pseudo-Keynesian thesis. The first may be called the 'supply-side case for Keynesian economics'. The second line of attack, stressing how savings may be deployed abroad, is more soundly 'classical'. *Secular* growth is undeniably determined by thrift and productivity. Keynes does not challenge that. Rather he argues – along lines Joan Robinson (1966) suggests are anticipated by Rosa Luxemberg – that aggregate demand in an unregulated private-ownership economy often, if not persistently, falls short of full-employment output, unless it is prodded by fiscal stimulus (which will be substantially self-financing since, in economies in Keynesian states, demand creates its own supply).

The Keynesian case for supply-side economics calls for the classical forces of thrift and productivity to be buttressed much of the time by fiscal stimulus and 'cheap' money'; and, what is more, the safety net thus woven stimulates animal spirits of entrepreneurs while reassuring timorous risk averters. The second line of attack implies that it may be attractive to direct savings flows towards overseas projects, so that gross-national-product effects may be nugatory. The prognosis for our workers is more guarded. (See the annotation of choice **80(c)**.) Domestic labour would be diverted towards 'pure services'; and productive processes would become less capital-intensive, Since the prime mover of this process is a deterioration of transformation possibilities, the standard of living will indeed deteriorate; but deterioration is damped by high elasticities of demand for services.

Finally, it cannot be surprising that non-human-capital ownership is relatively immune to the controlling adverse event: non-human capital is to be mobile and human capital immobile. Of course, in neoclassical theory, in stark contrast with the classics, economic agents are not assorted by class: each agent owns human and non-human capital, which he hires out at the same time he buys the services of others capital.

80(b) No! In both classical and neoclassical economics, real rates of interest are determined by real forces; see Irving Fisher's *thrift and productivity*; and go back to Ricardo and Thornton

(Thornton's *mercantile rate of profit* is an example). As neo-classical theory evolved, market rates of interest became resolved into real and nominal parts, the nominal part being explained by inflation-expectations in ways pioneered by Irving Fisher. Real parts of interest rates are dominated by the own rate of return on physical capital, governed by a process that is secularly invariant against monetary events.

As for Keynes:

> The principal discriminant between 'classical' and Keynesian economics is based on the following query. 'Do you accept monetary theories of the real rate of interest; or are real rates of interest determined by real causes?'. . . . What *is* the theory of money in the *General Theory*? In Chapter 13, Keynes categorically endorses the idea that the real rate of interest is determined by the quantity of money . . . His theory of *liquidity preference* supposedly links up the nominal quantity of money and the real rate of interest . . . The dénouement is starkly plain. Keynesians must live with it. '[Interest] is the reward for not hoarding (Keynes, 1936, p. 174)'.

Burstein, (1988a, pp. 162–3)

80(c) Would readers accept the choice if it had specified that GDP per head fell? One suspects many would. But they would be wrong. Say that huge *A* manufacturing complexes are allowed to run down and are replaced by complexes built by *A*-based multinationals in *Z* where wage rates are say 32¢ an hour. In the upshot, *Z*'s GDP increases massively; and effects on *Z* GNP may be but weakly positive. So long as displaced *A* manufacturing workers can be deployed so that values of their marginal products exceed 32¢ an hour, *A* GNP will increase. The lower the *Z* wage rate, the more attractive the proposition becomes.

Supplementary Remarks

1. The annotation of *choice* **80(c)** explains why say American MNCs did so well throughout the spurious 'deindustrialization' flap. And a related point is this. It is increasingly improper to associate overseas actions of Economy *E* companies

with E's trade account. IBM supplies an example. From a trade point of view, IBM Britain or IBM Germany are essentially British or German companies; merchandise flows across the Atlantic between these companies and IBM United States are quite balanced, as are those of comparable Ford entities. The important effects of such overseas activity are on overseas earnings of productive factors (see Lecture Two's y' variable).

2. The A/Z scenario may entail problems in distributive justice, since the net GNP gain may fall short of the gain in non-human-capital income; in the short run at least, labour income may fall. In a longer run, labour will benefit from amplified demand for services, resulting from higher GNP. Of course, in the neoclassical paradigm, everyone sells and buys services of human and non-human capital; and union pension funds are invested in shares, etc.

3. The A/Z scenario elides a significant gain for A: such external diseconomies as smog and acid rain are shifted from A to Z.

Problem 81

81(A) Refer back to the A/Z scenario in the annotation of choice **80(c)**. Obviously, the impact on GNP is greater if one's residents own the resources specialized to production of exports now in greater demand. Nor should the analysis be confined to *direct* impacts: local tennis professionals and restaurateurs will benefit more if the owners of now-more-valuable specialized resources reside 'here'.

81(b) No. Resources will be *absorbed* by the 'non-oil-export' sector. Resulting overabsorption of our GDP is partially offset by exchange-rate appreciation, making imports more attractive. Imports are also made more attractive by higher service-prices in our economy, as the expanding export sector bids up factor prices.

Now consider a corollary process. Say that the demand-shift causes assets specialized to exporting to be permanently upvalued and that we own such assets. The windfall pushes down our savings rate until our relative wealth position returns to its equilibrium level along the lines of Lecture Seven.

81(c) No. Continuing from the close of the annotation of choice **81(b)**, if the specialized assets are owned by non-residents, effects on demand for services are registered *abroad*.

Problem 82

82(a) Habitat bias imposes a binding constraint on the underlying wealth-maximization problem; the value of the solution of the more-heavily-constrained problem is lower. The correct analysis is illuminated by the following example from *antebellum* America. Slaveholders, especially in Mississippi and other 'western' sites, were allured by imperial prospects in South America, a lure that led to southern intransigence. If these 'dreams' had been realized, Southern GDP may have declined as resources flowed towards the newly-acquired realms; and GNP would have increased.

82(B) The annotation of choice **82(a)** controls **82(B)**. Think of Country C whose productive assets are owned by aliens, while C saving has always been placed abroad. Then C's GDP evolves sympathetically with GDP shifts in other countries. This stark result is moderated by switching to the less-stringent assumption that some productive resources sited in C are owned by C residents.

Now consider this outré possibility. C-owned assets may be concentrated in firms competing for the same specialized resources (aeronautical engineers or meteoric stones) as foreign-owned C firms (now assumed to be concentrated in selected sectors). Then intensified demand for products produced by the alien sector may cause our GNP to fall while our GDP rises.

82(c) Stalin exacted terrible sacrifices; and the resources he 'freed' were spent on inane projects and on military programmes that *did* make Russia a superpower. But public-sector absorption *may* enhance an economy's productive potential.

Moving onto a higher plane of generality, Lecture Four shows how policies imposing underabsorption map into wealth-accumulation.

Problem 83

83(B) At the simplest level of analysis, the E-dollar depreciates; imports become dearer. And there is apt to be downward pressure on E wages; pure services become relatively cheaper, especially if alternative consumption goods have high import content.

Caveat

'Maintenance' of the labour force – cf. closed Leontief models – may also entail substantial importing: the workers' wage-goods basket may have a high import-content. This makes it difficult for very open economies to execute exchange-depreciation strategies. (See Lecture Six.)

83(c) Strategy-choice pivots on whether the leftward shift of the demand schedule is temporary or permanent. Say that it is temporary. Then we should borrow against future receipts in order to maintain an orderly consumption-path. (See the discussion of the Laursen–Metzler effect in Chapter 6 for a related analysis.) The government might supply its notes, taking back private-sector IOUs; the loan proceeds support consumption and lead to an increase in public-sector debt held by foreigners. Or, the 'speculators' studied in Lecture Six may effectively lend foreign currency to the private sector; 'speculators' may be aliens.

If the adverse demand-shift is permanent, it is counter-productive for the government to buttress consumption by sell-offs of real wealth; then consumption is sustainable only by consumption of real capital.

Choice **83(c)** is framed with low cunning. Simplistically 'Keynesian' reasoning calls for fiscal stimulus to sustain aggregate demand. Classical/neoclassical analysis shows that the decay of export-demand requires reallocation of resources; and is indeed adverse, since equilibrium real income must fall when a constraint – here demand for E exports – tightens.

Note: The Stolper–Samuelson Factor Price Equalization Theorem

See Caves and Jones (1985, p. 511):

If two countries share the same technology and produce both goods in common [in this two good/two factor system, which has been successfully generalized] free trade in commodities will not only equate commodity prices, it will also result in *factor price equalization*.

8 Lecture Eight: Pure Theory of the Gold Standard: Commodity Money in Classical Economics

The lecture is partly based on Burstein (1986, Chapters 4 and 11). Also see Barsky and Summers (1988), Friedman (1951/1953) and Friedman and Schwartz (1982, esp. Chapter 10). The specie-flow mechanism and other properties of adjustment under fixed exchange rates have been studied in Lecture Six.

8.1 A DYNAMIC ANALYSIS OF A GENERIC COMMODITY-MONEY STANDARD

(See especially Burstein, 1986, pp. 52–3.)

Section 8.2 specializes the highly general discussion of Section 8.1; and Section 8.3 is still more specific. Section 8.4 concerns 'distributional' properties of gold stocks across economies.

A number of things promote stability in commodity-money systems. Excess supply of goods leads to increased money production, to an extent depending on elasticity of supply and reaction speeds of prices. And rising prices slow down money growth; real monetary balances shrink as inflation progresses. The following global system displays these properties (again, see Section 8.4 for properties of disaggregated systems):

$$Dp = \alpha(M - M^*) \tag{8.1}$$

$$M^* = ap - bDp \tag{8.1a}$$

$$DM = \Lambda - \gamma p \tag{8.2}$$

$$Dp = \alpha M - a\alpha p + \alpha b Dp \qquad (8.3)$$

$$D^2p = \alpha DM - a\alpha Dp + \alpha b D^2 p \qquad (8.4)$$

$$D^2 p(1-\alpha b) + a\alpha Dp + \alpha\gamma p = \alpha\Lambda \text{ (Recalling equation}$$
$$(8.2)) \qquad (8.5)$$

Equation (8.1) establishes the velocity of the price level as a lagged function of the excess of money supply over desired money supply, M^*. Equation (8.1a) determines the desired stock of money; money-demand increases with the price *level* and decreases as price-inflation increases, responding to a *de facto* tax on non-interest-yielding money balances. Equation (8.2), the model's power house, determines the planned rate of money-production; as prices increase, the real purchasing power of money falls and its cost of production increases.

Equations (8.3) and (8.4) manipulate the body of the model, leading to equation (8.5), a second-order differential equation. A particular solution of equation (8.5) is:

$$D^2 p = Dp = 0; \bar{p} = \Lambda|\gamma ; \bar{M} = \alpha\Lambda|\gamma \qquad (8.6)$$

The solution's remainder part is obtained from the characteristic equation:

$$\lambda^2 + \{a\alpha|1-\alpha b\}\lambda + \alpha\gamma|1-\alpha b = 0 \qquad (8.7)$$

The roots of the characteristic equation are:

$$\lambda_1, \lambda_2 = (1/2)[-\{\} \pm \sqrt{\{} \quad \{\}^2 - 4(\gamma\alpha|1-\alpha b)] \qquad (8.8)$$

Try: $\alpha = 1$; $b = 0.5$, $a = 2$; $\gamma = 3$. Where A and ε are arbitrary constants determined by initial conditions, the solution is:

$$\bar{p}_t = \Lambda|\gamma A e^{-2t} \cos(1.415t - \varepsilon) \qquad (8.9)$$

Damping is strong. Prices and gold production oscillate about stationary norms (that for gold production being nil). The amplitudes of the oscillations asymptotically approach zero.

8.2   THE PURCHASING POWER OF MONEY AS DETERMINED BY THE COST OF OBTAINING MONEY: A PRÉCIS OF THE CLASSICAL GOLD STANDARD

The section-head is suggested by the title of Nassau Senior's (1830) book, *The Cost of Obtaining Money*. And its *motif* was earlier stated by Adam Smith:

> The proportion between the value of gold and silver and that of goods of any other kind depends . . . [only] . . . upon that between the quantity of labour is necessary . . . to bring . . . gold and silver to market, and that which is necessary . . . to bring thither . . . other . . . goods.

> Smith (1910 / 1970, 1, p. 293)

Temporary Equilibrium of an Aggregated Global System

The schema is built up, step by step, starting with explication of equation (8.10),

$$x^s = f(\pi, S, \beta) \tag{8.10}$$

The rate of production of gold is symbolized by x^s; the purchasing power of gold is indexed by π; the stock of gold by S; and β is a shift parameter for the function $(f())$ determining gold production.

It is plausible that $\partial f / \partial S < 0$ – that the larger is the stock of gold, the less attractive are current mining prospects. (Although a parametric specification of β simplifies the analysis, it is more interesting to take β_t as the outcome of exploration activity; exploration activity at any time is a function of expected values of π; exploration for crude oil, especially since the 1973 oil shock, supplies a perfect example (a crude approximation to this approach is displayed *infra*).

$$S^d = g(\pi; y^\circ, \alpha, \ell) \tag{8.11}$$

Real economic activity (neglecting gold mining) is indexed by y° . 'α' is a shift parameter for industrial demand for gold, including jewellery; ' ℓ ' similarly parameterizes monetary demand for gold. And note the following points. (1)   Demand for monetary gold concerns a value-weighted quantity; what matters is the stock's purchasing power, not how much it weighs. (2)   For simplicity's sake, we ignore (admittedly substantial) money-substitute properties of golden jewellery, for example. (3)   Only the mint's buy–sell spread, together with private-sector charges for transforming specie into 'industrial' products, modify lockstep covariance of the purchasing power of monetary and non-monetary gold:

$$x^d = \phi[g(\ )-S] \tag{8.12}$$

$$x^d = x^s \tag{8.13}$$

Lower-case variables have the dimension of a flow.

The system comprising equations (8.10)–(8.13) determines the temporary-equilibrium vector $(\bar{\pi}, \bar{s}^d, \bar{x})$ – where $x^d = x^s = x$. In this way, temporary equilibrium is determined relative to S_t. (Subscripts are dropped when convenient). And the system can be reduced to a single equation in π:

$$\phi[g(\ ) - S] = f(\pi,s,\beta) \tag{8.14}$$

Stock-flow Equilibrium

The stock-quantity becomes an unknown; while $x^s = x^d = 0$ in equilibrium.

$$f(\pi,S,\beta) = 0 \tag{8.15}$$

$$g(\pi,y°,\alpha, \ell\,) = S \tag{8.16}$$

Equations (8.15) and (8.16) are in the unknowns (π,S). And if β is endogenized, we obtain the system comprising equations (8.17)–(8.19), three equations in (π,S,β):

$$f(\cdot) = 0 \tag{8.17}$$

$$g(\cdot) = S \tag{8.18}$$

$$\beta = \beta(\pi,S) \tag{8.19}$$

The reduced form of the system comprising equations (8.17)–(8.19), i.e. the set of equations expressing solution values of endogenous variables as functions of parameters, follows:

$$\bar{s} = \bar{s}(\alpha, y^{\circ}, \ell)$$ (8.20)

$$\bar{\pi} = \bar{\pi}(\cdot)$$ (8.21)

$$\bar{\beta} = \bar{\beta}(\cdot)$$ (8.22)

My colleague, S.-H. Chiang, points out that existence of a unique solution to the reduced form – equations (8.20)–(8.22) – requires that the implicit-function theorem hold, i.e. that the determinant of the following Jacobian be non-zero:

$$[J] = \begin{bmatrix} \partial f/\partial \pi & \partial f/\partial S & \partial f/\partial \beta \\ \partial(g-S)/\partial \pi & \partial(g-S)/\partial S & \partial(g-S)/\partial \beta \\ \partial \beta/\partial \pi & \partial \beta/\partial S & \partial \beta/\partial \beta \end{bmatrix} \neq 0$$ (8.23)

Some Casual Comparative Statics

If demand for monetary gold should shift upward (increasing in the schedule sense), the new stock-flow equilibrium entails an increased *physical* gold stock, i.e. $d\bar{S} > 0$. By way of proof, if increased monetary demand were accommodated solely by an increase in gold's purchasing power, so that gold production continued to be nil ($\bar{x} = 0$), although $d\bar{\pi} > 0$, the stock must have increased – so that the marginal cost of gold-production, starting from a nil rate, is higher.

A similar proof shows that the equilibrium stock of gold must increase when industrial demand for gold shifts upward, although the physical *monetary* stock then declines.

And S.-H. Chiang anticipates more rigorous comparative-statics demonstrations in the following way:

$$\begin{bmatrix} \partial f/\partial \pi & \partial f/\partial S \\ \partial g/\partial \pi & -1 \end{bmatrix} \begin{bmatrix} d\pi \\ dS \end{bmatrix} = \begin{bmatrix} 0 \\ (\partial g/\partial \ell)d\ell \end{bmatrix}$$ (8.24)

$$\partial \pi/\partial \ell = -\partial f/\partial S(\partial g/\partial \ell)/\Delta = (-)/(-) = (+)$$ (8.25)

$$\partial S/\partial \ell = (-\partial g/\partial \ell)(\partial f/\partial \pi)/\Delta = (-)/(-) = (+) \tag{8.26}$$

A Disaggregated Version of the Schema

$$L^i(\pi; y^\circ, \alpha_i, \ell_i) = S_i \qquad i = 1, \ldots, n \tag{8.27}$$

$$\Sigma S_i = S^* \tag{8.28}$$

Equations (8.27) and (8.28) comprise a system of $n+1$ equations in the $n+1$ variables (S_i) and π. In temporary equilibrium, the value of S at date t is predetermined (at S^*). And stock-flow equilibrium is at the rest point of the system:

$$\dot{S} = F(S) \qquad \text{(in vector notation)} \tag{8.29}$$

Solve equation (8.29) for $(\bar{S}_i)$ and so for $\Sigma \bar{S}_i$. Plug the resulting value for the global gold-stock into equation (8.28) – and solve as before.

Fleshing out '$F(S)$', if the purchasing power of gold exceeds marginal cost of production, measuring in Caesarae, at nil output, temporary equilibrium requires positive output; and the upshot is inconsistent with full (stock-flow) equilibrium. We thus uncover the criterion for the equilibrium level of stock.

A Sketch of Some Explicit Dynamics

(Symmetry would be served by introducing a leakage coefficient describing losses of gold and absorption by industrial processes.)

Switching notation so that the gold stock is represented by ξ, the analysis's canonical form is:

$$\dot{\xi} = \psi(\xi) \tag{8.30}$$

The dynamic system is stable: $\psi'(\ ) < 0$:

$$\dot{\xi} = \lambda_2 [g [\pi (\xi), y^\circ, \alpha, \ell] - \xi] \tag{8.31}$$

$$\partial \dot{\xi}/\partial \xi = \lambda_2 (\overset{(-)}{\partial g/\partial \xi} - 1) < 0! \tag{8.32}$$

Further Sketches of Dynamic Versions of the Model

The interesting discussion by Arrowsmith and Place (1982, pp.

200ff.) of Liapunov functions in connection with the behaviour of a non-linear system at one of its rest points repays study but is not deployed here.

The model yields more interesting implications if its variables are transformed into logs, so that resulting coefficients are elasticities, more or less. Define the transformed variables as follows:

$\chi_1 = \log(\bar{\xi}/\xi)$ = logarithm of the ratio of the equilibrium to the actual gold stock

$\chi_2 = \log(\bar{\pi}/\pi)$ = logarithm of the ratio of the equilibrium to the actual purchasing power of gold

The system comprising equations (8.33) and (8.34) is, of course, log linear:

$$\dot{\chi}_1 = a_{11}\chi_1 + a_{12}\chi_2 \tag{8.33}$$

$$\dot{\chi}_2 = a_{21}\chi_1 + a_{22}\chi_2 \tag{8.34}$$

Now consider the matrix (a_{ij}). The material above establishes the following sign pattern:

$$\begin{bmatrix} (-) & (+) \\ (-) & (-) \end{bmatrix}$$

Call this matrix A. Its trace is $a_{11} + a_{22} = (-)$ and its determinant, *DET*, is positive.

Stability hinges on the roots of the characteristic equation:

$\lambda_1 = 1/2 \, (Tr - \sqrt{\Delta})$
$\lambda_2 = 1/2 \, (Tr + \sqrt{\Delta})$ $\Delta = (Tr)^2 - 4DET$, thus being faithful to Arrowsmith–Place usage

Cycles are barred; imaginary roots are precluded. But saddle-point instability is *not* precluded; real roots (eigenvalues) of opposite sign are quite plausible.

The following case is not economically absurd:

Quantity adjustments are very slow and price adjustments quite *rapid: a_{11} and a_{12} are very small relative to a_{21} and a_{22}. The absolute value of the trace is large relative to DET.*

Stipulate a small value for *DET*, but it is not to vanish. Now the critical relationship concerns the absolute values of a_{22} and $\sqrt{\Delta}$. It is obvious that λ_2 is the dominant root; and that it is negative. λ_1 may be very small, but it must be negative. Stability is assured.

8.3 PROPERTIES OF SOPHISTICATED FINANCIAL SYSTEMS IN GOLD-STANDARD RÉGIMES

Equations (8.35) and (8.36) are in the unknowns (r', p), the deposit rate (r') and the general price level (p). The schema generates effects of changes in the 'mercantile rate of profit' (r^*), liquidity preference (ℓ), intensity of demand for non-monetary gold (α), the gold supply (k), etc.:

$$f(r^*,r',p) + g(r^*,r',p;\alpha) = k \tag{8.35}$$

$$\psi(r^*,r',p) = L(r^*,r',p;\ell) \tag{8.36}$$

Remarks

1. Demand for monetary gold $(G_M^d) = f(\ )$
2. Demand for non-monetary gold $(G_N^d) = g(\ )$
3. Money supply $(M^s) = \psi(\ )$
4. Demand for money $(M^d) = L(\ )$
5. In equations (8.35) and (8.36) the relation between G_M and M^s is implicit; the variables are rigidly linked up by Barsky and Summers (1988)
6. Price changes are once-over; the model does not accommodate inflation

Comparative Statics

First differentiate equations (8.35) and (8.36) with respect to α and r' and rearrange terms:

$$(f_{r'} + g_{r'})d\bar{r}' + (f_p + g_p)d\bar{p} = -g_\alpha d\alpha \tag{8.37}$$

$$(\psi_{r'} - L_{r'})d\bar{r}' + (\psi_p - L_p)d\bar{p} = 0 \tag{8.38}$$

Performing a sign analysis,

$$[(-)+(-)]d\bar{r}' + [(+)]d\bar{p} = (-)(+)d\alpha \tag{8.39}$$

$$[(-)-(+)]d\bar{r}' + [-(+)]d\bar{p} = 0 \tag{8.40}$$

Interpolation

$\partial f/r' = f_{r'} < 0$: a higher deposit rate makes gold-intake less attractive to banks; $\partial f/\partial p$ and $\partial \psi/\partial p$ reckon to be feeble and are neglected.

As for the system's determinant, cf:

$$\begin{vmatrix} (-) & (+) \\ (-) & (-) \end{vmatrix} = (+)$$

By Cramér's Rule:

$$d\bar{r}'/d\alpha = \begin{vmatrix} (-) & (+) \\ 0 & (-) \end{vmatrix} / (+) = (+) \tag{8.41}$$

The banks' spread narrows if demand for non-monetary gold (say, jewelry) increases: then a higher deposit rate is necessary to attract a given amount of gold (the non-banking public holds gold indirectly--via convertible bank obligations). But the need to pay a higher deposit rate(r') leads to lower planned money-supply; matched by a decrease in demand for money, induced by a lower price level:

$$d\bar{p}/d\alpha = \begin{vmatrix} (-) & (-) \\ (-) & 0 \end{vmatrix} / (+) = (-) \tag{8.42}$$

The purchasing power of gold (its Caesara price) increases in the wake of an increase in demand, in the schedule-sense, for non-industrial gold. There is incidental positive correlation between money and prices.

Now differentiate equations (8.35) and (8.36) with respect to the liquidity-preference parameter (ℓ); $\partial L/\partial \ell > 0$:

$$d\bar{p}/d\ell = \frac{\begin{vmatrix} (-) & (0) \\ (-) & (+) \end{vmatrix}}{(+)} = (-) \tag{8.43}$$

$$d\bar{r}'/d\ell \ = \ \begin{vmatrix} (0) \ (+) \\ (+) \ (-) \end{vmatrix} \ / \ (+) = (-) \tag{8.44}$$

If demand for money increases, the price level falls and the banks' spread widens.

Comparative Statics; Apposition to Barsky and Summers (1988)

Barsky and Summers introduce notation for the time rate of change of the general price level; but their concrete analysis is statical.

These are the Barsky–Summers results that interest us. (1) A rise in the *real* rate of interest – their model contains but one interest rate, equivalent to Thornton's mercantile rate of profit – leads to a decline in the purchasing power of gold (or its Caesara price). (2) A rise in *the* real rate of interest causes the stock of monetary gold to increase, subject to a caveat about interest elasticity of demand for money. There follow equivalent operations on our model – in which, of course, money yields interest:

$$\begin{bmatrix} (-) \ (+) \\ (-) \ (-) \end{bmatrix} \begin{bmatrix} d\bar{r}' \\ d\bar{p} \end{bmatrix} = \frac{(-f_{r^*} - g_{r^*})dr^*}{(-\psi_{r^*} + L_{r^*})dr^*} \tag{8.45}$$

Evaluating signs,

$$\partial f / \partial r^* = f_{r^*} \ = \ (+):$$ it is more attractive for banks to bid for gold when open-market yields increase

$$g_{r^*} \ = \ (-):$$ it is less attractive to hold non-monetary gold when open-market yields increase

$$\psi_{r^*} \ = \ (+):$$ see the analysis of 'f_{r^*}'

$$L_{r^*} \ = \ (-):$$ for $r_1 = r_1^\circ$, it is less attractive to hold money when 'r^*' increases

Therefore,

$$\begin{bmatrix} (-) \ (+) \\ (-) \ (-) \end{bmatrix} \begin{bmatrix} d\bar{r} \\ d\bar{p} \end{bmatrix} = \frac{[(-) - (-)]dr^* = (?)dr^*}{[(-) + (-)]dr^* = (-)dr^*}$$

It seems plausible that the absolute value of f_{r^*} exceeds that of g_{r^*}, since it is more sensible to hold convertible currency than jewellery in order to satisfy a liquidity motive. So we resolve the ambiguity so that $(?) \to (-)$:

$$d\bar{r}'/dr^* = \begin{vmatrix} (-) \ (+) \\ (-) \ (-) \end{vmatrix} / (+) = (+) \qquad \text{(as expected!)} \quad (8.47)$$

$$d\bar{p}/dr^* = \begin{vmatrix} (-) \ (-) \\ (-) \ (-) \end{vmatrix} / (+) = (?) \qquad (8.48)$$

Ambiguity, pursuant to 'interest on money', leaves the Gibson paradox (so to speak $d\bar{p}/dr^* > 0$) up in the air.

As for equation (8.48), ambiguity exists despite an assured decrease in the quantity of non-monetary gold – together with increased monetary gold – in the new equilibrium: the opportunity costs of holding 'G_N' are higher. The 'trick' is this. Monetary velocity must fall. There is less reason to economize on cash balances; and more reason to reduce transactions costs by increasing liquidity. Thus, if the absolute value of the partial elasticity of demand for money with respect to r' exceeds that with respect to r^*, monetary velocity may fall relatively more than money supply increases – when the bankers' spread is exactly maintained – so that $d\bar{p} < 0$. Equation (8.49) makes this point more rigorously. For $d\bar{r}/dr^* > 0$, it is necessary that

$$| (f_{r'} + g_{r'})(-\psi_{r^*} + L_{r^*}) | > | (\psi_{r'} - L_{r'})(-f_{r^*} - g_{r^*}) | \quad (8.49)$$

Inequality (8.49a) comprises a sign analysis of inequality (8.49):

$$|[(-) + (-)][(-)(+) + (-)]| > | [(-)-(+)][(-)(+) - (-)] | \quad (8.49a)$$

And consolidating the sign analysis,

$$(+) > | (-)[(-) - (-)] | \quad (8.49b)$$

Assume that $L_{r^*} \to 0$ and that $L_{r'}$ is substantial. Then it is quite plausible that the inequality is violated, that $d\bar{p}/dr^* < 0$.

Interpolation

When interest is *not* paid on money, and if we adopt Barsky and Summers's plausible assumption (p. 542) that an increase in *the* interest rate induces a switch from non-monetary to monetary gold, along with increased monetary velocity, then 'Gibson's result', $d\bar{p}/dr^* > 0$ is highly plausible. (See the annotation of Problem **87(a)**.)

Resumption of the Main Line of Argument

The ambiguity can be resolved in favour of the Gibson paradox ($d\bar{p}/dr^* > 0$) along a different line of reasoning.

Say that the long-run supply of money by the banking system is perfectly elastic relative to the spread $r^*/r' = \varkappa$. Then, in equilibrium, $dr'/r' = dr^*/r^*$. Next assume that demand for money is zero-order homogeneous with respect to the spread, i.e. for $dr^*/r^* = dr'/r'$, $dM^d = 0$. And, since the opportunity cost of holding non-monetary gold is thus higher 'in both directions', equilibrium requires $dG_M = -dG_N > 0$. The only *modus vivendi* for accomplishing this result is for the price level to increase. QED . . . When money yields interest, substitution effects-based investment opportunity can disappear. It is as simple as that. See Burstein (1986, Chapter 3).

If the partial elasticity of demand for money with respect to r' sufficiently exceeds that with respect to r^*, monetary velocity may fall relatively more than money supply increases, so that $d\bar{p}/dr^* < 0$. Thus examine the truistic equation (8.50):

$$d\bar{M}^d/\bar{M} = \eta_{M^d_{r'}}(dr'/r') - \eta_{M^d_{r^*}}(dr^*/r^*) + d\bar{p}/\bar{p} = \qquad (8.50)$$
$$d\bar{M}_s/\bar{M} = -d\bar{G}_N/\bar{G}_N$$

If $\eta_{M^d_{r'}}$ is large enough it is feasible for $d\bar{p} < 0$ to be the upshot of an increase in 'r^*'; then the Gibson paradox is violated.

Afterword on the Controlling Model of Section 8.3

The reader may have lost sight of the model's principal economic properties; she may be enveloped in algebraic fog. Collecting the economic properties, all monetary gold is held by banks. Nor do banks hold each other's paper; alternatively the banking system is consolidated for the analysis. Banks bid for gold by offering interest-yielding convertible paper. And real outcomes are *not* invariant against the inflation rate or the price-level: gold is numéraire, so that the relative price of gold falls as the price level rises, Granted, a more sophisticated model would measure all prices in Caesarae; then a uniform increase in *all* prices would preserve invariance.

Wicksell's (1898) System

Wicksell's banks form a cartel and deploy r' as a control. The cartel is prepared to supply the quantity of money demanded in the solution obtained relative to $\hat{r}'$. But Wicksell neglects to explain why agents should *hold* bank liabilities generated by his cumulative process. I tried to repair that neglect in 1988 (b).

In a mutant of Wicksell's system, the bank cartel discovers properties of general equilibria relative to alternative r' (control) values; and solves for its profit. It seeks the value of r' that maximizes aggregate net worth of its members. Put differently, it searches for a profit-maximizing *spread*: the wider the spread, the lower will be the volume of bank-mediation in equilibrium; and measured money-supply is affected covariantly with the volume of mediation.

In purely-competitive loan markets, banks have no power over their risk-adjusted lending rates; and Wicksell's scenario is untenable. Say that liquidity preference permanently increases. When money yields interest competitively, temporary competitive equilibrium is regained by widening of bank spreads: deposit rate can be negative (and has been in Switzerland from time to time). In the long run, the supply of mediation increases at a normal spread (see Marshallian *normal price*) at which bank capital earns a long-run equilibrium rate of return. (See Section 10.2 and Burstein, 1986, Chapter 3.)

In a properly open economy, banking markets are indeed competitive. And Chapters 6 and 7 show that in such an economy, say Economy E, an influx of specie (perhaps because of a more positive trade balance) importantly translates into additional lending abroad, and *not* into wider spreads: the world banking markets are then purely competitive. To the extent that there are preferred banking habitats, distribution of banking assets is at least transiently affected.

8.4   A NETWORK OR MATRIX APPROACH TO THE THEORY OF THE GOLD STANDARD

Girton and Roper (1978) make a striking point. The received notion of the quantity of money follows Irving Fisher; the principal model concerns a closed economy whose price level depends on the quantity of money made available by its authorities. Causality runs from money to prices. J. Laurence Laughlin, first professor of political economy in the University of Chicago and patron of Thorstein Veblen, opted for an open model in which perceived causality runs from prices to money so that the quantity of money in Economy E is determined by liquidity preference. Authorities exercise no control over money supply, prices or interest rates. Deviations of actual from desired aggregate monetary balances may trigger changes in current accounts of balances of payments; in a favourite paradigm, excess of actual over desired holdings stimulates expenditure, provoking trade-balance deterioration and so specie outflow – until portfolio balance is restored; and *vice versa per contra*. (See Lecture Nine.)

A Simple Mathematical System

(In the sequel, *gold* and *money* are used interchangeably.)

Let

M_j	=	the money supply of the jth economy
M^*	=	the global supply of money
y_j^*	=	real activity of the jth economy
ℓ_j	=	a shift parameter measuring the intensity of the jth liquidity preference
p	=	the global price level, parametric for the jth economy

And

$L^j(\cdot)$ determines demand for money in the jth economy; parameters include (y_j^*, M^*, ℓ_j)

$$L^j(p; \ell_j, y_j^*) = M_j \qquad j=1, 2, \ldots, n \qquad (8.51)$$

$$\Sigma M_j = M^* \qquad (8.52)$$

The $n+1$ equations comprising equations (8.51) and (8.52) determine $(\bar{M}_j, \bar{p})$.

Equations (8.53) and (8.54) comprise the reduced form of the model of equations (8.51) and (8.52) (ℓ and y^* are vectors):

$$\bar{M}_j = \phi^j(\ell, M^*, y^*) \qquad j = 1, 2, \ldots, n \qquad (8.53)$$

$$\bar{p} = \psi(\ell, M^*, y^*) \qquad (8.54)$$

It is to be shown that: $\partial \bar{p} / \ell_j < 0$; $\partial \bar{p} / \partial M^* > 0$; $\partial \bar{M}_r / \partial \ell_r < 0$; $\partial \bar{M}_s / \partial \ell_r$ < 0. And some illustrations are supplied; I have supplied others in 1986 (Chapter 11) and 1988b ('Alexander Hamilton').

$\partial \bar{p} / \partial \ell_j < 0$ *The* global price level falls if liquidity preference increases *anywhere*. Demand for money having increased in the *j*th economy, and not having fallen anywhere, there must be global excess demand for money. Lower commodity prices increase the real money supply. And the (David) Humean specie-flow mechanism operates to attract specie to the *j*th economy as its imports fall and its exports are stimulated by downward pressure on prices. (See Lecture Nine: monetary theories of balances of payments imply direct exchanges of securities for specie.)

$\partial \bar{p} / \partial M^* > 0$ (See Problem **85(b)**.) The primary demonstration is simple. Portfolio holders must be induced to hold more gold. The real quantity of monetary gold falls if the price level increases (relative to gold as numéraire). So a once-over price-level increase stimulates demand for 'physical' gold. And demand for non-monetary gold is obviously stimulated by a fall in its relative price.

A corollary issue, touched on in the annotation of Problem **85(b)**, is more interesting. Is the distribution of gold in full equilibrium invariant against *where* new mines are discovered? (Or, better, against ownership of the new sources(?).) Section 7.2 casts some light on the murky answer; it suffices here to say that the distribution of precious metals across economies will be relatively little affected by discovery-locale. Say that the relative share of world wealth of Economy *A* increases from 4 to 6% because of a gold-discovery windfall; and say that its share of the global gold stock rises from 4 to 6% *pari passu*. Obviously, *most* of the gold mined in the interval spanning the lives of the new mines will have flowed out; it will have been exchanged for non-golden assets, consumption goods, etc.

$\partial \bar{M}_r / \partial \ell_r > 0$ The proposition is that an increase in the *r*th liquidity preference leads to the *r*th economy holding a larger proportion of the global gold supply. Before proving the proposition (and indeed the fourth one as well), consider these remarks.

Remarks

1. Temin (1969) shows how Western price movements in the 19th century were affected by shifts of Oriental asset preferences.
2. Historically, gold preferences have significantly varied across economies; thus Indian and French precious-metal holdings have

long exceeded Scotland's (adjusting for population). And Adam Smith's *dead stock* analysis, picked up by Alexander Hamilton, interestingly illuminates the subject (see Burstein 1988b, 'Alexander Hamilton').

Resumption of the Proof

Differentiating around a solution point,

$$(\partial L^r/\partial \ell_r)d\ell_r + (\partial L^r/\partial p)d\bar{p} = d\bar{M}_r$$
$$r = 1,2,,,j-1,j+1, \ldots, n \qquad (8.55)$$

$$(\partial L^j/\partial p)d\bar{p} = d\bar{M}_j \qquad j \neq r \qquad (8.56)$$

$$\Sigma d\bar{M}_j + d\bar{M}_r = 0 \qquad (8.57)$$

Equations (8.55), (8.56) and (8.57) comprise a set of $n+1$ equations in the unknowns $(d\bar{M}_r)$, $d\bar{M}_j$, $d\bar{p}$). Assume that $d\ell_r > 0$ and that $d\ell_s = 0$ ($r \neq s$). As for $d\bar{p}$, if $d\bar{p} = 0$, demand for gold will increase in the rth economy and not change anywhere else. If $d\bar{p} > 0$, demand for gold will be higher everywhere. So $d\bar{p} < 0$ is necessary. Then demand for gold is lower in economies $1, 2, \ldots, r-1, r+1, \ldots, n$; but the sum of gold-holdings is unchanged. In the solution $\partial \bar{M}_r/\partial \ell_r > 0$.

$\partial \bar{M}_s/\partial \ell_r < 0$ This proposition has just been proved.

An Annotated Problem Set For Lecture Eight

PROBLEMS

84. If gold preference increases everywhere except in France:

(A) the world price level will decrease;
(b) French gold holdings will increase;
(c) France will run a more unfavourable trade account in the new long-run equilibrium;
(d) all of the above choices are correct;
(e) none of the above choices is correct.

85. In the long run:

(a) the purchasing power of money must be aligned with its marginal cost of production;
(b) the distribution of gold hinges on where gold fields are discovered;
(c) the global real rate of interest is a function of the nominal value of the global gold-stock;
(d) two of the above choices are correct;
(E) none of the above choices is correct.

86. Choose the correct statement:

(a) in the short run, an increase in demand for non-monetary gold leads to lower price levels everywhere;
(b) an increase in liquidity preference leads to an increase in the stock of monetary gold;
(c) the prospect of increased gold production, perhaps some years from now, leads to higher long-term nominal rates of interest now;
(d) two of the above choices are correct;
(E) choices (a), (b) and (c) are correct.

87. Which of the following lead(s) to a change in the rate of price inflation in the long run?

 (a) a new mining technique leads to a higher, but stationary, level of the stock of gold;
 (b) the global rate of growth of real output permanently increases;
 (c) the global propensity to save increases;
 (D) two of the above choices are correct;
 (e) none of the above choices is correct.

88. The global economy is on a gold standard. Global demand for liquidity, in the schedule sense, increases. Gold is not revalued. It follows, at least in the short run, that:

 (A) the rate of interest paid on monetary claims falls;
 (b) the value of jewellery, measured in terms of goods in general, falls and some monetary gold is converted into jewellery;
 (c) gold production falls;
 (d) two of the above choices are correct;
 (e) choices **(a)**, **(b)** and **(c)** are correct.

ANNOTATIONS

Problem 84

84(A) Take the *world* as a closed economy. The immediate effects of an increase in gold-preference make gold more valuable. Longer-run effects on prices depend on the elasticity of supply of gold-production and elasticities of substitution in demand between monetary and non-monetary gold.

84(b) No! French gold holdings will *decrease*. The lecture demonstrates this result with some rigour, confirming common sense. In each economy, *sauf* France, there is excess demand for gold initially; in France demand equals the gold stock initially. A higher value of gold will reconcile increased demand for gold, in the schedule sense, with the supply – in the short run, the global stock of monetary plus non-monetary gold is virtually a given – analogously to the minor increment that one year's investment makes to the stock of capital. And equilibrium requires the French stock to fall, since French demand is unchanged.

84(c) An egregious choice! It confuses the traverse to a new equilibrium distribution of gold with properties of the new full equilibrium (rest point) of the system. The specie-flow mechanism may compel France to run unfavourable (or less favourable) trade balances over the traverse. But the specie-flow mechanism shuts down once a rest point is attained. (In equilibrium-growth a rest point must be defined in a space spanned by basic vectors of *proportions* of gold stocks, etc.)

Problem 85

85(A) Assuming, as classical writers surely did, that the gold-mining industry is competitive, and deploying a standard of value defined on n commodities, so that one *Caesara* purchases an imaginary bundle composed of fragments of n commodities, temporary equilibrium of the gold-mining industry occurs at a rate of output for which the marginal cost of production, measured in Caesarae, is equal to price, also measured in Caesarae. In stationary equilibrium, marginal cost of production in the neighbourhood of *nil* output may be x Caesarae and the purchasing power of gold – i.e. the Caesarae price of gold – $\in (x-h)$. The mining industry is shut down.

85(b) (Lecture Seven includes a related discussion of the 'relative wealth of nations'.) Finessing the question whether equilibrium distribution is *strictly* invariant against locales of discovery, we can safely conclude from the lecture that discovery-locales do not dominate long-run outcomes. Think of the diffusion of metals throughout the world for many years after Spanish discovery of gold and silver mines in America.

85(c) A choice contradicting essential 'classical' reasoning. The supply of 'real liquidity' is floated up and down by price-level changes. But classical theory does not imply *monetary neutrality*: the lecture explains that a change in liquidity preference affects the equilibrium price of jewellery for example.

Problem 86

86(a) The purchasing power of an ounce of gold increases. And gold is the numéraire good. It is as simple as that.

86(b) Go back to choice **86(a)**. The increased value of a physical unit of gold stimulates gold production; and, as the lecture explains, heightened liquidity preference leads to transformation of some non-monetary gold into monetary gold; jewellery, etc. are imperfect *comme* liquid assets.

86(c) Students of rational expectations are familiar with this problem. Nominal interest rates reflect expectations of future inflation.

Problem 87

87(a) Wrong! It is unfailingly important to distinguish a higher price level from a higher inflation rate. In this connection see the *Gibson paradox* (Keynes's locution, 1930), interestingly discussed by Friedman and Schwartz (1982, Chapter 10) and by Barsky and Summers (1988), among many others. The Gibson paradox concerns 'the long observed positive correlation between interest rates and the *level* of prices' (Friedman and Schwartz, 1982, p. 478). Any serious attempt to probe the controlling literature requires at least a long essay (which would be a basis for an interesting course in applied monetary theory). So let Friedman and Schwartz's précis of 'an important paper by Benjamin Klein (1975)' suffice:

> There remains the problem of accounting for the apparent difference between pre-World War II relations and postwar relations, particularly after the mid-1960s, when the Gibson relation largely disappears and is replaced by a close relation between interest rates and the rate of change of prices . . .
>
> Klein argues that there has been a fundamental change in the character of the monetary system since World War II . . . Before World War II . . . the United States and the United Kingdom were regarded as being on specie standards which limited the price *level*. Prices might rise and fall over short periods, but the price level was widely expected

to revert to a roughly constant level, and it did. The price level in the United Kingdom in 1912 was roughly the same as in 1729 . . . Under this system, Klein argues, there was considerable short-term unpredictability of prices but much less long-term unpredictability. Current rates of price change contained little information about future rates of price change. On the other hand, the level of prices did contain such information. A price level that was high relative to 'normal' implied a subsequent decline in prices and conversely . . . [Now] it is rational to take this information into account, and interest rates now respond to recent rates of price change as they did not do so before.

Friedman and Schwartz (1982, p. 570)

Formerly, if the price level were above its norm at date t, interest rates at t would reflect an inflation premium imposed on the interval from $(t-h)$ when prices started to rise. And, by the time prices regain their norm at $(t+h)$, interest rates will regain *their* norm, although, along Fisherine (distributed lag) lines, interest rates will exhibit enough inertia so that *on average*, over the interval $(t) \rightarrow (t+h)$, interest rates and prices are above their norms. Similarly, if prices were below their norms at t, there would have been a deflationary traverse from $(t-h)$, so that, on average, lower prices were associated with lower interest rates, etc.

87(b) go back to the secular quantity theory of money formula:

$$\pi = m - \varrho$$

If money-growth is given at m^* and real growth (ϱ) increases, then the inflation rate (π) decreases *pari passu*. There was sustained deflation in the second half of the 19th century as real growth ran ahead of gold production – until gold was discovered in Alaska and South Africa. W. J. Bryan's (thou shalt not crucify mankind upon a) Cross of Gold speech concerned this episode.

87(c) the controlling reasoning is in two steps. Step One: the higher savings rate translates into a higher real growth rate. Step Two:

the higher growth rate maps into a lower inflation rate; see the annotation of **87(b)**.

Problem 88

88(A) The lecture dwells on this point; as do Barsky and Summers (1988). The deposit rate will fall if liquidity preference increases; banks will command wider spreads.

88(b) Some jewellery will be converted into monetary gold, or, in the Barsky–Summers model (which is commensurate with ours on the point) into claims against banks, the exclusive holders of monetary gold. So we want to evaluate $d\bar{p}/d\ell$. Confirming common sense, it has been shown to be negative.

88(c) Gold production is *stimulated* by gold's increased purchasing power (by a higher Caesara price of gold). The lecture's dynamic modelling supplies an analytic paradigm. But study the following, rather recherché, qualification. If, in the initial equilibrium, the marginal cost of production exceeds, perhaps substantially, the purchasing power of gold, the Caesara value of gold can increase, perhaps substantially, without gold-production being stimulated. The gold mines remain idle.

9 Lecture Nine: Monetary Theories of Balances-of-payment and Exchange-rate Fluctuations

Lecture Ten supplies a 'preferred theory' of financial innovation in open economies that treats the material of this lecture quite differently.

9.1 PRINCIPAL PROPERTIES OF MONETARY THEORIES OF BALANCES OF PAYMENT (MTBOP)

9.1.1 An Overview

In monetary theories of balances of payment under fixed exchange rates 'excessive' domestic credit engenders direct absorption effects that drain monetary reserves, braking money supply. The stable dynamic process also entails direct capital outflow: excess j-dollars are converted into specie or reserve currencies that are tendered for i-dollars. And influxes of specie and reserve currencies stimulate foreign economies unless their authorities sterilize reserve inflows.

Under floating rates, under MTBOP, monetary balances are rapidly adjusted by exchange-rate changes. However, if wages and prices are sticky, 'excessive' monetary expansion in Economy E may at first lead to a more positive trade account: prompt currency depreciation induces lower terms of trade. And, later, the trade account may fall into substantial deficit before finally stabilizing. *Overshooting* permeates this book.

The controlling mechanism pivots on narrowly-defined monetary assets: excess demand for (supply of) non-monetary assets, unaccompanied by disequilibrium in markets for monetary assets, is not to affect the trade account.

9.1.2 Alternative MTBOP Models; Explicit Dynamization of a MTBOP Paradigm

Perlman (1986) reminds us that MTBOP was quite fully developed by Ricardo. And the bullionist version of MTBOP easily transforms into a quite formal dynamic system.

Montiel (1984) shows that MTBOP can be interpreted truistically; but we finesse this peril by constructing a schema whose results are operationally distinguishable from those yielded by say strictly-Keynesian approaches.

Perlman (1986)

> [Ricardo] the hard-line bullionist, argued that a necessary and sufficient condition for a balance of trade deficit was a redundant currency. With convertibility this would lead to an outflow of gold; with inconvertibility . . . to a change in the exchange rate.
>
> Perlman (1986, p. 745)

This is an unmitigated version of MTBOP. And Thornton and Malthus properly pointed out that Ricardo went too far: 'they also believed that such a deficit could occur because of changes in the real sector of the economy' (Perlman, 1986, pp. 745–6).

Perlman's Appendices A and B (1986, pp. 759–61) are intriguing. Appendix A concerns Thornton's prescient analysis of *fiscal* theories of the balance of payments (see Section 9.3 below). Appendix B-2, concerning 'A Bad Harvest', brings out a tenuous line of argument that may prop up Ricardo:

> Ricardo was willing to concede to Malthus that a bad harvest will have an income effect on the demand for money and therefore will affect gold flows under convertibility or the price level and the exchange rate under inconvertibility . . . For Ricardo . . . effects of a bad harvest . . . would be [like those] of a change in the quantity of money.
>
> Perlman (1986, p. 761)

Montiel (1984)

> The monetary approach is not itself a structural model, but rather a framework of analysis that is compatible with diverse macroecon-

omic models, which in turn may possess quite different implications for the effects of stabilization policies on the balance of payments and on other macroeconomic variables.

Montiel (1984, p. 685)

Montiel goes on to assume that an economy's central bank is its only financial institution. Then,

$$F + D = M \tag{9.1}$$

F is the domestic currency value of the bank's net foreign assets; D, domestic credit extended by the bank; and M its monetary liabilities.

Since current account deficits must be financed,

$$BOP = \dot{F} = \dot{M} - \dot{D} \tag{9.2}$$

If the 'money market' is in continuous equilibrium, and P and L represent the domestic price level and real demand for money,

$$\dot{M} = d(PL)/dt \tag{9.3}$$

Substituting into equation (9.2),

$$BOP = \dot{F} = d(PL)/dt - \dot{D} \tag{9.4}$$

So the balance of payments of an economy in a fixed foreign exchange rate régime is equal to the difference between the rate of growth of money-demand and domestic-credit expansion; if domestic-credit expansion growth exceeds money-demand growth, the balance of payments must deteriorate. (And, for $d(PL)/dt = 0$, so that $\dot{M} = 0$, foreign assets must fall 1:1 with domestic credit expansion.)

Montiel calls equation (9.4) 'the fundamental equation of the monetary approach' (1984, p. 686). And he goes on to assert, and then to demonstrate, that

the monetary approach merely describes the effects of stabilization policies on the balance of payments in terms of effects on the flow demand for money, on the flow supply of domestic-source money, or on both; the monetary approach does not, however, commit one to any particular view about the effects of such policies on the balance of payments.

Montiel (1984, p. 686)

(Perhaps Montiel should characterize the 'fundamental equation' this way, rather than MTBOP.)

Confirming Montiel's assertion about the implications of equation (9.4), consider a crude hyper-Keynesian system's temporary-equilibrium properties. Its balance of payments is determined by equations (9.5) and (9.6):

$$\bar{y} = [1/(1-\beta_1)][x^\circ + G^\circ + I(r^\circ)] \tag{9.5}$$

$$BOP = x^\circ - \beta_2\bar{y} \tag{9.6}$$

where x = exports; β_1 = the propensity to consume home goods; β_2 = the propensity to import; G = government expenditure; and $I(r^\circ)$ determines investment.

As for money,

$$\bar{M} = L(r^\circ, \bar{y}) \tag{9.7}$$

The domestic price level is given throughout; and all values are on a scale supplied by the domestic numéraire.

Equation (9.8) describes the foreign-finance requirement (positive or negative):

$$\dot{F} = x^\circ - \beta_2\bar{y} \tag{9.8}$$

Continuous monetary equilibrium requires that $\dot{M} = 0$, since demand for money is constant. Therefore, when the trade account is in deficit, Montiel's bank must expand its credit at the rate $\beta_2\bar{y} - x^\circ$. Fresh credits are used to buy foreign assets from the central bank to finance imports. So:

$$BOP = \dot{F} = -\dot{D} \tag{9.9}$$

A hyper-Keynesian scheme strictly obeys a truistic fundamental

MTBOP equation. Think of a Fisherine quantity theory of money in which v in $Mv = PT$ is a slack variable.

Ricardo's version of MTBOP, and that of the late Harry Johnson, for example, are not empty. Nor is the following scheme:

$$z_j = z_j(\bar{\chi}_j - \chi_j) \tag{9.10}$$

where

z_j = the trade account of the jth BOP
χ_j = the proportion of the globally-available specie stock held in the jth economy
$\bar{\chi}_j$ = the equilibrium value of that proportion (see Burstein, 1986, Chapter 11)

Contact with the 'fundamental' equation (9.4) is regained in an obvious way.

Finally, it is possible to retain the principal properties of a non-empty MTBOP without requiring continuous equilibrium of the 'money market'. See the scheme represented by equations (9.11) and (9.12), tacitly adopting the 'law of one price':

$$z_j = \phi_j(L_j^* - M_j) \tag{9.11}$$

$$DM_j = \psi_j(\ell_j - \ell_j^*) \tag{9.12}$$

where

L_j^* = stipulated demand for money in the jth economy
ℓ_j = F/M = the bank's liquidity ratio
ℓ_j^* = the bank's desired liquidity ratio

The scheme reduces to:

$$\dot{F} = \dot{F}(F, M) \tag{9.13}$$

$$\dot{M} = \dot{M}(F, M) \tag{9.14}$$

Equations (9.13) and (9.14) comprise a canonical form; and study of the system's stability proceeds along exceptionally well defined lines.

Solve

$$0 = \dot{F}(F, M) \tag{9.15}$$

$$0 = \dot{M}(F, M) \tag{9.16}$$

Obtain the rest point $(\bar{F}, \bar{M})$. Then approximate the system linearly in the neighbourhood of its rest point. So, defining variables v and μ as deviations from $\bar{F}$ and $\bar{M}$,

$$\dot{v} = a_{11}v + a_{12}\mu \tag{9.17}$$

$$\dot{\mu} = a_{21}v + a_{22}\mu \tag{9.18}$$

Stability properties, relative to the transformed origin, $((\bar{F}, \bar{M}) = (0, 0))$, are determined by the eigenvalues of the quadratic characteristic equation in well known ways. (See Arrowsmith and Place, 1982.) Economic intuition suggests that, especially since the schema eschews autonomous speculation, phase portraits exhibit stable foci or attracting spirals.

The trade account of the balance of payments supplies the underlying motive power. When the rest point is achieved, when $(F, M) = (\bar{F}, \bar{M})$, the trade-account engine shuts itself off (see equation (9.11)).

The scheme based on equations (9.11) and (9.12) adequately represents Ricardo's and is likely to be strongly identifiable. Its implications are highly distinguishable observationally from those of, say, Keynesian models. The scheme carries the weight of serious MTBOP analysis; and is indeed the target of salvoes fired in Lecture Ten.

9.2 ABSORPTION AND MONETARY THEORIES OF BALANCES OF PAYMENTS

As for absorption,

> Another strand of the classical analysis has recently been revived under the title 'the monetary theory of the balance of payments'. This theory is logically equivalent to the specie-flow mechanism except that it makes quite different assumptions about adjustment speeds of the several variables . . . If the quantity of money in a country is 'too low', domestic nominal demand will not be adequate to absorb domestic output. Export of the surplus will produce a balance of payments surplus for that country, which will raise the

quantity of money. Specie flows are still the adjustment mechanism but they are produced not by discrepancies in prices but by differences between demand for output in nominal terms and the supply of output at world prices.

Friedman and Schwartz (1982, p. 28)

As for 'different assumptions about adjustment speeds', Friedman and Schwartz tacitly point out that MTBOP is a quasi-Keynesian mechanism. Reconstruction of flows is not triggered by price changes; indeed MTBOP tends to specify 'laws of one price'. *Absorption* differentials trigger trade-flow reconstruction.

Some Critique of Absorption in MTBOP

In the *General Theory*, Keynes acknowledges that *money* must be defined quite arbitrarily:

> We can draw the line between 'money' and debts at whatever point is most convenient in practice to include in *money* even such as *e.g.* treasury bills. As a rule I shall assume that money is coextensive with bank deposits.

Keynes (1936, p. 167)

So, in MTBOP, the quantity of money, whatever it may be, is to trigger balance of payment and exchange rate changes, just as, whatever it is, it determines the real rate of interest in Keynes's theory.

Doubtless the imprecision of operational definitions of *money* goes far to shatter MTBOP as a proper theory. But it remains useful to make the following point about implications of flexibly determined interest on 'monetary' assets. In closed economies, the upshot is that an increased quantity of money will be accommodated in portfolios if the yield on such balances increases relative to yields in general. The Keynesian paradigm simply crumbles. (See Burstein, 1986, Chapter 3.) An open-economy equivalent to this result is this. Globally, portfolios will accommodate heavier j-dollar concentration if interest yields on j-dollar-denominated monetary holdings increase relative to yields obtainable on alternatively denominated 'monetary' holdings. The situation is much less well defined than MTBOP would have it. (See Lecture Ten.)

Two Final Remarks

1. Following up on the muddle about the definition of *money*, excess demand for narrowly-defined money may imply nothing more than excess supply of time deposits and/or excess supply of debentures, etc. For MTBOP to have a ghost of a chance to explain absorption, *money* must be defined so broadly that it is congruent with *financial assets*. MTBOP advocates typically side-step this point by excluding non-monetary financial assets from the domain of discourse!
2. Perhaps *pace* Friedman and Schwartz, MTBOP also entails direct capital-account effects. See Frenkel and Johnson (1976, pp. 28–9).
   (I am indebted to John B. Beare in this connection.)

9.3   A STARK ALTERNATIVE TO MTBOP: FISCAL THEORY OF THE BALANCE OF PAYMENTS

In 'classical' economics, 'real' effects should have 'real' causes, making a *fiscal* theory of balances of payment more attractive:

$$j - x = (i+g) - (s' + \tau) \tag{9.19}$$

where

$$c + i + g + x - j = 1 \tag{9.20}$$

Glossing equations (9.19) and (9.20),

j = the proportion borne by imports to gross domestic product (GDP)
x = the proportion borne by exports to GDP
i = the proportion borne by investment expenditures to GDP
g = the proportion borne by government purchases to GDP
$(i+g)$ = the combined finance requirement of the private and public sectors; companies are to pay out all profits
s' = the proportion borne by savings to GDP
τ = the proportion borne by tax revenues to GDP
$(s'+\tau)$ = available domestic finance

Interpolation

In a closed economy in a Keynesian state, aggregate supply is perfectly elastic so that public spending is self-financing. In an open Keynesian economy, an increase in public spending induces deterioration in the trade balance (through multiplier effects on income, and so imports): incremental capital inflow must result.

The analysis is typically closed up by equation (9.21), requiring 'foreign-exchange market' equilibrium, in an obsolete locution; and requiring *external financial balance* in a better locution:

$$\phi = j - x \tag{9.21}$$

Ex post, capital inflow (ϕ) equals the trade deficit. Equation (9.21) may be treated trivially: a trade deficit must be financed. Or it may be infused with content – as equations (9.22) and (9.23), functionally active versions of equations (9.19) and (9.21), make clear:

$$j(r,\xi) - x(r,\xi) = i(r,\xi) + g^\circ - [s(r,\xi) + \tau^\circ] \tag{9.22}$$

$$\phi(r,\xi) = j(\cdot) - x(\cdot) \tag{9.23}$$

Equations (9.22) and (9.23) are in the unknowns (r, ξ), where ξ measures terms of trade. (For simplicity, we ignore 'y''', i.e. factor income earned abroad; see Lecture Two.) Traditionally, the right-hand side of equation (9.23) is taken to define excess supply of our currency generated by a trade deficit; so that foreign-exchange equilibrium appears to require foreigners to demand, on net, an equal volume of our securities, measured, and issued, in our money of account. This description is improper: the right-hand side of equation (9.23) merely states a finance requirement in *some* accounting unit. Of course, equation (9.19) requires that, if the aggregate finance requirement $((i+g)-(s'+\tau))$ should change, $(j-x)$ must change accordingly.

There is no necessary connection between trade-account situations and currency prices. The agents of the ith economy, including its government, may finance a trade deficit by selling securities denominated in j-dollars, or guaranteed in j-dollar value. Capital inflow does not entail foreign willingness to acquire assets denominated in our measure. True, foreigners must then be willing to extend credit, but that is consistent with acceptance of IOUs in *any* measure. (See Lecture Ten.)

Enlarging the Phase Space of the Analysis

If the analysis is dynamized, state variables include balance-sheet values. A flow equilibrium entailing a trade deficit and capital inflow may imply a deteriorating collective balance sheet: global claims against an economy may be increasing unsustainably rapidly.

Properties of Stock-Flow ('Long Run') Equilibrium

The rate at which an economy's foreign debt is increasing, if interest payments are financed by fresh borrowing, is given by:

$$rD + U \tag{9.24}$$

where D is foreign debt and U fresh borrowing beyond interest requirements. And the relative rate of increase is:

$$r + U/D \tag{9.25}$$

or

$$r + u/\delta \tag{9.26}$$

where $u = U/y$ and $\delta = D/y$

In a moving stock-flow equilibrium, real foreign debt per unit of output, foreign debt per unit of domestic wealth, etc. are constant. So, if the intrinsic real growth rate is $\varrho°$:

$$\varrho° = r + u/\delta \tag{9.27}$$

Specifying that the interest rate, as well as the real growth rate, is parametric, and rearranging terms,

$$u = \delta(\varrho° - r°) \tag{9.28}$$

As for δ, or, better, δ_j, an element of the vector system

$$\dot{\delta} = \dot{\delta}(\delta), \tag{9.29}$$

go on to solve for a rest point of that system,

$$0 = \dot{\delta}(\delta) \tag{9.30}$$

The solution of equation (9.30), $\bar{\delta}$, is a function of global asset preferences. Substituting the solution value of δ_j, $\bar{\delta}_j$, into equation (9.28), we discover the equilibrium value of capital inflow per unit of output. We are able to solve directly for $\bar{u}$. And interest payments per unit of output are $r°\bar{\delta}_j$. It only remains to solve for terms of trade consistent with a trade deficit per unit of output equal to the required capital inflow per unit of output.

The secular expansion-rate of the jth economy's money stock affects the evolution of its exchange rate (albeit, as Lecture Ten shows, not nearly as transparently as MTBOP suggests) but is neutral against its equilibrium trade position.

Seigneurage in the Extended Argument

An economy able to deploy its currency as a vehicle, and to earn seigneurage profits in other ways, operates a more benign calculus; the United States is an example. But seigneurage potential is exhausted at the point at which demand for seigneurage services is unit elastic, even if it is costless to supply such services. (A more sophisticated theory of seigneurage is supplied in Lecture Seven.)

Concluding Remarks, Section 9.3

1. Effects of changes in public-sector borrowing requirements or in financial-asset expansion may be invariant against choice of exchange-rate régime: a trade deficit of the jth economy may be denominated in i-dollars. If the trade deficit persists, it may strain the economy's credit-worthiness, but, if the deficit is financed by i-dollar-denominated issue, its effects will not spill over into foreign-exchange markets.
2. The position of the jth economy is not intrinsically different from that of a private agent. (And one way for either to pay for what it buys is to sell seigneurage services.) As the IMF drill displays so saliently, overextended debtors, public or private, must generate net credits from sales of goods and services. The canonical problem belongs to the theory of finance. It lacks substantial monetary content.

9.4 PORTFOLIO-MANAGEMENT IMPULSES AND BALANCES OF PAYMENTS: BEYOND MONETARY THEORIES OF BALANCES OF PAYMENTS (MTBOP)

Consider a sample of four events. In no case is the proper conjugate analysis monetary; but in each case a pseudo-monetary analysis is illuminating. The four events are:

1. Global excess demand for j-dollar-denominated assets.
2. Global excess demand for liquidity that is neutral against j-dollar (vs i-dollar) exposure.
3. Global excess demand for real assets, accompanied by excess supply of liquid assets.
4. A legitimate real-balance effect triggers disturbances, subject to the following remarks. A proper real-balance-effect-rooted sequence followed from the discovery of gold in America in the 16th century. But changes in quantities of narrowly-defined money typically reflect little more than asset-preference switches; while higher broadly-defined monetary magnitudes typically entail offsetting asset and liability changes.

Shifts in j-dollar-asset Preferences

If demand for real assets, sited in the jth economy, increases, their relative prices will increase. But there need not be capital flows: assets may simply be swapped; and in principle *no* transaction is required. Nor need foreign-exchange markets be affected: residents of the ith economy, purchasing assets of the jth economy 'for j-dollars', may issue j-dollar-denominated paper.

Anticipating Lecture Ten, assets can be 'metricized' to holders' tastes. The spectrum of options spans myriad convex combinations of 'currencies'. The familiar sequence – asset preference shift → exchange-rate movement → trade-account change → *financement* of capital flows – is a special case. Finally, temporary increases in demand for j-dollar finance of asset purchases are readily accommodated by currency traders, who will block substantial i-dollar depreciation; they know that, once the traverse is crossed (so that asset switches are completed), tiny changes in exchange rates will accommodate global asset portfolios to the miniscule relative magnitudes involved.

Global Excess Demand for Liquidity That is Neutral for the j-dollar

In the currency-competition régime of Lecture Ten, a global increase in liquidity preference induces 'currency writers' to increase supplies: writers can obtain wider spreads. An increase in demand for real liquidity induces a corresponding increase in supply.

Global Excess Demand for Real Assets That is Neutral for the j-dollar

Corporate treasurers will issue more shares, using the proceeds to retire debt. And the revised portfolios will be 'remetricized' to some extent, unless homogeneity properties are in complete control.

Legitimate Real-balance Effects

Central-bank actions confined to asset/liability switches, do not generate real-balance effects. (As for the Pesek–Saving fallacy, see Goodhart, 1975; and Burstein, 1986, Chapter 9.)

Current account surpluses (deficits) have wealth effects, which may have been planned for. But the upshot is problematical for MTBOP. Go back to the 'Japan Problem' of Lecture Four. Influxes in the form of sight claims on foreigners can be converted into foreign assets. Or portfolio managers may convert their claims into monetary assets (in *some* denomination). It is pointless to call this a problem of excess supply of money.

An Annotated Problem Set For Lecture Nine

PROBLEMS

89. Choose the correct statement:

(A) according to Perlman (1986), Ricardo argued that a necessary and sufficient condition for a balance-of-trade deficit is a redundant currency;

(b) MTBOP emphasizes the importance of options entitling holders to payments in foreign currencies;

(c) Montiel (1984) argues that Keynesian and MTBOP hypotheses are strictly observationally distinguishable;

(d) all of the above choices are correct;

(e) none of the above choices is correct.

90. According to MTBOP:

(a) under floating rates, monetary imbalance is adjusted by specie flows;

(B) under fixed rates, monetary imbalance is primarily corrected by effects on absorption;

(c) the controlling mechanism should pivot on a loose definition of *money*;

(d) all of the above choices are correct;

(e) none of the above choices is correct.

91. Choose the correct statement:

(a) Ricardo's statement of MTBOP, and that of Harry Johnson, are empty;

(b) it is possible to retain the principal properties of a nonempty MTBOP without requiring continuous equilibrium of the money market;

(c) Friedman and Schwartz (1982) argue that MTBOP is logically equivalent to the specie-flow mechanism;

(D) two of the above choices are correct;

(e) choices **(a)**, **(b)** and **(c)** are correct.

92. Which of the following characterize(s) MTBOP?:

(a) it is highly dependent on relative-price discrepancies across economies;

(B) it relies on 'absorption' effects;

(c) it virtually erases distinction of *money* from *debt*;

(d) all of the above choices are correct;

(e) none of the above choices is correct.

93. If interest is flexibly paid on monetary balances:

(a) MTBOP is buttressed;

(b) the Keynesian model is valid, but not otherwise;

(c) 'money' cannot become denationalized to all intents and purposes;

(d) all of the above choices are correct;

(E) none of the above choices is correct.

94. Under our *fiscal theory of the balance of payments*, if an economy's external finance requirement increases:

(a) capital inflow depends on foreign willingness to acquire assets denominated in its 'currency';

(B) exchange rates need not change;

(c) its exchange rate will be affected unless it monetizes its finance requirement;

(d) all of the above choices are correct;

(e) none of the above choices is correct.

95. Choose the correct statement:

(a) in stock-flow equilibrium, foreign debt is constant;

(b) the *j*th economy's money growth determines its equilibrium real trade position;

(c) an increase in an economy's trade-surplus maps into increased money-supply 1:1;

(d) all of the above choices are correct;

(E) none of the above choices is correct.

96. Choose the correct statement:

- **(a)** increased demand for assets sited in the *j*th economy maps into increased demand for *j*-dollars 1:1;
- **(b)** MTBOP emphasizes ways in which increased demand for *j*-dollars provokes corresponding supply-increases;
- **(C)** current-account surpluses need not map into monetary-base increases;
- **(d)** two of the above choices are correct;
- **(e)** none of the above choices is correct.

SELECTIVE ANNOTATIONS

Problem 89

89(b) Regrettably monetary theory, including MTBOP, centres on a primitive model in which each economy's (nation's) monetary assets consist of paper with its sovereign's (or father figure's) image engraved on it. The models of Lecture Ten may still be rather futuristic, but they are portentous: denationalization of money proceeds apace. The book explains the modalities again and again.

Problem 90

90(B) Another *bêtise* translates monetary imbalance directly into changes in absorption. Of course, it is absurd to stipulate that because a claim against a bank not defined as *money* is switched into one that is defined as *money*, the holder's demand for goods and services increases. And surely the great bulk of transactions generating money-supply changes entail 'washes', i.e. balance-sheet switches that do not affect net worth.

Problem 91

91(c) See the annotation of Problem **90(B)**. Alas, this *bêtise* is true. The operative material is subsumed under the head, 'the transmission mechanism of the quantity theory of money'. (See Brunner and Meltzer, 1974, for example.) The more plausible adjustment mechanism, when liquidity is excessive, is for balance-sheet switches to transform liquid holdings into less-liquid ones; for example, companies may buy back notes and issue shares.

Problem 92

Problem 92 calls for review of already developed material. Choice **92(c)** reminds us of the fragility of MTBOP: the *money* of MTBOP is undefined: the underlying hypothesis is that *money*, whatever it is, is supremely important.

Problem 93

93(a) No! Then portfolio imbalances, including differences between actual and desired liquidity, are corrected by relative-price changes within economies; in particular by changes in the relative yields of 'monetary' assets.

93(b) Recall that Keynes claims that the *General Theory* establishes a monetary theory of the real rate of interest, *via* substitution effects between monetary assets and non-monetary ones. (See Leijonhufvud, 1968.) If money flexibly yields interest, there is no *a priori* basis for assuming that an increase in the quantity of money, for example, compels lower yields of real assets.

93(c) Plans to transform one's *j*-dollar-denominated holdings into *i*-dollar-denominated ones may well be triggered by changes in relative yields against a background of exchange-rate expectations. The analyses, in Lecture Three, of interest parities establish properties of 'denationalized' portfolio management when *all* assets flexibly yield interest.

Problem 94

94(a) Lecture Ten establishes an analytical foundation for a contrary conclusion. And we have seen that, in practice, most international debt is denominated in 'foreign currencies'; *that* lies at the bottom of the third world debt problem.

94(B) Confirmation is implicit in the annotation of Problem **94(a)**:

if Economy *E* obtains finance denominated and payable in United States legal tender and plans to use the proceeds to pay finance charges on existing debt, the script works itself out without exerting impact on foreign exchange markets.

Problem 95

95(a) Realistic stock-flow-equilibrium analysis belongs to the *genre*, *models of equilibrium growth*. On an equilibrium growth-path, the ratio of external debt to wealth is constant, for example.

95(b) This rather asinine choice may fruitfully lead to review of Lecture Six.

95(c) And *this* rather asinine choice may fruitfully lead to review of Lecture Four (in particular, its 'Japan Problem').

Problem 96

Problem 96 transists into Lecture Ten.

96(a) Choice **96(a)** concerns the first of the four 'events' studied in Section 9.4.

96(b) Substitute 'the theory of Lecture Ten' for 'MTBOP'. In MTBOP money-supply processes strictly imitate those of closed models: British authorities 'create' pounds; American authorities 'create' dollars, etc. In the preferred theory, stimulated by innovated financial practice virtual monetary assets are generated by spontaneous market action; textures of portfolios shift kaleidoscopically independently of official action.

96(C) Choice **96(C)** is a reprise of choice **95(c)**, which in turn reviews results established earlier in the book. Choice **96(C)** perhaps comprises an epigram of the counterattack on the thrust of MTBOP.

10 Lecture Ten: Monetary Theory in Innovated Open Economies

10.1 PRINCIPAL PROPERTIES OF THE THEORY

The theory pivots on generalized portfolio analysis. And it entails *quasi-banking*: an agent prepared to be a quasi-banker warps his portfolio, for a fee, to accommodate others' plans to revise their portfolios. In innovated open economies, shifts in asset preference lead to counter-switches in balance sheets of financial intermediaries. And the theory's financial space is amorphous so that monetary disequilibrium is not different from disequilibrium in *any* asset market. Finally, the theory bars 'monetary' theories of balances of payments and exchange rate movements.

10.1.1 Monetary Disequilibrium

Even in a closed system, faster growth of the reserve base does not lead to faster growth of well-defined monetary stocks in any simple way. Monetary assets are readily transformed into non-monetary ones (think of demand deposits being transformed into non-monetary deposits). And options commitments are reversible: for example, put options written on non-monetary stocks (that are thus eligible to be transformed into money) may be unwound.

Turning to open systems, distinguish effects on exchange rates from direct balance-of-payments (BOP) effects. As for the former, if transactors rigidly adhere to prior views on the evolution of central *j*-dollar rates, they will be prepared to absorb large quantities of monetary *j*-dollar assets, while widening their spreads. But the theory accommodates effects of monetary events on exchange rates – while denying that monetary explanations are properly exclusive.

As for BOP effects, consider the aftermath of a spurt in growth of *j*-dollar base money. Increases in 'local' money supply incited by base-money growth will be at least partially countered: e.g. options entitling holders to *j*-dollar payments will run off without being replaced (or will be closed out prematurely). And $i(\neq j)$ dollar 'issues' will increase as dealers take advantage of wider spreads. The following transaction – not entailing deals in underlying stocks – is revealing. Holders of options to put assets for *j*-dollars will trade them to dealers in exchange for options to put assets for *i*-dollars, thus extinguishing the *j*-dollar puts.

Continuing discussion of BOP effects, but along a new azimuth, whatever are called *monetary j*-dollar-denominated assets comprise a small, perhaps miniscule, part of the proper domain of discourse; and distinctions between 'monetary' and 'non-monetary' sub-sets may be chimerical when monetary assets flexibly yield interest. Nor is that all. Say that virtual monetary stocks (selected Euro-dollar holdings, equities in options deals, commitments by foreign banks to redeem in *j*-dollars or equivalents to *j*-dollars, etc.) are initially equal in mass to conventionally-defined *j*-dollar monetary stocks. Say that these stocks have been growing at 10% per annum. Now authorities step up growth of the 'conventional' stock to 15%. If virtual money stocks now increase at only 5%, the aggregate expansion rate does not change.

The controlling point is this. The ambient environment features very high elasticities of substitution of both demand and supply.

10.1.2   Non-monetary Disequilibrium

MTBOP adherents deny that excess demand for Suffolk land significantly affects the British balance of payments. So do we. MTBOP and our theory are *d'accord* on the point. But there is an important difference: in our theory, monetary and non-monetary asset market vibrations are *equivalent* for balance-of-payments effects.

Say that investors *partout* plan to switch towards Suffolk land. Restoration of equilibrium requires that the relative price of such land increase, something that can be accomplished without any flows of funds. If there are flows of funds, foreign purchasers need not commit themselves to increased exposure to sterling-risk (to larger net sterling sensitive positions): they can buy a sort of portfolio insurance by maintaining short positions in sterling futures.

Shifts in monetary and non-monetary asset preferences are symmetrical in the theory. A surge in global demand for the monetary assets of large American banks will – in a simplistic analysis ignoring option dealing – lead to lower yields for such assets, just as prices of Suffolk land rise in the scenario just above. (The huge accumulation of *petro-dollars*, following the oil shocks of 1973 and 1979, evolved in ways suggested by this paragraph.) Changes in relative yields accomplish necessary accommodation to the revised demand conditions even if exchange-rate and balance-of-payments effects are blocked out.

10.1.3 Choice of Currency

On an abstract plane, there is no reason why a borrower resident in the *j*th economy should issue *j*-dollar-denominated securities. In an economy in which choice of measure is open in all transactions, contracts are written in a variety of measures independently of what currencies are used to discharge debts. (The *res* is choice of *measure*, not currency.)

10.1.4 Innovated Responses to Asset-preference Shifts

In the preferred theory, an increase in liquidity preference among agents of the *j*th economy is accommodated by small increases in spreads obtainable by agents (anywhere) prepared to sell liquid *j*-dollar-denominated claims (perhaps against themselves) for illiquid ones. The settlement medium is immaterial.

The market's responses may defy conventional analysis: put options may be written on *i*-dollar assets held by agents of the *j*th economy, perhaps monetizing their assets in a *j*-dollar measure. Or *i*-economy agents may purchase calls on *j*-dollar assets, simultaneously buying put options entitling them to convert *j*-dollar profits (or, if they stand for delivery, proceeds of securities sales) into *i*-dollars on stated terms. Speculators easily absorb resulting pressure. (See McKinnon, 1979, on the adequacy of the 'supply of speculation'.)

In a small open economy, in which agents mostly hold foreign currency, changes in liquidity preferences are accommodated by switches within (x_{ij}), a vector of *i*-dollar securities held by *j*-agents $(i = 1, 2, \ldots, j-1, j+1, \ldots)$.

10.1.5 Consolidating Comments

The pith of the theory contains two clusters.

The 'supply of money' cannot be precisely defined under innovated conditions. Nor is the linkage between central-bank purchases and sales of securities and changes in balance sheets of financial institutions well defined. The first cluster suffices to block MTBOP: the *money* of MTBOP cannot be operationally defined.

The second cluster leads towards generalized portfolio theory. Disequilibrium in *any* asset market may, or may not, activate disturbances to current accounts of balances of payments. In the upshot:

1. Absorption-based adjustment mechanisms are eschewed.
2. Forces affecting demand cannot be disentangled from those affecting supply – importantly because in quasi-banking many agents monetize-assets. Modigliani–Miller-like theorems lie close to the surface: agents 'roll their own' liquidity profiles.
3. Spreads between agents' borrowing and lending rates are critically important. Say that expectations of exchange rates are quite rigid. Now assume that currency preferences shift: the public want to increase their virtual dollar exposure and reduce exposure to sterling. Options writers must shorten their net dollar positions in order to accommodate the public. Competitive writers will require larger risk premia: buy–sell spreads will widen. But, if writers' expectations are firmly planted, central rates may be little affected by switches in asset preferences.

    The concept of excess supplies of or demand for 'currencies' becomes untenable. One can increase one's dollar exposure by purchasing a put option entitling one to put a stock for a quantity of sterling equivalent to x^* at maturity. Or one can sell a call option entitling the buyer to call away one's dollar stock for a quantity of dollars equal to £y on the call day – if one wants to lock in a profit obtained from a higher dollar.

10.1.6 An Application of the Theory: A Security Market Problem

A company's cost of capital may be measured by the price of its shares relative to its 'true' earnings potential. And the share price is sensitive to autonomous speculative processes capable of producing bubbles or implosions. Share-price movements obviously influence real costs of capital and so real economic action.

As for the supply of shares:

1. The supply of shares is functionally related to *demand*: demand vibrations affect new issue, in part *via* changes in debt/equity ratios.
2. Forward and futures transactions, together with options writing, affect virtual supplies independently of the actions of the firm's board, comparable to a central bank.
3. If the supply of stock (of the 'underlying commodity') increases, the equilibrium share price plausibly falls. But, just as in monetary models, quasi-issue may be negatively correlated with the supply of underlying stock.

Consider two corollaries to point 3. (i). Projecting the analysis onto open-economy theory, *j*-dollar securities may be issued by the *r*th authority or agent: positive and negative positions will be taken across the whole spectrum of 'issue', so that each agent's balance sheet displays a hodge-podge of 'denominations'. (ii). An increase in an underlying stock makes it easier to sustain short positions, dangers of delivery squeezes thus being reduced.

10.2 MONETARY INNOVATIONS AND MONEY-SUPPLY THEORY

Denationalization

The representative agent contracts for liabilities (obtains 'resources') in various measures and arranges for cover like agents with short commodity positions. The underlying stock includes government bonds as well as central-bank liabilities; delivery-squeeze peril is exiguous. In the upshot, the *j*th monetary authority cannot exercise control over the volume of *j*-dollar-denominated liquid assets (liabilities).

In the theory, banks' assets and liabilities are written up in any number of monies of account. True, *j*-dollar obligations of *j*-banks may be preferred: *j*-banks are apt to have privileged access to the *j*th central bank. But Lloyds Bank can obtain overdraft facility from Chase (perhaps as part of a swap) so that it can surely meet US dollar demands on sight.

In the upshot, the stock of money in the *j*th economy cannot be properly defined in terms of liquid liabilities of selected *j*-institutions expressed in *j*-dollars.

Interest on Money

All financial assets are to yield interest flexibly in competitive markets – although transactions costs and convenience yield factors may lead to the *r*th asset's nominal yield being *nil* in equilibrium.

'Interest on money' may confuse operators of ISLM schemes. If the model is defined in r/y space, so that there is *an* interest rate (and a baby model), *interest on money* erases the substitution effect of a change in *the* interest rate: the LM curve becomes vertical: equilibrium income is determined by the quantity of money, so that a monetary theory of the real rate of interest is amplified up to a monetary theory of real income. If r is a *vector*, substitution effects are regained; LM vibration is largely absorbed by changes in spreads, a line of argument that is intensified if the equilibrium real cost of capital is an invariant (see Burstein, 1986, Chapter 3).

Another 'paradox' is this. An increase in Bank Rate implies faster money-growth: the rate at which paper breeds paper increases. And since the equilibrium real rate of interest is determined by real factors outside the ambit of central-bank action, higher Bank Rate maps into a higher steady rate of inflation – in a proper model of equilibrium growth. True, the *impact* of an unexpected increase in Bank Rate (or of an expected one when prices are sufficiently inertial, perhaps because of embedded contracts) is contractionary: price-inertia then induces a sympathetic increase in real interest rates. So, to the extent that buoyancy of aggregate demand influences price-acceleration, temporary effects of higher Bank Rate may be deflationary; and indeed Bank Rate-policy is typically an exercise in transient closed-loop control; changes in Bank Rate are typically meant to be temporary.

Interpolation: Bank Rate Policy, Credit Flows and Money Supply

The *Financial Times* and the *Wall Street Journal* for 23 June 1988 reported that the Bank of England increased its base lending rate to 9% from 8.5% in order to resist inflationary pressures on British prices. And 'British monetary officials are thought to be particularly concerned about the high level of borrowing, much of which is for property purchases' (*Wall Street Journal*). And 'the Government, while wanting rates higher, is afraid of sparking a pound rally' (*Wall*

Street Journal – see Lecture Three). So it is: the concepts of *money* and *credit* are intertwined in any analysis of central-bank policy.

As for deployment of Bank Rate as a control of price-inflation, typical analyses run along two paths. The first follows the *Phillips Curve*. Higher interest rates are to deter aggregate demand, leading to exploitation of a discredited employment/inflation trade off; the 'Phillips Curve' path does not traverse monetary territory.

The second path exploits the fact that, in Bank Rate régimes, banks' reserves elastically accommodate their lending; and their lending is the motor force for monetary growth or contraction. Indeed most analyses end at this point: higher Bank Rate deters demand for loans and so monetary expansion. But a correct analysis *begins* at this point: the valid channel of *monetary* influence concerns the volume of *intermediation*: *overall* demand for credit may fall while bank lending rises. The controlling idea is, once again, the *spread*. If market rates of interest rise relative to Bank Rate (say that Bank Rate laggardly chases market rates), banks will acquire more reserves from the Bank, in order to place more funds in the market (purchasing T-Bills, gilts, etc.); in this way, the non-banking public substitutes intermediate for direct asset holdings.

The analysis can be extended in a number of directions. Increased liquidity preference leads to more mediation (and so to faster money growth) at a wider spread between deposit rate and market rate. If the central bank were simultaneously to increase its lending and borrowing rates – in a reformed régime in which bank deposits with the Bank yield interest – banks would seek to curtail their loans and investments, planning to use divestment proceeds to repay the Bank and/or increase deposits at the Bank. In the upshot, measured money supply contracts; and the credit markets are squeezed; and indeed real economic growth may come to a screeching stop.

Wicksell's (1898) analysis – which I discussed in 1988 – is the most famous contribution to an influential Bank Rate/money supply/ price-behaviour literature initiated by Thornton (1802). (See Section 8.3).

A Remark on Competing Currencies

Currency competition or, better, competition between metrics, is pervasive. Why 'competition between *metrics*'? Debts expressed in the ith metric (money of account) can be discharged by j-dollar tenders; an economy can be i-dollarized without switching to the *i*-dollar as a payments medium. The upshot is inimical to aspirations of monetary authorities to manage 'their' currencies: e.g. liquid holdings in the *k*th economy cannot properly be assigned an exclusive *k*-dollar metric; and options transactions transform apparent *k*-dollar holdings into virtual *j*-dollar ones in ways that cannot be tracked.

Quasi-banking (see Burstein, 1986, Chapter 11)

Banking functions are distributed over a continuous field, rather than clustering at nodes. But quasi-banks imitate the banks of orthodox theory in that they distort their balance sheets to supply liquidity services – for a fee.

Options markets illustrate quasi-banking: *B* can monetize *A*'s assets (in any measure) by selling *A* a put option. The upshot is important in at least two ways. First, even in closed economies, money supply is ill defined. Secondly, in an innovated open economy, agents' operations cannot be properly classified by 'economy of origin'. For one thing, options and futures contracts need not be settled in any particular currency: a *j*-dollar option may be settled by an *i*-dollar tender, or by a 'cocktail' of tenders.

Applying the Quasi-banking Model

Say that there is a basic shift in currency preferences against the *j*-dollar.

The Orthodox Scenario   Specialists must take in stock (*j*-dollars). They will lower the price (in an *i*-dollar measure) they are prepared to pay for *j*-dollars. And they will widen their buy–sell spreads for *j*-dollar transactions.

The Innovated Scenario   Under quasi-banking, the effective supply of highly-liquid *j*-dollar assets responds to demand. When demand shifts towards the *i*-dollar, *j*-dollar options are converted into *i*-dollar ones, with some adjustment of spreads. And an increase in the supply of 'conventional' *j*-dollars induces contraction of *j*-dollar options writing; just as contraction of *j*-dollar supply stimulates quasi issue.

Quasi-banking in Future   A proper theory of an innovated economy may elide banks; see Burstein (1988b: 'Beyond the Banking Principle'). Once regulatory obstructions are cleared away, 'issuers' of short-term liquid obligations cannot properly be perceived to expand

and contract their balance sheets in discrete steps, responding to intermittent official stimuli. The quasi-banks of the theory continuously expand and contract in profit-seeking response to stimuli received from the market. Money-supply, however defined, evolves in a closed loop.

10.3 FACETS OF THE THEORY

10.3.1 Denationalization of Money Redux

Sophisticated trading nexi in open economies project the practices of Einaudi's medieval fairs onto a plane featuring inconvertible paper money. In an open jth economy, various i-dollar claims ($i \neq j$) freely circulate alongside j-dollar ones. Metrics are freely elected. (Hayek, 1976, shows that governments, jealous of seigneurage profits, systematically obstruct spontaneous evolution of monetary modalities – surely including denationalization of money – in order to preserve predominant demand for official money.)

In the economy of the preferred theory, French francs may be borrowed in the form of French 'currency'; and the proceeds may be injected directly into the British economy. The loan may be repayable in a variety of currencies. Convex combinations of n basic vectors are admissible; n currencies discharge debt cast up in any number of metrical combinations. A debt denominated in j-dollars need not be discharged by a j-dollar tender. Nor need 'currency baskets' in the jth economy contain 'j-dollars'.

Denationalization of Money and Monetary Measurements

Conventional measurements of the stock of j-dollars are deceiving. Holders of j-dollars may have i-dollar guarantees; they may have bought put options; j-dollar holdings may be subordinated to strategies keyed on 'the i-dollar'. In the limit, j-dollar holdings of 'j' residents may be open-valued on a j-dollar scale and fixed in i-dollar value.

10.3.2 Speculative and Other Private-sector Intervention in the Money-supply Process

Perhaps the supply of j-dollar-denominated monetary assets – e.g.

treasury currency and selected bank liabilities – is less than demand. Wider spreads will induce options writers elastically to supply enlarged stocks of monetized *j*-dollar assets, i.e. to write options virtually monetizing stocks in a *j*-dollar metric. If there has been a *once-over* shift in asset preferences, agents, forming expectations rationally, may demand wider spreads: their portfolios will be more distended. But a bubble will not form; it will be seen that there has been a 'permanent' preference-shift.

In the innovated model, virtual money-supply is endogenous in open and closed systems.

Speculative Support of Exchange Rates and Endogeneity of the Stock of Money (See Lecture Six)

Speculators, defending exchange rates, become quasi-monetary authorities, adjusting global stocks of monetary (monetized) assets to demands. Will not speculators' balance sheets ultimately break down as their obligations to deliver *i*-dollar paper grow relative to deliverable stocks? At least two factors mitigate such qualms. (1) Available stocks are massive – encompassing stocks of government debt for example. (2) A commitment to guarantee the *i*-dollar value of a stock need not be dischargable by an '*i*-dollar substance'. Contracts based on future values of the Dow Jones Industrial Average or Standard and Poors's '500' are an example.

10.4   A PRÉCIS OF THE THEORY: CONTRASTS WITH MTBOP

Theme

The asset subset, M, has no special importance for current-account fluctuations. All that survives of MTBOP are traces of a pseudo-monetary theory based on a broad spectrum of assets.

Money Supply

Even these trace quantities are suspect. The 'supply side' of the analysis is amorphous. Portfolio switches are induced by miniscule changes in spreads; elasticities of substitution are high. So energy released by asset-preference shifts and central-bank strategies is mostly absorbed within the global financial sector, without escaping into 'real economic space'. Under innovated conditions, the 'supply of money' cannot be operationally defined.

The Upshot

Disequilibrium in *any* asset market may affect balances of payments – but need not do so. In the upshot: (1) absorption is rejected; (2) forces affecting demand cannot be disentangled from those affecting supply; (3) under quasi-banking, currency-preference shocks are absorbed by (perhaps very small) changes in writers' spreads.

Absorption paradigms break down for at least two reasons: (1) 'money' becomes an evanescent idea; (2) real-balance effects, never robust, are inadmissible in innovated modelling.

There are a number of valid channels of influence of asset-market shifts or shocks on the real economy. (i) Autonomous speculative processes may induce foreign-exchange-rate vibrations, leading to correlated vibration of terms of trade. (ii) Net global excess demand for (supply of) j-dollar-denominated assets also transmits to the terms of trade in most cases. (iii) vibrations in real-asset preferences (between economies) may communicate to the current account of the balance of payments, primarily *via* effects on the terms of trade. In the theory, free-market processes swamp out official-sector monetary actions and freely cross national borders. And these processes often have unobservable effects: a British purchaser of a put option may monetize a real British asset in a US dollar measure. In short, innovations break down the fibre of nationalized money.

Innovations include the following

1. *Denationalization of Monetary and Quasi-monetary Issue*   Agents arrange for cover of exposure to a variety of foreign-exchange-rooted risks like agents with short commodity positions; and assets and liabilities of financial institutions are written up in any number of accounting units. Money-supply cannot be defined in terms of liquid liabilities of selected local institutions, expressed in a single measure.
2. *Interest on Money*   Excess supply of money no longer implies downward pressure on interest rates.
3. *Central Bank Lending and Borrowing*   Monetary policy is operated by manipulating central-bank lending and borrowing rates – with problematic effects.
4. *Quasi-banking*   In régimes of quasi-banking, central banks merely

make ripples on surfaces of lakes made up of underlying stocks that include government debt. Quantities of monetary, or monetized, assets evolve from spontaneous free-market transactions. Thus B can monetize A's asset, in any measure, by selling A a put option. In the innovated economy, monetary disequilibrium is corrected by changes in writers' portfolios (books). Adjustment processes unfold within the financial sector without impinging on balances of payments.

Further Applications of the Theory

Fiscal Perturbation   If an economy's public-sector borrowing requirement increases, its current account may deteriorate, especially if it is fully employed. Borrowings may be denominated in foreign measures: the jth economy can finance a current-account (or trade) deficit by selling securities redeemable or guaranteed in i-dollars. Exchange rates need not be affected.

Portfolio-management Impulses   Enhanced preference for assets sited in the jth economy may lead to capital inflow. But 'metricization' is open: hedging opportunities span myriad convex combinations of 'currencies'; i-economy agents purchasing j-economy assets may issue j-dollar-denominated paper that need not be redeemable in j-dollars; the paper may call for payment of the number of i-dollars that will, on maturity, purchase x^* j-dollars. There are many ways in which agents anywhere can write j-dollar claims.

Coda: Analysis of McKinnon (1979)

A domestic money supply operation is always the dual of a purchase or sale of foreign exchange, and the fixed exchange rate requires that the domestic dual not be undone.

In contrast an *inconsistent* domestic monetary *cum* foreign exchange policy would be where excess guilders (at the existing price level) are pumped into the economy . . . Then, under a fixed exchange rate *and* free convertibility, this excess would quickly appear as a deficit in the balance of payments, leading to a loss of exchange reserves that may well be unsustainable.

McKinnon (1979, p. 43)

Marginalia: Modifications of McKinnon's Text

1. If guilders are convertible, elasticities of substitution should be high. The upshot may merely be that guilder securities are priced to yield slightly more.

   If more 'Dutch money' is to be 'created', Dutch banks must pay more on their liabilities. That done, in innovated models, demand for 'local money' is continuously aligned with supply (including the virtual supplies discussed above) by the flexibility of money's relative yield, whatever *money* is.

2. The proper scale factor is the entire guilder-asset stock.

3. Point 1 leads to higher relative yields of monetary guilder assets and their close substitutes. Dutch companies will refinance their debt, offering longer-term, and less liquid, guilder securities for liquid ones. And guilder-denominated private issue will be called in and replaced with *x*-denominated stock (*x* = pound, dollar, mark, yen, franc, lira, peso, etc.). And calls will be written, allowing guilder-holders to call away *x*-denominated assets at a guaranteed guilder rate. Countervailing decreases in guilder stocks are generated.

   McKinnon may be disingenuous in confusing effects of increased guilder-issue with those resulting from a putative decay in the ratio of Dutch reserves to Dutch monetary liabilities. If Dutch monetary assets increase (inevitably accompanied by some increase in yield) *and* if Dutch gold and other reserves increase *pari passu* it is hard to see why global portfolio managers should so stubbornly resist the blandishments (including slightly higher yields) of the Dutch – who, for some reason, want to increase their share of global monetary issue.

   Granted, dealers, more exposed in principle to guilder risk, will widen spreads and increase holdings of assets negatively covariant with guilder ones.

An Equivalent Scenario, Concerning Non-monetary Assets

There is to be excess supply of Dutch shares, bonds, etc., i.e. of non-monetary Dutch assets. Dealers' books become laden with guilder commitments; dealers, defending the guilder, act like quasi-monetary authorities. They will widen spreads and, under flexible exchange, mark down central guilder rates.

Fixed Foreign-exchange Rates   (Demand for non-guilder funds to complete foreign purchases will be at least partially offset by foreign offers to swap ex-Dutch properties for now-relatively-cheaper Dutch property.) There may be a net transitional imbalance, generating ephemeral excess supply of 'guilders'. Dealers, recognizing that the situation is ephemeral, will issue non-guilder claims, or offer to sell non-guilder assets, to finance the switch. If the upshot looks like a 'permanent' skewing of their books, spreads may 'permanently' widen – keeping in mind that the scenario plays itself out against vast asset/liability stocks.

Flexible Exchange Rates   Here an increase in, say, demand for American assets generates effects in two directions. (1) Demand schedules for US-sited assets (e.g. Manhattan real estate) shift rightward. (2) There may be increased demand for 'dollarization' of portfolio positions.

It is easy to construct a script in which there are excess tenders of foreign 'currencies' for American funds wanted to finance transactions. Then specialists supply US funds from stocks *à la* Wall Street specialists (but not on 19 October 1987). Dollar rates commanded by foreign currencies may be marked down to some extent. And, again, dealers' books are rewritten. But the controlling forces are not monetary; nor is the initial disturbance.

Coda: Further Applications of the Preferred Theory in Innovated Economies

Bank $\propto$ sells medium- or long-term debentures (unsecured obligations) for A-dollars, committing itself to pay A-dollar consideration equivalent to x^* ECU on maturity. The A-dollar proceeds are invested in A-dollar-denominated paper.

Bank $\propto$'s book is thus skewed. It will seek to lay off its ECU exposure by buying options to put A-dollar assets for ECU equivalents. Any resulting depreciation of the A-dollar will be along lines that do not intersect MTBOP: there is no demand for 'foreign currency', only for cover.

Related Examples   Sellers of securities to the A central bank deposit the proceeds (central-bank drafts) with A banks in exchange for ECU-guaranteed claims – reminiscently of related Euro-market analyses. If A banks buy A-dollar assets with the proceeds, their foreign-exchange books will be unbalanced, and they may lay off the fresh exposure by options dealings. Or they may seek to buy ECU-related securities, offering *A*-dollar bank drafts. Acceptors of these offers may seek to lay off *their* incremental *A*-dollar exposure. Or *A* banks may offer higher deposit rates, enabling them to acquire the ECU-related securities at lower prices, since supply prices will be higher if options-costs (cover-costs) are not in play; securities sellers will plan to hold the higher-yielding *A*-dollar deposits.

All the scenarios work themselves out without direct (or perhaps indirect) effects on prices or quantities in goods-and-services markets; *absorption* is elided.

An Annotated Problem Set For Lecture Ten

PROBLEMS

Problems **97–101** comprise a quiz, or pseudo-quiz, on the lecture; this sub-set is readily answered by referencing the lecture, although there is some overlap with subsequent Problems.

The theory developed in the lecture is often called 'the preferred theory' *infra*.

97. The preferred theory:

- **(a)** pivots on generalized portfolio analysis;
- **(b)** posits that agents are prepared to warp their portfolios for fees;
- **(c)** finds shifts in asset preferences leading to countervailing switches in balance sheets of financial intermediaries;
- **(d)** two of the above choices are correct;
- **(E)** choices **(a)**, **(b)** and **(c)** are correct.

98. Quasi-bankers:

- **(a)** maintain portfolios in assets confined to the currency of the economy they reside in;
- **(b)** buy and sell options and make forward transactions;
- **(c)** respond elastically to small changes in spreads;
- **(D)** two of the above choices are correct;
- **(e)** choices **(a)**, **(b)** and **(c)** are correct.

99. In the preferred theory:

- **(a)** borrowers resident in the jth economy issue only j-dollar-denominated securities;
- **(b)** contracts are written in a variety of measures, independently of currencies used to discharge debt;

(c) an increase in liquidity preference in the jth economy is accommodated by small increases in spreads of agents (anywhere) prepared to sell liquid j-dollar-denominated claims for illiquid ones – the settlement medium being immaterial;

(D) two of the above choices are correct;

(e) choices (a), (b) and (c) are correct.

100. In the preferred theory, denationalization of money leads to:

(a) free election of metrics;

(b) conventional measurements of the stock of j-dollars losing importance;

(c) j-dollar holdings of 'j' residents possibly becoming open-valued on a j-dollar scale and fixed in i-dollar measure;

(d) two of the above choices are correct;

(E) choices (a), (b) and (c) are correct.

101. As for shifts in j-dollar-asset preferences:

(a) increased global preference for real assets sited in the jth economy leads to massive changes in j-dollar exchange rates;

(B) a temporary increase in demand for j-dollar finance is readily accommodated by currency traders – who may simply revise their commitments, as in quasi-banking;

(c) risks generated in a stochastically-stationary environment are indistinguishable from those in stochastically-volatile ones;

(d) all of the above choices are correct

(e) none of the above choices is correct.

****

102. In the preferred theory:

(a) monetary theories of the balance of payments are validated;

(b) the supply of j-dollar-based paper is closely keyed to the growth rate of base money in the *j*th economy;

(c) an increase in liquidity preference in the *j*th economy leads to a sharp increase in real interest rates in that economy;

(d) all of the above choices are correct;

(E) none of the above choices is correct.

103. Which of the following are among the principal features of Lecture Nine's analysis of MTBOP (carried over into Lecture Ten)?:

(A) under innovated conditions, the supply of money cannot be precisely defined, let alone measured;

(b) only money-market disequilibrium affects the current account of the balance of payments;

(c) forces affecting supply are sharply distinguished from those affecting demand for financial assets;

(d) spreads between agents' borrowing and lending rates vary only randomly;

(e) none of the above choices is correct.

104. Which of the following are among the principal arguments of Lecture Ten?:

(a) if currency preferences shift, foreign-exchange rates fluctuate violently;

(b) foreign exchange rates do not fluctuate violently unless dealers' expectations are firmly planted;

(c) exposure to sterling risk is increased by purchase of a put option entitling one to put stock for sterling equivalent to x^* on the day – thereby reducing one's dollar exposure;

(d) if money flexibly yields interest, changes in monetary preferences powerfully affect exchange rates;

(E) none of the above choices is correct.

105. Which of the following correctly characterize(s) the 'security market' problem?:

(a) the supply of shares is uncorrelated with demand shifts;

(b) options transactions affect virtual supplies of stocks;

(c) quasi-issue may be negatively correlated with supply of the underlying stock;

(D) two of the above choices are correct;

(e) choices (a), (b) and (c) are correct.

106. In the preferred theory, if there is a basic shift in currency preference against the *j*-dollar:

(a) specialists take in stock and narrow buy – sell spreads for *j*-dollars;

(B) *j*-dollar options are converted into *i*-dollar ones;

(c) bubbles are barred;

(d) two of the above choices are correct;

(e) none of the above choices is correct.

107. In the preferred theory:

(A) an increase in conventional *j*-dollar supply induces contraction of *j*-dollar options writing;

(b) denationalization of money may result in *j*-dollar holdings of *j*-residents that are open-valued on a *j*-dollar scale only if the international gold standard is in full force;

(c) if an economy's external finance requirement increases, foreigners must be induced to hold more claims strictly denominated in that economy's currency;

(d) two of the above choices are correct;

(e) choices (a), (b) and (c) are correct.

108. Choose the correct statement about valid channels of influence of asset-market shifts or shocks on the real economy:

(A) autonomous speculative forces may induce exchange-rate vibrations, leading to sympathetic vibration of the terms of trade;

(b) in an innovated economy, money-supply is best defined in terms of liquid liabilities of its institutions, measured relative to its dollar;

(c) the rigid control exercised by central banks over money supplies enables them to offset financial shocks' effects on terms of trade, etc. quite precisely;

(d) all of the above choices are correct;

(e) none of the above choices is correct.

109. In the preferred theory:

(a) assets and liabilities of *j*-economy financial institutions are written up only in *j*-dollars;

(b) quantities of monetary, or monetized, assets evolve mechanically from central-bank decisions on paths of their credit;

(C) central banks merely make ripples on surfaces of lakes comprising underlying stocks that include government debt;

(d) two of the above choices are correct;

(e) choices **(a)**, **(b)** and **(c)** are correct.

110. Which of the following situations is(are) consistent with the preferred theory, following a global increase in preference for US dollar sensitive situations?:

(a) exporters to the US are more likely to bill in US dollars, partly because US dollar trade acceptances now command higher prices (are subject to lower discounts) than before;

(b) prices of Fifth Avenue condominium properties increase;

(c) the American trade account becomes more positive;

(D) two of the above choices are correct;

(e) choices **(a)**, **(b)** and **(c)** are correct.

111. In the preferred theory:

(a) borrowers resident in the *j*th economy issue only *j*-dollar-denominated securities;

(B) contracts are written in a variety of measures, independently of which currencies discharge debt;

(c) fiscal factors cannot explain balance-of-payments data;

(d) all of the above choices are correct;

(e) none of the above choices is correct.

112. Choose the correct statement:

    (A) by way of innovated response to asset-preference shifts, put options may be written on i-dollar assets held by agents of the jth economy, perhaps monetizing their assets in a j-dollar measure;

    (b) put, but not call, options writers always stand for delivery;

    (c) in our Swiss franc example (see Burstein, 1986, Chapter 11), the controlling tabular standard sensitizes Swiss trade to fluctuations in the Swiss franc;

    (d) all of the above choices are correct;

    (e) none of the above choices is correct.

113. Choose the correct statement about valid channels of influence of asset-market shifts or shocks on the real economy:

    (A) autonomous speculative forces may induce exchange-rate vibrations, leading to sympathetic vibration of the terms of trade;

    (b) the validity of monetary theories of balances of payments (MTBOP) hinges on free-market processes that may swamp out effects of official monetary actions;

    (c) in an innovated economy, money-supply is properly defined in terms of liquid liabilities of its financial institutions, measured relative to its dollar;

    (d) in régimes of quasi-banking, central banks rigidly control virtual money supplies and, perhaps more problematically, exchange rates;

    (e) all of the above choices are correct.

114. In the preferred theory:

    (a) agents arrange for cover of exposure to foreign-exchange-rooted risks like agents with short commodity positions;

    (b) assets and liabilities of j-economy financial institutions are written up in any number of accounting units;

    (c) quantities of monetary, or monetized, assets evolve from spontaneous free-market transactions;

(d) two of the above choices are correct;
(E) choices **(a)**, **(b)** and **(c)** are correct.

SELECTIVE ANNOTATIONS

Problem 103

103(b) Consider the following counter-example. A switch in foreign preference in favour of American shares leads to stock sales by Americans. This cannot be accomplished unless aliens accumulate corresponding claims against American residents: American holdings of American stock are to fall. There must be a corresponding deterioration in the American trade account. Nothing 'monetary' is entailed.

A Second Counter-example

Aliens wish to increase their US dollar sensitive positions. Barclays Bank may 'issue' dollar-linked paper. Such issue creates an open short position in American dollars. So the bank may increase lending for which repayment is keyed to the US dollar (USD) – see sterling loans calling for repayment in sterling equal in value to x^* on the due date. Or it may buy put options, effectively 'dollarizing' some of its assets. The second counter-example also shows how a change in demand for USD triggers effects not registered in monetary statistics.

103(d) No! The theory requires such spreads to expand and contract as market makers' books become distorted in various directions.

The controlling theme of choices **103(c)**, **104(c)**, **108(c)**, **109** and **114(c)** concerns laissez-faire banking.

Focus on how a bank anywhere can 'issue' monetary liabilities in *j*-dollars, covering these by selling long securities, including its shares, in *j*-land, thus acquiring *j*-dollar assets. In the scenario, *j*-land residents simply shift the structure of their equity holdings: they buy obligations of financial intermediaries – obligations that are strictly non-monetary if the institution does not belong to the *j*-land clearing house. The processes dilute the *j*th central bank's influence on 'its' economy.

An Example

If Italians want to become 'dollarized', it pays to raise dollar capital and use the proceeds to back the equivalent to Eurodollar issue in Italy.

Other Examples

See the following hypothetical British scenarios, more or less under laissez-faire:

1. British banks transform some sterling liability, some of which may be monetary, into USD liability, so to speak at the stroke of a pen. From a portfolio-balance standpoint, the banks are now too long sterling and too short USD. They can redeem equity by selling debt-correcting excessive length on the sterling side. And they can lengthen their USD position by selling equity for USD. So far as we have gone, nothing need happen to the dollar/pound exchange rate.
2. Under laissez faire, British depositors may want to reduce sterling claims in favour of USD ones. So British banks convert such claims into ones redeemable in USD, or in sterling on a guaranteed-USD-equivalent basis. Liquid American securities qualify as reserves. It may be attractive to capitalize the new banking business: since claims can be floated with an attractive spread (given the intensified demand for USD), 'seigneurage profit' can be capitalized. In the simplest case, British houses sell shares in the United States.

Still Another Example

Japanese investors acquire vast quantities of American assets (including cheques drawn on American banks) sold by Japanese exporters. The dollar claims may be sold for ECU-type obligations, even if these are discharged by US dollar tenders (in an ECU measure). Banks may raise capital by selling shares and long bonds in Britain, Germany, etc. until books are evened up.

And Another Example

French companies may demand more liquidity. The *liquides* may be denominated in French francs. Guaranties (to indemnify in French franc equivalents) are given by banks everywhere. The banks may raise capital by selling equities in France – obviously a central idea in the analysis.

Another Example!

Italians borrow from Citicorp in the United States. Proceeds are used to buy e.g. capital equipment. The Italian borrowers may be obligated to pay back in lire. Then Citicorp may make short sales of lire – leading to a fall of lire in foreign-exchange markets, it is true.

Problem 104

The problem reminds us that the degree to which exchange rates fluctuate covariantly with fluctuations in currency preference partly depends on the firmness of market makers' beliefs and their willingness and/or ability to back up 'belief'.

104(d) When monetary assets flexibly yield interest, changes in preference across currencies are absorbed by changes in relative yields of monetary liabilities, i.e. in spreads. So fixed exchange rates are consistent with variations in yields across economies – subject to what used to be called the *susceptibility* of funds to such differentials.

Problem 105

105(b) *An Illustration*. What if Englishmen want to assure the USD value of their assets – e.g. USD equivalence of property values – so that they are left only with 'intrinsic' property risk? Think of a Belgravia-property owner who buys put options. Sellers of such options have shorted the dollar; but they may have substantial USD sensitized holdings (think of IBM or Eastman Kodak selling such options). Underlying stocks are immense.

Problem 106

106(a) Specialists – market makers, dealers, etc – distort their books in the exercise of their office. Here they widen their spreads, equivalently to an increase in supply price. Indeed it is unlikely that specialists' confidence in the j-dollar is firm enough for the j-dollar not to fall.

As for 'currency preference', the desire to change i-dollar exposure has nothing to do with 'money'. That said, an increase in the expansion-rate of the jth monetary base may lead to a fall in the j-dollar. One should not succumb to an obsession to deny monetary influence on exchange rates.

106(b) The market wants to convert options to switch into j-dollars into ones calling for i-dollars. Settlement does *not* typically entail actual delivery; and, on the plane of this abstract discussion in which transactions costs are suppressed, the settlement-medium is immaterial.

106(c) Asset-market processes are typically autonomous. Bubbles cannot be precluded.

Problem 107

107(b)/111(a) No! The standard literature tends to reflect the continental, and still intellectually insular, American economy. And the Brazilians, Mexicans *et al.* are in parlous condition because they have had to issue securities both denominated and payable in USD. Ideally (see choice **111(a)**), instruments are denominated in 'imaginary' units or in a potential infinity of convex combinations of 'real' ones, reflecting exposures of issuers everywhere.

Referring to Problem **112**, and to Burstein (1986, Chapter 11) the *Swiss franc* of the problem is an investment currency; transactors contract in terms of cocktails of currencies.

Continuing annotation of choice **107(b)**, the literal choice is preposterous; but it provokes a stimulating line of thought.

One reads of 'dollarization' of South American economies. And the fall of the Israeli finance minister (Mr Horowitz) a few years ago is instructive: he proposed to make the USD Israel's accounting unit. The proposal, and its unfortunate author, were harshly condemned: it was widely believed that it entailed a derogation of sovereignty; sovereign nations should be free to ruin themselves (and indeed there is a proper sense in which liberty does require that!). The controlling insight, leading to a correct analysis, concerns the partition separating choice of payments media from choice of monetary *measure*.

Transactions costs may puncture such partitioning; see costs entailed by reckoning in one currency and using another as the settlement medium; in particular the cost of obtaining accurate quotations may be high.

Problems **108** and **109** are readily referenced from the lecture.

Problem 110

110(a) The following material embellishes the theme, 'interaction of industrial/commercial with financial modalities'. Think of financial counterparts, or duals, to industrial/commercial situations. Label the latter A_i, and the former B_j:

A–1 A European company sells to the United States and buys materials and factor services elsewhere. The company, as an exporter to the US, has USD risk exposure: it is typically long USD.

B–1 The company issues USD-denominated debt – thus balancing its exposure to the dollar.

A–2 A British company regularly imports substantial quantities of inputs from the US. It typically owes USD.

B–2 The company raises Euro-sterling capital, investing the proceeds in USD or USD-guaranteed assets – shortening its sterling position and lengthening its USD position. McKinnon (1979) shows that there are many ways to accomplish this result.

B–3 USA–Ajax floats a huge DM Eurobond loan.

A–3 USA–Ajax diverts its sales towards Germany and invests in German companies, or in positions covariant with the

DM. Proper evaluation of the *n*-dimensional financial position of an economic agent considers the agent's *entire* position – including sensitivity of transactions to various currencies (and the variance/covariance matrix controlling multinational currency fluctuation); and disaggregated balance sheet positions.

B–4 British portfolio managers (*any* agent is a portfolio manager) want to increase their USD exposure.

A–4 British exporters invoice in USD and retain proceeds in that form. Cover against dollar-appreciation relative to sterling becomes more expensive. There is pressure on the pound – although, in general, the British do *not* plan to increase their *monetary* dollar positions. In an outlying case, Britain may become 'dollarized' to a degree; it may become attractive to bill in USD in domestic British situations.

Problem 111

111(a) Contrast American and Brazilian foreign-debt characteristics *circa* 1988–9. Brazil must service immense debt denominated and payable in US dollars. American foreign debt is predominantly denominated and payable in USD – and so can be discharged by the American 'printing press'.

Over the 1981–9 interval, foreigners bought huge amounts of US paper, including United States Government (USG) debt, in exchange for goods. If the United States could confine foreign creditors to nursing piles of paper, growing at interest rates determining the paper-rate on paper, it could extract huge seigneurage profit perpetually. By 1988 foreigners appeared to play other cards, however: they increased their rate of purchase of *real* American assets.

Problem 112

112(c) (See the Swiss franc problem in Burstein, 1986, Chapter 11.) The crux is in divorce of the problem of choice-of-preferred-liquid-assets from that of settling trade accounts. In the theory Swiss francs are held only by non-Swiss (!); and Swiss transactors metricize their deals in a composite unit, the Pfolmar; and settle only in non-Swiss-issued paper. The Swiss franc is then a liquid asset whose properties are studied in the theory of currency competition; but the Swiss franc does not serve as a means of payment.

Problem 113

113(d) (See also **114(c)**.) Now consider attempts by central banks to control credit flows within their jurisdictions. Consider France in particular – and indeed the analysis supplies a *raison d'être* for the French proclivity for controls (cf. *dirigisme*; 17th-century France became the prototype centralized state).

Citicorp may barge in. ('The day after tomorrow' Citicorp may be a fully qualified player on foreign giros. But accounts chequeable in France are readily swapped for liquid short-term Citicorp liabilities.) And note that banks other than central banks may make swap arrangements like those between central banks: banks can provide against risks of having to redeem liabilities subject to alien tenders on short notice; cf. swaps between Citicorp and Lloyds bank. Of course, underlying stocks include mountains of government debt, high quality corporate bonds and debentures, etc.

In the above script, in which Citicorp massively increases its French lending, it would doubtless plan to raise capital in France along now-familiar lines. Frenchmen, holding shares in Compagnie de *X*, effectively sell these shares to Citicorp for Citicorp shares: Citicorp invests the proceeds of sales of its shares in French franc (FF) securities markets; evening up its book. (Banks typically overtrade on their capital more than the script suggests.)

Relating the annotation of (**113d**) to Problem **103**, as well as to **114(c)**, the principal new idea developed by this material concerns the way in which a bank anywhere can 'issue' monetary liabilities in *j*-dollars, covering these by selling long securities, including its shares, in '*J*' security markets, thus evening up *j*-dollar exposure on its books. In the upshot residents of the *j*th economy simply alter the texture of their collective equity portfolio; *inter alia*, they buy non-monetary obligations of financial intermediaries. It is hard to see how central banks can exercise control in an innovated global economy.

Additional Hypothetical Cases

Multinational Companies (MNCs) Beyond Central Banking
IBM's balance sheet is titanic. One envisages link ups between
banks and industrial companies leading to useful buttressing
of bank balance sheets. Or, along vaguely 19th-century lines,
IBM would conduct banking, or quasi-banking, operations,
accepting drafts on itself by way of granting credits. Its
obligations would be backed by its vast global holdings, some
almost perfectly liquid.

*Concluding Reflection on Ways in Which Alien Banks May
Intrude Upon Central-bank Control-efforts* Barclays Bank
can easily attract lendable USD funds by paying over the
market for deposits and then lending out the placements
(inflows) as they come in. So attempts by the Banca d'Italia,
for example, to restrain 'member bank' lending are likely to
fail.

Problem 114

114(a) The analogy to forward markets in commodities is very
attractive. So the divorce of positions in actual (underlying)
stocks from, say, options positions is decisive. Recall the
purchase of a put option by a Belgravia real estate holder
who wants to sensitize his portfolio to the dollar.

114(b) Such procedures are intrinsic to open economies. Holland is a
good example.

114(c) The analysis builds up to the compelling conclusion that
central banks have little, if any, control over credit emission
or effective stocks of monetary holdings in *laissez faire* en-
vironments. So the analysis goes far to explain why central
banks so much prefer *dirigisme* to *laissez faire*. The real world
upshot finds central banks exercising tenuous control over
credit emission *via* Regulation.

114(E) Ergo: **114(E)**.

Bibliography

AGHEVIL, B. *et al.* (1977) *The Monetary Approach to the Balance of Payments* (Washington, DC: International Monetary Fund).

ALLEN, R. G. D. (1938) *Mathematical Analysis for Economists* (London: Macmillan).

ALLEN, R. G. D. (1963) *Mathematical Economics* (London: Macmillan) 2nd edn.

ALLEN, R. G. D. (1967) *Macro-Economic Theory: A Mathematical Treatment* (London: Macmillan).

ALLINGHAM, M. G. and M. L. BURSTEIN (eds) (1976) *Resource Allocation and Economic Policy* (London: Macmillan).

ARCHIBALD, G. C. and R. G. LIPSEY (1958) 'Monetary and Value Theory: A Critique of Lange and Patinkin', *Review of Economic Studies*, 26, p. 1.

ARROWSMITH, D. K. and C. M. PLACE (1982) *Ordinary Differential Equations* (London: Chapman & Hall).

BARRO, R. J. (1974) 'Are Government Bonds Net Wealth?', *Journal of Political Economy*, 82.

BARRO, R. J. (1984) *Macroeconomics* (New York: John Wiley).

BARSKY, R. B. and L. H. SUMMERS (1988) 'Gibson's Paradox and the Gold Standard', *Journal of Political Economy*, 96, p. 528.

BECKER, G. S. (1971) *The Economics of Discrimination* (Chicago: University of Chicago Press) 2nd edn.

BILSON, J. F. (1979) 'Recent Developments in Monetary Models of Foreign Exchange Rate Determination', *IMF Staff Papers*, 26.

BLAUG, M. (1978) *Economic Theory in Retrospect* (Cambridge: Cambridge University Press) 3rd edn.

BLEJER, M. I. and L. LEIDERMAN (1981) 'A Monetary Approach to the Crawling Peg System: Theory and Evidence', *Journal of Political Economy*, 89.

BRANSON, W. H. (1979) *Macroeconomic Theory and Policy* (New York: Harper & Row) 2nd edn.

BRUNNER, K. and A. MELTZER (1974) 'Friedman's Monetary Theory' in Gordon (ed.) (1974).

BRUNNER, K. and A. MELTZER (eds) (1976) *The Phillips Curve and Labour Markets* (Amsterdam: North Holland)–supplement to *Journal of Monetary Economics*, 4, pp. 19–46.

BUITER, W. H. (1980) 'The Rôle of Economic Policy after the New Classical Economics', in Currie and Peel (eds) (1980).

BUITER, W. H. and M. MILLER (1981) 'Monetary Policy and International Competitiveness: The Problems of Adjustment', in Eltis and Sinclair (eds) (1981).

BURSTEIN, M. L. (1963) *Money* (Cambridge, MA.: Schenkman).

BURSTEIN, M. L. (1968) *Economic Theory: Equilibrium and Change* (London: John Wiley).

BURSTEIN, M. L. (1978) *New Directions in Economic Policy* (London: Macmillan).

BURSTEIN, M. L. (1986) *Modern Monetary Theory* (London: Macmillan).

BURSTEIN, M. L. (1988a) 'Keynes and the Rate of Interest', in Hamouda and Smithin (eds) (1988) 2, *Theories and Method*, p. 162.

BURSTEIN, M. L. (1988b) *Studies in Banking Theory, Financial History and Vertical Control* (London: Macmillan).

CAGAN, P. (1972) *The Channels of Monetary Effects on Interest Rates* (New York: Columbia University Press–for the National Bureau of Economic Research).

CAVES, R. E. and R. W. JONES (1985) *World Trade and Payments* (Boston: Little, Brown) 4th edn.

CLINTON, K. (1988) 'Transactions Costs and Covered Interest Arbitrage: Theory and Evidence', *Journal of Political Economy*, 96, p. 358.

CLOWER, R. W. and M. L. BURSTEIN (1960) 'On the Invariance of Demand for Cash and Other Assets', *Review of Economic Studies*, 28.

CORDEN, W. M. (1977) *Inflation, Exchange Rates and the World Economy* (Chicago: University of Chicago Press).

CURRIE, D. and A. PEEL (eds) (1980) *Contemporary Economic Analysis* (Beckenham: Croom Helm).

DIXIT, A. K. (1976) *The Theory of Equilibrium Growth* (Oxford: Oxford University Press).

DORNBUSCH, R. (1975) 'A Portfolio Balance Model of the Open Economy', *Journal of Monetary Economics*, 1.

DORNBUSCH, R. (1976) 'Expectations and Exchange Rate Dynamics', *Journal of Political Economy*, 84.

DORNBUSCH, R. (1980) *Open Economy Macroeconomics* (New York: Basic Books).

DUESENBERRY, J. S. (1949) *Income, Saving and the Theory of Consumer Behaviour* (Cambridge, MA.: Harvard University Press).

The Economist (1962) 10 February, pp. 541–2; 28 April, pp. 366–8.

EINAUDI, L. (1936) 'Teoria della moneta imaginaria nel tempo da Carlomagno alla rivoluzione francese', *Revista di Storia Economica*, 1.

EINAUDI, L. (1952–reprint) 'The Theory of Imaginary Money', in *Enterprise and Secular Change* (Homewood, Ill.: Richard D. Irwin).

EINZIG, P. (1961) *A Dynamic Theory of Forward Exchange* (London: Macmillan).

EINZIG, P. (1969) *The Euro-bond Market* (London: Macmillan) 2nd edn.

EINZIG, P. (1970) *The History of Foreign Exchange* (London: Macmillan) 2nd edn.

ELLIS, H. S. (ed.) (1948) *A Survey of Contemporary Economics* (Homewood, Ill.: Richard D. Irwin).

ELTIS, W. A. and P. J. N. SINCLAIR (eds) (1981) *The Money Supply and the Exchange Rate* (Oxford: Clarendon Press).

FETTER, F. W. (1965) *The Development of British Monetary Orthodoxy* (Cambridge, MA.: Harvard University Press).

FISHER, I. (1930/1954) *The Theory of Interest* (New York: Kelley and Millman).

FLEMING, M. (1962) 'Domestic Financial Policies Under Fixed and Floating Exchange Rates', *IMF Staff Papers*, 9.

FRENKEL, J. A. (1976) 'A Monetary Approach to the Exchange Rate', *Scandinavian Journal of Economics*, 2.

FRENKEL, J. A. and H. G. Johnson (eds) (1976) *The Monetary Approach to the Balance of Payments* (London: Allen & Unwin).

FRENKEL, J. A. and H. G. Johnson (1978) *The Economics of Exchange Rates: Selected Studies* (Reading, MA.: Addison Wesley).

FRENKEL, J. A. and A. RAZIN (1987) 'The Mundell–Fleming Model, a Quarter Century Later: A Unified Exposition', IMF *Staff Papers*, 34.

FRENKEL, J. A. and C. A. RODRIGUEZ (eds) (1975) 'Portfolio Equilibrium and the Balance of Payments', *American Economic Review*, 65.

FRIEDMAN, D. (1977) 'The Size and Shape of Nations', *Journal of Political Economy*, 85.

FRIEDMAN, M. (1946/1953) 'Lange on Price Flexibility and Employment: A Methodological Criticism', *American Economic Review*, 36, p. 613–reprinted in Friedman (1953a).

FRIEDMAN, M. (1951/1953) 'Commodity Reserve Currency', *Journal of Political Economy*, 59, p. 203–reprinted in Friedman (1953a).

FRIEDMAN, M. (1953a) *Essays in Positive Economics* (Chicago: University of Chicago Press).

FRIEDMAN, M. (1953b) 'The Case for Flexible Exchange Rates', in Friedman (1953a, pp. 157–203).

FRIEDMAN, M. (1962) *Price Theory: A Provisional Text* (Chicago: Aldine Press).

FRIEDMAN, M. (1968) 'The Rôle of Monetary Policy', *American Economic Review*, 58, p. 1.

FRIEDMAN, M. (1969) *The Optimal Quantity of Money and Other Essays* (Chicago: University of Chicago Press).

FRIEDMAN, M. (1984a) 'Financial Futures Markets and Tabular Standards', *Journal of Political Economy*, 92, p. 165.

FRIEDMAN, M. (1984b) 'The Taxes Called Deficits', *Wall Street Journal*, 26 April.

FRIEDMAN, M. (1986) 'The Resource Cost of Irredeemable Paper Money', *Journal of Political Economy*, 94.

FRIEDMAN, M. and A. J. SCHWARTZ (1963) *A Monetary History of the United States* (Princeton, N.J.: Princeton University Press).

FRIEDMAN, M. and A. J. SCHWARTZ (1982) *Monetary Trends in the United States and the United Kingdom* (Chicago: University of Chicago Press).

FRIEDMAN, M. and A. J. SCHWARTZ (1986) 'Has Government any Rôle in Money?', *Journal of Monetary Economics*, 17.

FRISCH, H. (1983) *Theories of Inflation* (Cambridge: Cambridge University Press).

FRYDMAN, R. and E. S. PHELPS (eds) (1983) *Individual Forecasting and Aggregate Outcomes: Rational Expectations Examined* (Cambridge: Cambridge University Press).

GIRTON, L. and D. ROPER (1978) 'J. Laurence Laughlin and the Quantity Theory of Money', *Journal of Political Economy*, 86, p. 599.

GOODHART, C. A. E. (1975) *Money, Information and Uncertainty* (London: Macmillan).

GOODHART, C. A. E. (1984) *Monetary Theory and Practice: The U. K. Experience* (London: Macmillan).

GORDON, R. J. (ed.) (1974) *Milton Friedman's Monetary Framework* (Chicago: University of Chicago Press).

HAIGH, C. (ed.) (1985) *The Cambridge Historical Encyclopedia of Great Britain and Ireland* (Cambridge: Cambridge University Press).

HALL, R. E. (1978) 'Stochastic Implications of the Life Cycle-Permanent Income Hypothesis: Theory and Evidence', *Journal of Political Economy*, 86, p. 971.

HAMOUDA, O. and J. N. SMITHIN (eds) (1988) *Keynes and Public Policy After Fifty Years*, 2 vols (Aldershot: Edward Elgar).

HAYEK, F. A. (1960) *The Constitution of Liberty* (Chicago: University of Chicago Press).

HAYEK, F. A. (1976) *Denationalization of Money* (London: Institute of Economic Affairs).

HICKS, J. R. (1946) *Value and Capital* (Oxford: Clarendon Press) 2nd edn.

HICKS, J. R. (1986) 'Managing without Money', in *Chung-Hua Series of Lectures by Invited Eminent Economists*, 11 (Tapei: Institute of Economics, Academia Sinica) pp. 19–29.

HIMMELFARB, G. (1959) *Darwin and the Darwinian Revolution* (Garden City, N.Y.: Doubleday).

HIRSHLEIFER, J. (1978/1987) 'Natural Economy versus Political Economy', *Journal of Social and Biological Structures*, 1, p. 319–reprinted in Hirshleifer (1987).

HIRSHLEIFER, J. (1987) *Economic Behaviour in Adversity* (Chicago and Brighton: University of Chicago Press and Wheatsheaf Books).

JASAY, A. E. (1959) 'Memoranda of Evidence', in *Principal Memoranda of Evidence*, III, pp. 129–32, issued by the Committee on the Working of the Monetary System (Radcliffe Committee) (London: HMSO).

JOHNSON, H. G. (1972a) *Further Essays in Monetary Theory* (London: Allen & Unwin).

JOHNSON, H. G. (1972b) 'The Monetary Approach to Balance-of-Payments Theory', *Journal of Financial and Quantitative Analysis*, 7.

JOHNSON, H. G. (1977) 'The Monetary Approach to the Balance of Payments: A Non-Technical Guide', *Journal of International Economics*, 7.

KALDOR, N. (1960) *Essays on Economic Stability and Growth* (London: Duckworth).

KAMIEN, M. I. and NANCY L. SCHWARTZ (1981) *Dynamic Optimization* (New York: North Holland).

KEYNES, J. M. (1923) *A Tract on Monetary Reform* (London: Macmillan).

KEYNES, J. M. (1930) *A Treatise on Money*, 2 vols (London: Macmillan).

KEYNES, J. M. (1936) *The General Theory of Employment, Interest and Money* (London: Macmillan).

KINDLEBERGER, C. (1958) *International Economics* (Homewood, Ill.: Richard D. Irwin) rev. edn.

KLEIN, B. (1974) 'The Competitive Supply of Money', *Journal of Money, Credit and Banking*, 6.

KLEIN, B. (1975) 'Our New Monetary Standard: The Measurement and

Effect of Price Uncertainty, 1880–1973', *Economic Inquiry*, 13 (April) pp. 461–84.

KOURI, P. and M. G. PORTER (1974) 'International Capital Flows and Portfolio Equilibrium', *Journal of Political Economy*, 82.

KREINEN, P. and L. H. OFFICER (1978) *The Monetary Approach to the Balance of Payments: A Survey* (Princeton Studies in International Finance, 43, Princeton, N. J.: Princeton University Press).

KRUEGER, A. O. (1983) *Exchange Rate Determination* (Cambridge: Cambridge University Press).

KRUGMAN, P. (1983) 'Oil and the Dollar', in Bhandari, J. S. and B. H. Putnam (eds), *Economic Interdependence and Flexible Exchange Rates* (Cambridge, MA.:MIT Press) p. 179.

KYDLAND, F. E. and E. C. PRESCOTT (1977) 'Rules Rather Than Discretion: The Inconsistency of Optimal Plans', *Journal of Political Economy*, 85, p. 473.

LAURSEN, S. and L. METZLER (1950) 'Flexible Exchange Rates and the Theory of Employment', *Review of Economics and Statistics*, 32.

LEIJONHUFVUD, A. (1968) *On Keynesian Economics and the Economics of Keynes* (New York: Oxford University Press).

LEIJONHUFVUD, A. (1981) *Information and Coordination* (New York: Oxford University Press).

LEONTIEF, W. (1958) 'Theoretical Note on Time-Preference, Productivity of Capital, Stagnation and Economic Growth', *American Economic Review*, 48.

LEONTIEF, W. (1959) 'Time Preference and Economic Growth', *American Economic Review*, 49.

LERNER, A. P. (1953) *Essays in Economic Analysis* (London: Macmillan).

LERNER, A. P. (1952/1953) 'The Essential Properties of Interest and Money', *Quarterly Journal of Economics*, 66–reprinted in Lerner (1953).

LUCAS, R. E. (1976) 'Econometric Policy Evaluation: A Critique', in BRUNNER and MELTZER (eds) (1976).

McKINNON, R. I. (1979) *Money in International Exchange*: *The Convertible Currency System* (New York: Oxford University Press).

MEADE, J. (1951) *The Balance of Payments* (London: Oxford University Press).

METZLER, L. A. (1942) 'Underemployment Equilibrium in International Trade', *Econometrica*, 10.

METZLER, L. A. (1948) 'The Theory of International Trade', in Ellis (ed) (1948).

MINTS, L. A. (1945) *A History of Banking Theory* (Chicago: University of Chicago Press).

MONTIEL, P. (1984) 'Credit and Fiscal Policies in a "Global Monetarist" Model of the Balance of Payments', *IMF Staff Papers*, 31.

MONTIEL, P. (1985) 'A Monetary Analysis of a Small Open Economy with a Keynesian Structure', *IMF Staff Papers*, 32.

MUNDELL, R. A. (1960) 'The Monetary Dynamics of International Adjustment under Fixed and Flexible Exchange Rates', *Quarterly Journal of Economics*, 74, p. 227.

MUNDELL, R. A. (1961) 'A Theory of Optimal Currency Areas', *American Economic Review*, 51, p. 657.

MUNDELL, R. A. (1968) *International Economics* (New York: Macmillan).

MUNDELL, R. A. and A. K. SWOBODA (eds), *Monetary Problems of the International Economy* (Chicago: University of Chicago Press).

MUSSA, M. (1976a) 'The Exchange Rate, the Balance of Payments and Monetary and Fiscal Policy under a Régime of Controlled Floating', *Scandinavian Journal of Economics*, 2.

MUSSA, M. (1976b) 'Tariffs and the Balance of Payments: A Monetary Approach', in Frenkel and Johnson (eds) (1976).

NELSON, R. R. (1956) 'A Theory of the Low Equilibrium Trap in Underdeveloped Countries', *American Economic Review*, 46.

NEWLYN, W. T. and R. P. BOOTLE (1978) *Theory of Money* (Oxford: Clarendon Press) 3rd edn.

Oxford Classical Dictionary, N. G. L. Hammond and HH. Scullard (eds), (1970) (Oxford: Clarendon Press) 2nd edn.

PAYNE, P. L. (1985) 'The British Economy: Growth and Structural Change', in Haigh, C. (ed) (1985) p. 269.

PERLMAN, M. (1986) 'The Bullionist Controversy Revisited', *Journal of Political Economy*, 94.

PHELPS, E. S. (1968) 'Money Wage Dynamics and Labour Market Equilibrium', *Journal of Political Economy*, 76.

RICARDO, D. (1817/1951–1955) *The Principles of Political Economy and Taxation*–see Sraffa, P. and M. Dobb (eds), *The Works and Correspondence of David Ricardo*, 10 vols (Cambridge: Cambridge University Press) vol. 1.

RIVERA-BATIZ, F. L. and L. R. RIVERA-BATIZ (1985) *International Finance and Open Economy Macroeconomics* (New York: Macmillan).

ROBINSON, J. (1966) *An Essay in Marxian Economics* (London: Macmillan) 2nd edn.

ROBINSON J. (1969) *The Accumulation of Capital* (London: Macmillan) 3rd edn.

RODRIGUEZ, C. A. (1976) 'Money and Wealth in an Open Economy Income-Expenditure Model', in Frenkel and Johnson (eds) 1976).

SALANT, S. W. (1983) 'The Vulnerability of Price Stabilization Schemes to Speculative Attack', *Journal of Political Economy*, 91.

SAMUELSON, P. A. (1947/1983) *Foundations of Economic Analysis*, (Cambridge, MA.: Harvard University Press) 1st and 2nd edns.

SARGENT, T. J. and N. WALLACE (1976) 'Rational Expectations and the Theory of Monetary Policy', *Journal of Monetary Economics*, 2, p. 169.

SARGENT, T. J. and N. WALLACE (1981) 'Some Unpleasant Monetarist Arithmetic', *Federal Reserve Bank of Minneapolis Quarterly Review*, 5, p. 1.

SAYERS, R. S. (1957) *Central Banking After Bagehot* (Oxford: Clarendon Press).

SCHUMPETER, J. (1954) *History of Economic Analysis* (New York: Oxford University Press).

SENIOR, N. (1830) *The Cost of Obtaining Money*, reprinted in the Scarce Tract Series, published by the London School of Economics.

SHEFFRIN, S. (1983) *Rational Expectations* (New York: Cambridge University Press).

SMITH, A. (1776/1910/1970) *An Inquiry into the Nature and Causes of the Wealth of Nations*, 2 vols (London: Dent–Everyman's Library edn, E. A. Seligman (ed.)).

SOHMEN, E. (1958) Appendix D of Kindleberger (1958), pp. 610–12.

SPRAOS, J. (1959) 'Speculation, Arbitrage and Sterling', *Economic Journal*, 69.

STOLPER, F. and P. A. SAMUELSON (1941) 'Protection and Real Wages', *Review of Economic Studies*, 9, p. 58.

SVENSSON, L. E. O. (1988) 'Trade in Risky Assets', *American Economic Review*, 78, p. 375.

SWEEZY, P. M. (1942/1970) *The Theory of Capitalist Development* (New York: Modern Reader Paperbacks).

SWOBODA, A. K. (1983) 'Exchange Rate Régimes and European – U.S. Policy Interdependence', *IMF Staff Papers*, 30.

TELSER, L. G. (1981) 'Why There Are Organized Futures Markets', *Journal of Law and Economics*, 24.

TELSER, L. G. (1986) 'Futures and Actual Markets: How They are Related', *Journal of Business*, 59.

TEMIN, P. (1969) *The Jacksonian Economy* (New York: Norton).

THIRLWALL, A. P. (1988) 'What is Wrong with Balance of Payment Adjustment Theory?', *Royal Bank of Scotland Review*, 15, (March) pp. 3–19.

THORNTON, H. (1802/1939/1962) *An Enquiry into the Nature and Effects of the Paper Credit of Great Britain* (London: Allen & Unwin; 1939). The 1962 edn (London: Frank Cass) reprints the 1939 edn which contains an introduction by F. A. Hayek. The 1802 edn was published in London by Hatchard.

TIEBOUT, C. M. (1956) 'A Pure Theory of Local Expenditures', *Journal of Political Economy*, 64, p. 416.

TINBERGEN, J. (1963) *On the Theory of Economic Policy* (Amsterdam: North Holland) 2nd edn.

TRIFFIN, R. (1957) *Europe and the Money Muddle* (New Haven, CT: Yale University Press).

TRIFFIN, R. (1961) *Gold and the Dollar Crisis* (New Haven: Yale University Press) rev. edn.

VINER, J. (1937) *Studies in the Theory of International Trade* (New York: Harper & Row).

WALLACE, N. (1979) 'Why Markets in Foreign Exchange are Different From Other Markets', *Federal Reserve Bank of Minneapolis Quarterly Review*, 3.

WHITE, L. H. (1984) 'Competitive Payments Systems and the Unit of Account', *American Economic Review*, 74.

WHITMAN, M. von N. (1975) 'Global Monetarism and the Monetary Approach to the Balance of Payments', *Brookings Papers on Economic Activity*, 3.

WICKSELL, K. (1898/1936) *Geldzin und Güterpreise* (Jena: Gustav Fischer), translated by R. F. Kahn and published as *Interest and Prices* (London: Macmillan).

WILLIAMSON, J. (1981) *Exchange Rate Rules: The Theory, Performance and Prospects of the Crawling Peg* (New York: St Martin's Press).

WORKING, H. (1948) 'Theory of the Inverse Carrying Charge in Futures Markets', *Journal of Farm Economics*, 30, p. 1.

WORKING, H. (1962) 'New Concepts Concerning Futures Markets and Prices', *American Economic Review*, 52, p. 431.

Index of Names

Index of Subjects